Crime and Justice
1750–1950

**Barry S. Godfrey and
Paul Lawrence**

WILLAN
PUBLISHING

Published by

Willan Publishing
Culmcott House
Mill Street, Uffculme
Cullompton, Devon
EX15 3AT, UK
Tel: +44(0)1884 840337
Fax: +44(0)1884 840251
e-mail: info@willanpublishing.co.uk
website: www.willanpublishing.co.uk

Published simultaneously in the USA and Canada by

Willan Publishing
c/o ISBS, 920 NE 58th Ave, Suite 300,
Portland, Oregon 97213-3786, USA
Tel: +001(0)503 287 3093
Fax: +001(0)503 280 8832
e-mail: info@isbs.com
website: www.isbs.com

First published 2005

Reprinted 2010

ISBN 978-1-84392-116-5 paperback
      978-1-84392-117-2 hardback

British Library Cataloguing-in-Publication Data

A catalogue record for this book is available from the British Library

FSC
Mixed Sources
Product group from well-managed
forests and other controlled sources
Cert no. SGS-COC-2482
www.fsc.org
© 1996 Forest Stewardship Council

Project managed by Deer Park Productions, Tavistock, Devon
Typeset by GCS, Leighton Buzzard, Bedfordshire, LU7 1AR
Printed and bound by TJI Digital, Padstow, Cornwall

Contents

Crime and Justice 1750–1950

List of figures, tables and illustrations

Figures

Tables

Illustrations

This book developed out of a collaborative teaching project between Keele University and The Open University. The authors would like to thank Chris A. Williams for providing valuable feedback and a first draft of parts of Chapters 2 and 3, and Gerry Oram for providing a first draft of parts of Chapters 3 and 8.

1. Introduction

William Sanders stated that: 'In the course of their work, both detectives and sociologists must gather and analyse information. For detectives, the object is to identify and locate criminals and to collect evidence to ensure that the identification is correct. Sociologists, on the other hand, develop theories and methods to help understand social behaviour' (Sanders 1974: 1). But how important is it to gain an understanding of how criminal behaviour and society's reactions to it have changed over time? What part does history play in understanding criminality, and what tools can we use to recover evidence from one or two centuries ago? Whether you are interested in modern history, criminology or sociology, you will be questioning which areas of knowledge are important to you and your work, and which are not. This book will explain how a critical appreciation of the history of crime can inform current understandings of offending, and why historical events in the past two hundred years will continue to affect crime and criminal justice for many years to come.

If we were designing a criminal justice system to meet the needs of today's society, would it look like the one we actually have? Almost certainly it would not, and that is because the institutions of criminal justice – the police, prisons and the courts – have all been shaped and influenced by events and ideas over a long period of time. For example, the growth of police services from a private force employed and run for the benefit of the social elite to recover stolen property to a professional, uniformed and preventative public service is complex. We can only fully understand why the police force works the way it does (prioritizing the maintenance of public order, being organized in counties rather than being 'The British Police Force', being largely unarmed, and so on) by looking at the changes made over two hundred years of history. In addition to institutional changes, historical research can also reveal attitudinal changes towards crime and risk in contemporary society. For example, youth crime appears to be a persistent problem for modern society. Media debates about joy riding and the drug/rave culture have recently given way to celebrations of Anti-Social Behaviour Orders (ASBOs) and their effectiveness against youth 'yob culture'. However, when did juvenile delinquency become a pressing problem, what particular sets of anxieties or events made it so, and are those factors still present today? Was delinquency always waiting to be discovered, or was it 'invented' – can crime be 'manufactured' in this way? If so, what are the conditions that allow us to manufacture crime, and do fears about particular types of offenders reflect rising crime or do they feed a system which creates rises in crime?

Do we live in a safer society now than our parents and grandparents did? Statistics tell us that violence fell to its lowest prosecuted level about a century ago, and that the rates of violence are now much higher (they peaked around the 1990s and are currently declining). Why is this? Are we safer now? Do we care more about violence now? Are we more worried about violence than we ever were? We are not going to find the answers to such questions by just looking at the situation as it stands today. We need to find meaningful comparisons with the recent and far past. We also need to question the assumptions that people readily make about the past – that it was a golden age where police officers clipped unruly teenagers around the ear and people did not need to lock their doors. Was that really true and, if so, how do we know?

It is also clear that the past has a future. Perceptions of crime and changes in the Victorian criminal justice system have left their legacy. For example, why do we imprison women and children in separate prisons to men? Why are men and women sentenced in different ways? What is it about the persistence of eighteenth- and nineteenth-century constructions of femininity that means that we still feel their impact today? These kinds of questions remain relevant to modern criminology and social policy, and they remain pertinent to anyone wanting to understand the social world.

Does crime history have a history?

Crime history itself has created a history – a 'historiography'. Since the subject began to develop out of the general upsurge in popularity of social history generally – mainly through the work of Leon Radzinowicz (1948–86), Doug Hay *et al.* (1975), Edward Thompson (1975) – it has now grown to be a substantial subdiscipline in its own right. Whether the subject is properly situated within 'history' or 'criminology' is an interesting question, and you will find crime history articles in both historical and criminological journals (and if you are interested in the development of crime history itself as a subject there are a number of interesting review articles listed at the end of this chapter in 'further reading'). Where once one would struggle to find a course containing a history of crime element, it is now extremely common for criminal justice and criminology courses to include modules on crime history or the history of deviance, as well as on the foundations of criminology itself.[1] History degree courses too, even when not specifically addressing the issue of crime, usually include modules on large-scale disorders (industrial disputes and labour relations, food riots and the economy, political movements which were heavily policed, and so on). The extraordinary growth in interest in lawbreakers and the policing of society has been matched with a growing body of academic literature. Peter King (1999) has provided a guide to navigating the various sources that can be explored (on the Web, in bibliographic databases and in journals, for example). However, the wealth and diversity of literature can be bewildering. A small number of authors have attempted to review the field and construct a narrative of crime and its control from the mid-eighteenth to the mid-twentieth centuries. Notable among these are Jim Sharpe (1999), David Taylor (1998), Philip Rawlings (1999) and perhaps the person who has done most to popularize this subject, Clive Emsley (2005). Those authors have all described crime in what might be termed 'the modern world'. Why is there a concentration on this period?

Why the period 1750 to 1950?

Put simply, during this period the 'modern world' was shaped. The dynamic development of new forms of industrial production, the rise of the great urban towns and cities and unprecedented population growth all changed the appearance of the British Isles. They also created new social conditions and problems that policy-makers attempted to ameliorate, control or eradicate. The period witnessed the end of capital punishment and the transportation of convicts overseas, and the rise of a system of mass imprisonment which is now culminating in the highest number of people ever imprisoned in this country and the largest prison population in Europe. It saw the beginning of public uniformed policing, the first mass-media moral panics about violent crime (from the 'garotters' to Jack the Ripper), and changes to the court system which ensured the rapid processing of offenders. During this period the systematic recording of levels of crime was begun by the Home Office (an organization which itself grew impressively from six clerks in 1817 to a vast bureaucracy in the twentieth century). Perhaps most importantly, this period witnessed the beginnings of the 'science' of criminology, and when 'crime' moved from being considered an accepted part of life – like the weather – to a subject which today commands the highest political and press attention.

The structure of the book

This book has been written with researchers of crime, criminology and social policy in mind. It intends to give a broad historical overview of crime, policing and punishment within the context of historical processes such as urbanization and industrialization, and it will present different perspectives on a number of 'issues' and debates in current criminological and historical research. By drawing on primary source materials it aims to show how historical knowledge is constructed, and also suggest ways in which researchers can investigate primary source materials for themselves.

The book itself is divided into two sections. The first section contains chapters which describe changes to the criminal justice system in this period. It explores the development of the main institutions and charts procedural and legal changes – from the means of detection, through the changing prosecution and court formats, and onto the punishment of offenders. The second section contains chapters describing how conceptions of crime and criminals altered between 1750 and 1950. These two thematic strands are, of course, closely related. Each chapter contains suggestions for preliminary reading, three sections which explore different facets of the topic, a full bibliography and suggestions for further reading. For those who want to explore the subject in more detail, we have posed some key questions. We have suggested how the first question can be approached. For questions two and three we have listed some of the main texts you may need to answer the questions, but you should consult the main Bibliography at the end of the book. After the conclusion, there is a glossary of terms (with brief explanations of legal and historical terms used in this book), and a 'timeline' of significant events. These are designed to make a difficult and complex subject easier to navigate. There are also some suggested websites that provide additional information on crime and offending.

Following this introduction, Chapter 2 describes the development of policing in England from 1750 to 1950. During this period there were three phases of development. Initially, from 1750 up to about 1850, there was an amateur or semi-professional parish system organized by local authorities, a system that varied in quality. Then, following the setting up of the Metropolitan Police in 1829, a more consistently professional system of uniformed 'New' Police was developed. It took almost thirty years of experimentation to consolidate this new style of policing, and there have been numerous debates about its purpose among historians. Some argue that it was a rational response to rising crime in rapidly growing cities, while others claim that it was in fact a tool via which the middle classes ensured the sanctity of their newly-earned property, and point to its 'social control' function. By 1870, however, the new system was firmly established, leading eventually to what has often popularly been conceived of as a 'golden age' of policing, between about 1890 and 1950. This chapter gives an account of the historical development of the English police, starting at a point (1750) where almost all its modern features had yet to appear, and critically explores the nature of enforcement for two hundred years. In doing so it considers arguments around the introduction of the New Police, and debates whether any 'golden age' of policing ever really existed.

While, as detailed in Chapter 2, the New Police gradually developed into the default mechanism for enforcing the law and apprehending criminals, this process took a long time and was only partially complete by the 1850s. Chapter 3 deals with the role of the victim in the criminal justice process – a role which was initially far more instrumental than it is today – and begins with a consideration of victims, the prosecution of crime and the changing face of the prosecutor. At the beginning of our period it was largely through individual or private actions, not through police involvement, that cases were prosecuted. Prosecutions could be expensive as well as difficult and this chapter will examine the various ways by which private individuals were able to bring cases to court. The emotive subject of self-defence will then be discussed. 'The Englishman's home is his castle' is not just a modern sentiment but is a long-established view. Accordingly, we will take a close look at how the use of 'reasonable force' has been variously interpreted and the underlying causes of any shifts in attitudes. Finally, there have always been measures that private individuals could – and were expected to – take in order to safeguard their own property and prevent crime. The route to court was therefore a dynamically changing situation with some essential elements remaining fixed. This could also be said of the court system itself.

The period 1750–1950 witnessed far-reaching changes in trial procedures, in court jurisdictions and in the administration of justice more generally. Significant change also occurred in the way in which trials were run, with increasing ceremony and more meticulous analysis of evidence becoming the norm. Chapter 4 firstly provides a broad, largely factual, overview of some of these changes, then moves on to consider debates about the accessibility, efficiency and legitimacy of the court system. The major question will be whether the courts acted as unbiased arbiters of justice or whether they primarily served the interests of a small, privileged elite. If the latter, how long did that situation persist?

It is not the permanence of situations but the rapidity and extent of change that dominates the chapter on punishment. For example, in the late-eighteenth century, execution or transportation (initially to America and then to Australia) were the norm for serious (and even minor) offences. Prisons were used sparingly, and then only to detain offenders before and after trial and to imprison debtors who could not pay their fines. By 1950, however, prison was used almost exclusively for all serious criminal cases. While the death penalty was not finally abolished until 1969, transportation had ended in the 1860s along with public executions, and the prison had long been the primary punishment inflicted by the courts. By the start of the twenty-first century, England and Wales would have their highest ever prison population – over 75,000 people. Historians, criminologists and social commentators have all debated these dramatic changes. They question whether the rise of the prison indicates a growth of 'humanitarianism', or just a switch to a different (but similarly severe) method of discipline. Was there a relationship between changing modes of punishment and the rise of industrial society and (later) the welfare state? When precisely did the 'rise of the prison' occur? Chapter 5 provides a basis for answering these questions by first outlining the extent of the changes in managing offenders before exploring why these changes took place.

The chapter on punishment marks the end of the first section on the workings of the criminal justice system. The second section of the book considers specific issues within the history of *crime* – such as the changing perceptions of criminality and the changing nature of crime over our period. How were criminals portrayed in society? How was criminality explained? Why was there a connection made between poverty and crime in this period?

Chapter 6 will discuss why and in which ways the putative 'site' of criminality changed over time. In the eighteenth century, criminality was related to a deficiency in morality. Criminals were seen as simply too greedy or lazy to control their most base desires, as individuals who *chose* to steal rather than earning money through honest work. Those who did not work, or who worked in low-earning occupations, were associated with crime, but the role of poverty in engendering crime often went unacknowledged. By the turn of the twentieth century, however, this view of crime as a 'choice' taken by rational individuals had declined. Instead, early criminologists, psychologists and social commentators had shifted towards the view that crime was often the product of either inbuilt hereditary deficiencies, or the exhausting and degrading urban environment in which much of the population now lived. This change in turn altered the dominant perceptions of criminals themselves, and this chapter will initially consider the different ways in which criminals and criminality were conceptualized and represented. It will question why some groups (particularly among the poor) were often perceived to be inherently 'criminal', while certain types of middle-class ('white-collar') crime were often virtually ignored. It will then propose some broad explanations for the changes which took place in the way criminals were viewed during the nineteenth century, and consider the input of popular culture, scientific debate and crime fiction. Finally, an overview of the interactions between changing perceptions of criminals and the evolution of Victorian penal policy will be provided. The following chapter will also question perceptions of criminals, this time with regard to age and gender.

From 1750 to today, men have always formed the vast majority of offenders. Indeed Home Office figures published in 2004 suggest that men are responsible for 80 per cent of recorded crime, and that one-third of men will have a conviction by their thirtieth birthday (this does not include motoring offences). The history of offending has therefore tended to be a history of *male* offending. Chapter 7 examines the criminological 'others' – women and children – and shows how expectations about behaviour and the 'natural' character of women underpinned penal reactions towards 'deviant' women and children. In addition to considering the 'reality' of juvenile and female offending, therefore, this chapter will also discuss how conceptions of 'respectable femininity' and 'ideal childhood' conditioned criminal justice responses. It will question whether the propensity or opportunity of women and children to commit crime affected prosecution figures, or the way that offending women and children were policed and punished. These issues are critical because the differential treatment they received throws light not only on conceptions of female and child criminals, but on the status of all women and children in society and how their positions have changed over time.

Some of the most important and interesting questions that we can ask about ourselves involve 'violence'. Chapter 8 discusses whether levels of violence have changed over time, and examines how we might go about answering that question. The media and older generations of society constantly tell us that violent crime and public disorder are now much higher than they were at some (usually undefined) point in the past. We are also familiar with historical reconstructions of Victorian streets where murderers lurk around every murky fog-laden London street corner. Neither myths of a putative 'golden age' in the 'peaceable kingdom' nor media depictions (past and present) of ever-escalating social violence seem entirely convincing or particularly analytical. This chapter will take a more rigorous approach – firstly considering the statistics of violent crime from 1857 (when annual statistical measures started) through to 1950 and asking when the figures rose or fell. Then it will question the reliability of those statistics and investigate what alternatives there are to governmental statistics.

After discussing whether the level of violence in society has changed, it will discuss whether the 'meaning' of violence has also changed. Despite queries about the accuracy of the statistics of murder and assault, the changing amounts of prosecuted violence are often used to suggest that societal attitudes have also shifted considerably since the Victorian period. This chapter will explore what these changes might be and how they were brought about, and offers a critical view of the apparent decline and subsequent rise in violence over the last hundred years. The efficacy of using different statistical and qualitative measures of crime will again be raised in Chapter 9. However, this chapter will mainly deal with the use of criminal law in private spaces and the use of the criminal code against employees (taking the example of Worsted Act prosecutions against textile factory workers).

The workplace has long been a battleground between the rights of custom and tradition and the rights of property. The 'rights' of workers to work at their own pace, take home waste material and have some autonomy over the conditions of their employment have been gradually eroded from the eighteenth century onwards. The introduction of the factory system has been seen as a key weapon in the employers' fight to control workers in their employ. In the eighteenth and nineteenth centuries, the workplace proved the battleground for the conceptual battle between the entitlements granted to employees by custom and tradition, and the rights of property enjoyed by employers. This chapter therefore describes how employers tried to limit and eradicate the workers' traditional entitlement to 'appropriate' waste materials created in manufacture using legislation (particularly the 1777 Worsted Acts) and changes in the organization of work (particularly the factory system). In particular it focuses on the possibilities that this new system of production offered employers for increased powers of surveillance over workers. Lastly, the chapter will briefly discuss the general rise of surveillance in society, and pose the question 'are we now living in a "Big Brother" society and, if so, how and when did that come about?'

Note

1. The new 'science' of criminology has done much to increase attention on crime and criminality. Criminology itself has a history which stretches back to the late nineteenth century – building on classical approaches, and leading to positivism, and biological determinism (see Garland 2002: 7–50). As the 'science' became more sophisticated and developed more nuanced and less crude theories to explain crime, some authors began to chart its progress (and still do). This is, of course, a different thing from a history of crime. Crime history attempts to understand the processes and interactions between how people perceived crime and its impact at particular moments in history, how it was represented in sources of information such as newspapers, how the authorities reacted, and what changed over time. Nevertheless, the history of crime and the history of criminology interact with each other and should be studied in tandem.

Further reading

The references for this chapter can be found in the Bibliography at the back of the book. If you wish to pursue this topic, however, below is a list of publications which could be consulted.

Innes, J. and Styles, J. (1986) 'The crime wave: recent writing on crime and criminal justice in eighteenth-century England', *Journal of British Studies*, 25, 4, October, pp. 380–435.

Monkkonen, E. (2002) *Crime, Justice, History*. Columbus, OH: Ohio State University.

Philips, D. (1983) 'A just measure of crime, authority, hunters and blue locusts: the "revisionist" social history of crime and the law in Britain 1780–1850', in S. Cohen and A. Scull (eds), *Social Control and the State*. Oxford: Robertson, pp. 50–74.

Pratt, J. (2002) *Punishment and Civilization. Penal Tolerance and Intolerance in Modern Society*. London: Sage.

Sheldon, R.G. (2001) *Controlling the Dangerous Classes. A Critical Introduction to the History of Criminal Justice*. Boston: Allyn & Bacon.

Part 1 Institutions and Processes

2. The development of policing, 1750–1950

Introduction

The development of policing in England from 1750 can be roughly divided into three phases. Initially, from 1750 up to about 1850, what has become known as the 'old' police was in operation. This was a system of amateur or semi-professional parish constables and nightwatchmen. While reputedly ineffective at enforcing legislation, this system actually worked remarkably well in many places. Then, in the latter half of the nineteenth century, following the setting up of the Metropolitan Police in 1829, a more consistently professional system – the so-called New Police – was developed. This featured uniformed officers, a hierarchy of ranks, and a pattern of operation based on patrol and prevention. It took almost thirty years of experimentation to consolidate this new style of policing, and there have been numerous debates about its purpose among historians. Some argue that it was a rational response to rising crime in rapidly growing cities, while others claim that it was in fact a tool via which the middle classes ensured the sanctity of their newly earned property, and point to its 'social control' function. By 1870, however, the new system was firmly established. Following a period of social turbulence in the 1880s, what has often popularly been conceived of as a 'golden age' of policing began, which lasted from about 1890 to around 1950. Yet police forces went through many further changes during this period, too, and arguments with the Home Office over centralization, often violent clashes with demonstrators and pickets, and disputes over pay were at least as typical as the amiable approach of *Dixon of Dock Green* (a long-running TV series depicting a kind, fatherly and friendly policeman who was supported by all the law-abiding people on his beat).

Throughout the history of policing, therefore, there has been a marked divergence between the image and reality of policing – between what the police have been asked to do and the extent to which they have actually done this. This divergence in enforcement, and the nature of police discretion, is a key theme in current research into the history of policing. This chapter gives an account of the historical development of the English police, starting at a point (1750) where almost all its modern features had yet to appear, and will thus help you to think critically about the nature of enforcement. It will also introduce you to a specific academic debate over the development of the New

Police during the nineteenth century, and will debate whether any Golden Age of policing ever really existed.

Introductory reading

Emsley, C. (1996) *The English Police: A Political and Social History*. Harlow: Longman.

Gattrell, V. (1990) 'Crime, authority and the policeman-state', in F.M.L. Thompson (ed.), *The Cambridge Social History of Britain 1750–1950: Vol. 3 Social Agencies and Institutions*, Cambridge: Cambridge University Press, pp. 243–310.

Steedman, C. (1984) *Policing the Victorian Community: The Formation of English Provincial Police Forces, 1856–80*. London: Routledge.

Storch, R. and Philips, D. (1999) 'The wreck only of an ancient system', in *Policing Provincial England, 1829–1856: The Politics of Reform*. London: Leicester University Press, pp. 11–35.

The 'old' police

The 'old' police system, which operated until the middle of the nineteenth century, consisted of three elements: the rural and urban 'amateur parish constables', the (mainly urban) semi-professional or professional 'acting constables' and the urban 'watch forces'. This loose 'system' of policing had evolved gradually over a considerable period of time and was only gradually dismantled (under protest in some cases) during the nineteenth century. The 'old' police system varied considerably from area to area, however, and the different components (parish constables, acting constables and night watches) operated in very different ways. Hence, it is perhaps easiest to consider each element in turn.

The parish constable's authority derived from a large number of laws, some dating from the Middle Ages and many more from the seventeenth and eighteenth centuries. In theory he was an amateur – a free-born Englishman of the 'middling sort' carrying out a number of essential public duties. He was an expression of an ideology of government which saw a small, cheap national state as desirable and assigned essential administrative tasks whenever possible to local government. For example, the Select Committee on the Police of 1822 (investigating the possibility of police reform) concluded that:

> It is difficult to reconcile an effective system of police, with that perfect freedom of action and exemption from interference, which are the great privileges and blessings of society in this country; and Your Committee think that the forfeiture or curtailment of such advantages would be too great a sacrifice for improvements in police, of facilities in detection of crime, however desirable in themselves if abstractly considered.

Such sentiments clearly indicate a desire for minimal central interference in local affairs. The constable was under a form of supervision by the Justices of the Peace, who were in this period not merely the basic judicial authority, but also the main institution of local government when they met periodically in quarter sessions. This relationship was often a tense one, and thus has left a succession of orders and exhortations from magistrates for the parish constables to be more vigilant.

Parish constables were usually simply householders, picked every year to serve. In some cases the constable was selected by the vestry, the body elected by all the property-owners who ran the affairs of the parish. In others he was picked at the local baronial court leet, an annual assembly of the ratepayers. If he refused to serve, or to find a substitute willing to take his place, he could be prosecuted and fined. He had a responsibility, through his powers of arrest and entry, to assist in the working of the criminal law, but his job also involved administrative tasks such as preparing the militia lists, fixing the rates for billeting soldiers and moving paupers through the parish.

When it came to coercion, the parish constable had a variety of powers, but most of these depended on the specific offence that he was dealing with. For example, in the case of vagrants he was empowered to arrest them and convey them to a magistrate. If a witness could be found who was prepared to go to a magistrate and swear that the constable had failed to apprehend a vagrant, he was subject to a fine of ten shillings for dereliction of his duty. In felony cases he had wider powers. He could enter houses to search for suspects, stop, search and arrest if he thought that a serious crime had been committed. 'Felony' in the late eighteenth century consisted of the crimes of theft, robbery and burglary, murder and attempted murder, rape, and other offences involving the stealing of property or serious violence. Assault was not a felony but fell into the category of misdemeanour. The constable could only arrest for an assault if he saw it committed: otherwise his role was to advise the victim or their friends to get a warrant against the perpetrator from the justices. He did have power to intervene if he thought there was likely to be a breach of the peace.

Constables were obliged to serve all kinds of justices' warrants, for non-payment of rates or failure to perform legally mandated duties, as well as for criminal offences. In most cases their power was derivative: the initiative lay with the private citizen. The constable mainly acted when called upon: he would chase up cases of theft, arrest suspects or receive them into custody, take them before the magistrates and collect evidence for the prosecution, but it was up to the victim to ask him to do so and to promise to reimburse his expenses.

In the main, the system seems to have worked adequately (Morgan and Rushton 1998: 29). However, the rural constable, alone in his community and knowing that he would need to live and trade there as a private citizen after his term of office was over, could find it difficult to enforce legislation dealing with 'victimless crimes'. He certainly tended to turn a blind eye to laws against drunkenness and swearing. Some constables even connived in 'social crimes' – like the rural constable in Devon who recorded in his diary how he took part in smuggling trips during his year in office (Sayers 1997: 24–6). But the pattern of authority and work revealed by this man – Michael Evans – is complex. On one single day in 1836, he bought a bottle of smuggled brandy, took part in an unpopular eviction and suffered community disapproval for it, and helped to investigate a theft. He also applied himself to his day-job as a tailor. So here we have a man who was quite capable of conniving at some illegal activity that had community support, but was in other contexts quite willing to uphold the letter of the law even if it led to his unpopularity. It is difficult, therefore, to label this one man – let alone the whole institution – as 'efficient' or 'inefficient'.

Not all constables were 'amateur', however. Let us now consider the semi-professional or professional 'acting constables'. Often, the job of constable was taken year after year by the same man, who used the income from fees to supplement his trade at another occupation. In this way, as John Beattie has shown (2001: 151), he would be in a position to gain expertise as a constable over the years. In many towns there was too much business for the average householder to perform the duties adequately – especially if he did not want to neglect his day job while he was occupied with it. But business also meant rewards and expenses: enough income to maintain a number of constables. The rewards of thief-taking could be large: there were statutory rewards of up to one hundred pounds given out for the conviction of robbers in London. So if the same man volunteered as substitute every time, the post of constable could become full-time. Some of these men were the subject of accusations that they operated rackets for their own benefit, notably allowing young thieves to get away with crime until they were old and reckless enough to commit a capital crime, in which case the thief-taker would arrest them, prosecute them and earn a large reward when they were executed. One such thief-taker, the notorious Jonathan Wild, while highly successful at recovering stolen property also became a major receiver and was eventually executed for this in 1725.

These men were called 'acting constables' to distinguish them from the 'constable', which became an honorary post for a member of the middle classes. Often they were attended by assistant constables. Acting constables were men of some standing who had to be literate and trustworthy. Their assistants could only succeed them if they were literate; if not, they had to stay as 'runner' to another man once their masters retired.

In the early nineteenth century, the acting constables of the large towns in England were powerful men. They could and did travel round the country in search of stolen property. Joseph Nadin, who acted in Manchester during the early years of the nineteenth century and was in charge at the Peterloo Massacre of 1818, was reputed to be one of the most powerful men in the town. It is hard to estimate exactly how much they earned, but it is likely that their income put them in the class of respectable tradesmen. When Sheffield created a new police force in 1843, the town took on its two acting constables as officers to serve warrants for the magistrates. Their salary replaced their fee income: it was £150 a year, over three times what a policeman got, and only one hundred pounds less than the head of Sheffield's new police.

Aside from the two types of constable discussed above, the final element of the 'old' police system was the night watch. Watch forces were an exclusively urban phenomenon. They were financed by a tax on the wealthy inhabitants of a particular limited area, and generally they were controlled by a committee elected from these ratepayers or from a subsection of them. Their job was to patrol the streets of their area, from a fixed box, often taking turns to stand still while their mate walked the rounds. They had more limited powers of arrest than constables, restricted to apprehending suspicious 'night walkers'.

Many called the hour of the night to announce their arrival; in some places they alternated calling – thus acting as a deterrent – with walking their beats silently so as not to warn malefactors of their approach. Especially before the arrival of gas light in the early years of the nineteenth century, English towns generally had an informal curfew even when the old seventeenth-century curfew laws were no longer enforced. Chester, for example, bolted the doors to the city walls every night at nine o'clock up until 1914. If a watchman encountered anyone on the streets after dark, the onus was on the stranger to prove his business or he would be searched as a matter of course for stolen property.

Watchmen were potentially the weak link in the chain of the old police. It was hard to make a decent living on their wages, and correspondingly difficult to attract able-bodied men. On the other hand, it provided steady employment in an age where most jobs of work were highly susceptible to fluctuations in the economy. Night watches were no pushover. There are documented cases of the City of London's Watch getting involved in fights with would-be burglars, robbers and thieves on the streets. In 1820s Sheffield, the approach of the watch often scared off miscreants, and they were regularly willing to risk injuries to make arrests (as the following extract demonstrates).

A stereotypical depiction of a night-watchman. In fact, watchmen were reasonably effective at preventing crime in some towns and cities.
Source: The Police Journal, Vol. V, 1932.

A person by the name of Monk was stopped by two men in Garden Street on Saturday night last, who took his neckcloth off, and attempted to cut his throat; but on hearing the approach of the watchmen, they decamped, after robbing him of a few shillings, and otherwise ill-using him. (*Sheffield and Rotherham Independent*, 14 October 1820)

By the end of the eighteenth century, many watch forces had become highly sophisticated. Elaine Reynolds (1998: 63, 120) has shown that the Marylebone Watch, in northern Westminster, introduced a three-tier command structure in 1775, a uniform and a system of beats. It served as a starting point for the plan for Peel's Metropolitan Police. The beginning of our period saw the creation of a variety of small forces of constables in London. These followed the model of the professional 'thief-taking' constable, but they were created by laws that put them under the direct control of stipendiary magistrates – full-time paid magistrates, appointed by the government. The pioneers were the Bow Street Runners, created in the 1750s on the initiative of the novelist and magistrate Henry Fielding. These men followed the money: they were often sent outside London on errands for the rich – up to and including the monarch – who needed police services to be performed for whatever reason. In 1792 a group of police offices on the Bow Street model, each under the control of a full-time paid magistrate, was created covering much of London's suburbs.

In summary, it is important to realize that the 'old' police were by no means a uniform institution. Parish constables in highly populated areas had a chance to make a good living at their job, once fees and rewards were taken into account. On the other hand, they did not have a guaranteed steady income. This may have led to a rather 'entrepreneurial' approach to crime-fighting. The night watch did receive a wage, but it was rather a poor one. Hence, they may well have been less willing to act on their own initiative and more willing simply to do the minimum required of them. Overall, the 'old' police appear to have been reasonably good at catching criminals and reasonably good at patrolling the streets at night. However, they were not very effective at dealing with public disorder and were very bad at imposing legislation which did not have public support (such as anti-smuggling laws). In such instances, a 'live and let live' approach was very much the order of the day. It should also be noted that this survey has only considered the constituent parts of what might be called the 'official' police system. There were, of course, other private police agencies, usually concerned with the regulation of trade and industry. Some of these, such as the Worsted Inspectorate, are discussed in Chapter 9.

The transition to the New Police

As we have seen, the 'old' police were probably quite good at enforcing some types of legislation, and less good at implementing other types. However, from the end of the eighteenth century, many people were condemning the old police system as inadequate. For example, the magistrate and police commentator Patrick Colquhoun, in his widely-read *Treatise on the Police of the Metropolis* (1800: 107) argued that night watches were 'without energy, disjointed, and governed by almost as many Acts of Parliament, as there are Parishes, Hamlets, Liberties and Precincts'. He believed that:

> Watchmen and Patroles, instead of being, as now, comparatively of little use, from their *age, infirmity, inability, inattention,* or *corrupt practices,* might almost at the present expense, by a proper selection, and a more correct mode of discipline, by means of a general superintendence over the whole to regulate their conduct, and keep them to their duty, be rendered of great utility in preventing Crimes, and in detecting Offenders.

Criticism intensified during the early part of the nineteenth century, and eventually led to a variety of Royal Commissions and Acts of Parliament which established the New Police – a shorthand term used by historians to signify a markedly different approach to the control of crime and the regulation of society. The New Police were greater in number than the old police, were uniformed and were supposedly both more efficient and more professional than their eighteenth-century counterparts. Essentially, they evolved into the police we know today. But the various New Police forces were often very dissimilar from one another. Initially, the development of new forms of policing was marked by contesting visions of appropriate duties and by a tussle between local and national authorities as to who should control these new forces. Subsequently, the relative effectiveness of the New Police has been the subject of very different interpretations by historians.

The first step in the construction of the New Police was the establishment of the Metropolitan Police in 1829. Sir Robert Peel had become Home Secretary in 1822 and, partly reacting to concerns over radical demonstrations, argued the need for a new 'vigorous system of police'. At this stage many, even within the establishment, were concerned that this would lead to the development of a centralized 'state' police (such as was perceived to exist on the Continent). However, Peel handled the political dangers of this sensitive topic very skilfully. As David Philips (1980: 186) has noted, Peel took care 'to conceal the fact that he had already made up his mind about the form the reform should take'. He made shrewd use of crime statistics, newly available for the first time, which appeared to show a tide of rising criminality. Taking the seven-year periods 1811 to 1818 and 1821 to 1828, he had figures to show a population increase of 19 per cent in London and Middlesex, but an increase in crime of 55 per cent. Although the validity of these statistics was probably minimal, in 1829 the Metropolitan Police Improvement Bill was passed and 3,000 uniformed constables replaced the various local watch forces and took to their beats. Initially there was a period of confusion, as the new and the old forces worked in parallel. Then, the Metropolitan Police Bill of 1839 transformed the old police offices into police courts and offered the remaining Bow Street patrolmen the opportunity of transferring into the Metropolitan Police. However, throughout the 1830s there had been vociferous criticism of Peel's new force, and this by no means abated in 1839. Many commentators felt the uniforms of the new police betrayed their essentially 'military' character, associating them with the gendarmeries of the Continent which were seen to serve political ends. Others griped at the cost of the new system, which was more expensive than the old but which still had to be paid for out of the rates.

Moreover, a new kind of permanent police force in the provinces was to prove much harder to accomplish, due largely to a marked aversion to central government interference on the part of regional authorities. Many towns had been reforming their police piecemeal before the Act of 1835 that obliged them to set up a police force. There was still concern over a perceived rise in crime in the countryside, as is perhaps evidenced by the increase in private prosecution societies (Philips 1989: 113–70). The Luddite disturbances of 1811–12 also acted to fuel fears of rural unrest. As Philips (1980: 180) notes, such events 'caused men of property to think more favourably of a strong police force which might protect their persons and property from such attacks', and some counties thus began their own initiatives, usually based on an extension of the old system of policing.

Then, in 1836, the Home Secretary Lord Russell agreed to Sir Edwin Chadwick's requests for a Royal Commission to investigate rural policing. Chadwick, a disciple of Jeremy Bentham, was always keen to extend the influence of central government. He unhesitatingly asked leading questions and distorted the evidence presented to the Commission (Storch and Philips 1999: 111–35). Drawn from anecdotal materials, and ignoring the detailed evidence presented concerning policing experiments in various parts of the country, the Commission's report was damning about the quality of policing in rural England. However, due to the delicate nature of the central/regional power balance, the Rural Constabulary Act of 1839 omitted most of the Commission's more contentious centralizing recommendations. It left the decision to establish a rural police and the control of that police in the hands of the county magistrates, although that year the government did take control out of the hands of local authorities in three large industrial cities: Birmingham, Bolton and Manchester. Thus, as Emsley (1996: 43) notes, 'as the 1840s dawned there was still no single model of policing dominant in England'.

In fact, wrangling continued even as late as the 1850s, when not only was there still a variety of different models, there were still local authorities who had yet to set up any new provision at all (Hart 1955). Thus, in the mid-1850s, more legislation was drawn up with the aim of ending the consolidation of traditional systems of policing. Home Secretary Lord Palmerston was the driving force behind the 1853 Select Committee appointed to consider the issue. Again, as in 1839, the Committee was far from open-minded. It recommended a more centralized system, with closer contact between Chief Constables and the Home Office, and some amalgamations of the small towns. Resistance to this was again strong, and hence the new bill introduced by Grey in 1856 was designed 'to provide an efficient police force, for both counties and boroughs, *as is possible under the existing system of local management*'. Local control was retained, but the establishment of a force was made mandatory, and a degree of central influence was secured by the appointment of three Inspectors who would authorize a quarter of the authority's police costs to be met from central funds if they were satisfied with the force's efficiency.

Even after 1856, policing in England was subject to change and development. Certainly, as Carolyn Steedman (1984) has shown, it would be wrong to interpret the evolution of the New Police as merely the gradual export of an urban-metropolitan model to the provinces. However, by the late-1850s the main contours of the new system were in place. Yet to know this is only half the story – many more important questions remain. Why had this new system been deemed necessary at this particular time? What role did the New Police serve? These are questions to which different historians have provided very different answers.

Initially, twentieth-century historians considering issues of crime and policing accepted fairly uncritically the ideas in vogue at the beginning of the nineteenth century. They accepted that crime *had* been rising at an alarming level, that the old system of police *had* been unable to cope and that the more efficient New Police *had* eventually reversed this situation. Many of these early accounts of the New Police were written by ex-officers and they produced an uncritical, linear account in which the development of the New Police was viewed as 'progressive' (because it was seen to lead to our contemporary system, which they believed to be excellent), and in which those who opposed it were by implication 'regressive', myopic and foolish. This interpretation has subsequently been labelled the 'Whig' view of policing.[1]

Charles Reith (1943: 3), for example, claimed that:

In the eighteenth century orderliness in London was almost non-existent, and its endurance in other areas was unreliable. This period and that of the early decades of the nineteenth century are notorious for the absence of public order. [...] It is an unquestionable historical fact that the appearance of public orderliness in Britain, and of individual willingness to co-operate in securing and maintaining it, coincides with the successful establishment of the police institution which was inaugurated experimentally in London, in 1839, and was copied throughout the entire area of the country, and of the empire, in the short space of thirty years.

Similarly, T. A. Critchley (1967: 22) argued that the early nineteenth century was a period in which there had been a 'danger of a total relapse into barbarity' (due to the corruption of the old constables and the social and economic upheaval of the eighteenth century), which was only averted by the far-sightedness of police reformers such as Henry Fielding, Patrick Colquhoun and Sir Robert Peel.

However, there are many problems with this interpretation of events. Firstly, there is no real way of measuring whether crime and disorder were actually rising in England immediately prior to the creation of the Metropolitan Police. Certainly, there was a widespread fear of crime, but this is rather different from proving that crime was actually on the increase. Secondly, these 'Whig' historians fell into the trap of accepting the distorted reports of the nineteenth-century Royal Commissions. For example, one of the questions asked by the 1839 Commission was 'To what causes do you ascribe the failure to bring offenders to justice; and have such failures been ascribable in any cases to the inefficiency of the constables?' This is clearly a leading question, as it assumed, in advance of any evidence, that there had been such a failure.

During the 1970s, an alternative interpretation of the New Police, inspired by Marxist theory, was formulated. This has subsequently been termed the 'revisionist view' of policing. Put simply, the revisionists argued that the way in which societies develop is not determined by consensus (by what is best for everyone) but by class conflict. In other words, those with power in society arrange things to suit themselves. Thus, according to the revisionists, the New Police were established essentially for purposes of control and surveillance in a society experiencing the upheavals of massive economic change and the need for a more compliant workforce.

Robert Storch (1976: 481), for example, argued that the New Police did far more than prevent and fight crime, claiming that

> The police had a broader mission in the nineteenth century, however, to act as an all-purpose lever of urban discipline. The imposition of the police brought the arm of municipal and state authority directly to bear upon key institutions of daily life in working-class neighbourhoods, touching off a running battle with local custom and popular culture which lasted at least until the end of the century [...] the monitoring and control of the streets, pubs, racecourses, wakes, and popular fêtes was a daily function of the new police [...] In the northern industrial towns of England these police functions must be viewed as a direct complement to the attempts of urban middle-class elites – by means of educational, temperance, and recreational reform – to mould a labouring class amenable to new disciplines of both work and leisure [...] In this respect the policeman was perhaps every bit as important a 'domestic missionary' as the earnest and often sympathetic men high-minded Unitarians dispatched into darkest Leeds or Manchester in the 1830s and 1840s.

It is certainly true that a whole host of non-criminal activities was brought under police control during the nineteenth century, from street-trading to fairs, from common lodging houses to licensing legislation. Revisionist historians argued that the police thus did far more than catch criminals, and that these extra activities were part of a drive to mould the behaviour of the working classes, to render them malleable and docile.

In some ways this revisionist view is more convincing than the Whig interpretation outlined above, but it still suffers from numerous problems. Firstly, if the police were established to control the new working class, why were they first established in London, since this was not an industrial centre in the new sense, like Manchester or Oldham? Moreover, the revisionists, like the Whig historians before them, underplayed the extent of resistance to the development of the New Police. If they were there for the benefit of the propertied classes, why were there so many complaints from county magistrates and ratepayers about the cost of the new system? Finally, it can be argued that this interpretation omits any notion of police discretion. Recent research on the origins of police officers shows that many of them in fact had working-class backgrounds, and hence had a degree of sympathy and tolerance for those living in the poor areas they policed (Emsley and Clapson 1994; Lawrence 2000).

Thus any interpretation of the New Police which attempts to provide a single coherent explanation for this development is bound to prove unconvincing. Current historical research tends to emphasize the contingent and multifaceted nature of the new police, building on some elements from both 'Whig' and 'revisionist' histories. On the one hand, it is not hard to argue that the massive explosion of industrial capitalism during the nineteenth century would eventually have required a more structured and regulated police force than previously existed. Moreover, some historians do contend that crime statistics (when viewed critically) do show an overall rise and then a decline over the course of the nineteenth century, seeming perhaps to indicate the success of the New Police in preventing and controlling crime. On the other hand, it is also certainly true that the New Police were initially resented by the working classes, and that violence both against, and on the part of, the police was often a feature of policing during the mid-nineteenth century.

During recent years, more historians have looked at the first few years of the new police forces, and the last few years of the 'old' police systems which it replaced. They have reached conclusions which are very different from the accepted view which was advanced by most traditional writers on the early years of the New Police. By looking at accounts, report books and other surviving records from 'old' police forces, they have come to the conclusion that most of them were reasonably efficient and popular. Many have recently advanced the idea that the new system of policing developed in the nineteenth century was not actually such a break with the past as had previously been thought, and that the much-vaunted 'professionalism' of the New Police existed more in their image than as reality. Elaine Reynolds (1998: 164), among others, notes that:

> When we combine our better understanding of the elements, process, personnel, and motivations that were involved in police reform in London during the whole period from 1735 to 1829, it becomes clear that Robert Peel's reform in 1829 was not revolutionary. It rationalized and extended but did not alter existing practices. Centralization, by 1829, seemed logical and worth attempting. The change was carried out with the input and cooperation of local authorities, although not all were confident as to its benefits. The new police took on the functions of the old and did them in much the same fashion, drawing on the experience and expertise of the parish watch system. Many of the people who staffed the new police had staffed the parochial police. The continuity, then, between the 'Charlies' of the night watch and the 'bobbies' of the Metropolitan Police may help to explain the relatively rapid acceptance of the new force.

What is undeniable, however, is that by the final quarter of the nineteenth century, 'both the idea and experience of policing had undergone a dramatic transformation from what had been (and had been accepted as) the norm in the 1820s' (Storch and Philips 1999). What has subsequently been popularly perceived as a 'golden age' of policing had begun.

A golden age of policing?

In 1900 the Radical Independent MP John Burns said: 'I believe that the Metropolitan Police, after the City [of London] police, are the best police force in the world' (Emsley 1993: 124). This view persisted in many quarters of British society – not least in the self-image of the police themselves – until at least the 1950s. The works of the rather uncritical historians, like Critchley, discussed above, meant the idea still has currency today. The idea of a 'golden age' of policing, when the public fully supported a professional and efficient police service which did its best to enforce legislation fairly and equally, is seductive. Television programmes such as *Heartbeat* (in fact set in the 1960s but in a provincial part of England that suggests earlier times) demonstrate that this notion is still prevalent today. Despite this comfortable image, however, the police underwent a range of significant changes during the period spanning the end of the nineteenth century and the first half of

Metropolitan Police marching to work. It was common practice during the nineteenth century to parade through the streets dropping constables off at their beats, thus reinforcing the authority of the police.
Source: European Centre for the Study of Policing Archive, The Open University.

the twentieth. For example, police corruption had a profound impact on the organization of police forces in England and Wales. The two world wars produced challenges leading to significant changes such as the introduction of female police officers. Public order issues surrounding the policing of fascist and anti-fascist demonstrations called police impartiality into question. Despite the persistence of views of a golden age, tensions and confrontations (both internal and external) which marked the police service in this period are at least as typical as the image of a friendly bobby on the beat.

With the notable exception of the Metropolitan Police, jurisdiction over police affairs remained largely a local affair and was jealously guarded. The period 1870–1950 was characterized by an increased centralization of government, but in the matter of policing the municipalities were able to resist this process – at least until 1964. Centralization had been a desire of the Home Office since the very beginning of the police and the debate had re-emerged at regular intervals throughout the nineteenth century. But it was largely through the police that the boroughs were able to exercise genuine control over the public spaces and even on occasions the private affairs of those living, trading or working in the area. The police were an effective means of controlling the free flow of the highway, either facilitating or hampering trade as desired and many police powers and practices reflected the exigencies and concerns of local trade and commerce. Morality was also regulated through the police by enforcing laws that restricted or banned gambling, drinking or keeping brothels. A less tangible reason for the retention of local control was its symbolic significance and police uniforms often bore unique insignia to reflect the identity of the borough to which they belonged. The true autonomy of the boroughs, though, was compromised by financial considerations. The Police (Expenses) Act of 1874 allowed for half the cost of police wages to be met by the exchequer, but this was conditional on boroughs keeping a force of an approved strength. Although much lower than desired most seem to have been able to accommodate this. Boroughs wishing to avoid this indirect control could do so only by increasing the rates and raising money locally.

The most serious threat to local control came in 1914. The First World War brought wide-ranging centralization of British society as the government took control of raw materials, the means of production and human resources. It signalled a shift in relations between central and local government that would see the ascendancy of the former. The police were not immune from this process and local borough watch committees could be dispensed with and their forces amalgamated with county forces – all for the sake of increased efficiency. Many of the incursions of central government were retained after 1918, but formal control of the police was returned to its pre-war status. However, the precedent had been established and served to clarify Home Office planning. Moreover, tussles over who should control police forces were not the only challenges produced by the war.

The war itself had resulted in extra responsibilities for the police. Firstly, national security issues such as the threat of espionage, the monitoring and arrest of aliens, the 'threat' of pacifist agitation or conscientious objectors and implementing the requirements of the Defence of the Realm Act (DORA) all redefined the police role as national rather than local. For example, Special

Branch (originally set up to counter Irish Fenian activities and later involved in monitoring suffragettes) was requested by the War Office to monitor the personal advertisements in the *Times* newspaper because it was widely believed that spies were using these to pass cryptic messages about troop and ship movements. For the majority, though, there was probably little change in routine. Police were required to act in support of the armed forces by visiting the home addresses of deserters and pass them to the military authorities for trial. A number of men who had successfully deserted the front and made it home were transported back to France or Belgium to be executed by their army comrades.

The war also brought about the 'dilution' of the workforce – topping up by untrained, or at least less trained, staff covered for those who had enlisted. For the police this meant replacing male officers with women and greater use of the part-time Special Constabulary. In this respect the police were little different to most other workers who tended to resent the arrival among them of relatively untrained personnel. Special Constables were initially issued with armbands to wear on their civilian clothing to denote their status. But this resulted in an unfortunate incident in London's East End when, during the anti-German riots that followed the sinking of the *Lusitania* in 1915, a number of 'Specials' found themselves on the receiving end of regular officers' truncheons. Henceforth they were issued with proper uniforms so that they could be more readily identified in a crowd.

Once fears of a German invasion had died down the most serious threat to national security was thought to be the rise of Bolshevism. The monitoring of suspected Bolshevik agents was carried out by a select few police officers. Industrial unrest was often blamed on communist agitators whose role was usually exaggerated by the government, but the policing of these disputes could also have a damaging effect on the relationship between police and workers. Arguably, though, the most important development of the war for the police was the increased membership of its own union, which had been formed prior to the First World War. This contributed to the police strikes in 1918 and 1919. On 31 August 1918 12,000 police officers went on strike over the non-recognition of the newly formed Police and Prison Officers Union as well as demands for a £1 a week pay rise and a 12 per cent war bonus and to protest at the dismissal of a union official. The dispute was only resolved when the Prime Minister, Lloyd-George, intervened.

Lingering discontent over pay and conditions and union recognition were the main causes of the strikes by police in London and Liverpool in 1919. These resulted in the setting up of the Desborough Committee. Under the 1919 Police Act police trade unions were prohibited and the Police Federation set up to safeguard members' interests. Significantly, the Home Secretary was given powers to make police pay and conditions the same across the country. The Act simultaneously removed the police from the sphere of labour relations and dealt a blow to local control of the police when responsibility for pay and conditions was centralized. During the 1920s the Home Office also began to intervene in the appointment of Chief Constables.

Further threats to this autonomy followed with the prospect of Labour-controlled local authorities. In Monmouthshire and St Helens disputes between

Labour authorities and their Chief Constables were settled by the Home Office, which sided with the Chief Constables on both occasions. The need for an independent and professional police service had never appeared greater. Local executive control of the police was castigated as political and open to abuse. Sir John Anderson, Home Office Permanent Secretary expressed this view forcefully in 1928 when he declared that 'the policeman is nobody's servant. He is not appointed merely as an agent of some higher authority' (Anderson 1929: 192).

It is difficult to measure how this affected policing itself or the impartiality of 'the bobby on the beat', but deployment at industrial disputes during this period often resulted in the police acting in the interests of the state. Strikes (including the General Strike of 1926), marches and demonstrations in London, and the often violent struggles between different political movements were a problematic issue for the police who were commonly seen as a repressive tool of the state during this period. A march to Downing Street in 1920 by unemployed London ex-servicemen was the first serious test for the Metropolitan Police. It earned them much criticism and resentment. A baton charge into the crowd by mounted police was described by the (Labour-supporting) *Daily Herald* as 'charging up and down Whitehall running down and clubbing men, women and children'. The response of the police to the 'Hunger Marches' of the early 1930s perpetuated this friction and, during 1931 alone, more than 30 British towns and cities experienced serious battles between police and unemployed demonstrators. Calls for investigation into police actions were often brushed aside by both government and police who argued that actions were justified and there was no case to answer.

However, it was the clashes between fascist and anti-fascist agitators in the 1930s which provided the police with their most decisive test, upon which historians have written extensively. Sir Oswald Mosley formed the British Union of Fascists in 1932. While never coming close to matching the political upheaval created by fascism in Italy and Germany, they were at the centre of some of the worst political violence in Britain in the twentieth century, and were a key factor in the introduction of the 1936 Public Order Act. Wearing distinctive uniforms, Mosley's fascists organized huge meetings where inflammatory anti-communist and anti-Semitic speeches were given. Violence often broke out both inside and outside the venues as communist and anti-fascist activists tried to disrupt proceedings. Some historians, such as Robert Benewick (1969) have argued that, because the fascists wore uniforms and marched to and from their meetings in an orderly fashion, the police were inclined to treat them leniently. Others, such as Barbara Weinberger (1991, 1995), have added that the police were biased against the political left, deeply distrusted communists and acted harshly against them. Other historians (such as Robert Skidelsky 1990) have argued that the police were in fact merely 'pro-police' – aiming to retain control of the streets with the minimum possible violence. This is a complex debate for which there is not space here. It is certain, however, that during this period the police were often unable to control the huge public demonstrations of the time without resorting to violent, authoritarian tactics. Clearly, however, the notion that policing during the period to 1950 was characterized solely by the cheerful 'bobby on the beat' is erroneous.

The outbreak of the Second World War once again placed additional strains on the police. Added to the duties that had characterized policing during the First World War was the considerable extra burden caused by German air raids, including the threat of gas attacks. Broadly speaking, the police benefited from an increase in public esteem and an enhanced self-image because of the role they performed in connection with air raids. They were also the first point of contact for the bereaved, for those searching for missing relatives or for families made homeless. There were also factors that might have lowered public esteem such as the role played by the police in suppressing industrial disputes (which increased during the war) and monitoring unpopular rationing laws. In particular, enforcing restrictions on petrol supplies brought the police into conflict with the motoring middle class. Nevertheless, public opinion surveys conducted at the end of the war indicate a highly positive attitude towards the police. The wartime role and the experiences of police and public alike between 1939 and 1945 did much to shape the image of the English 'bobby' personified in the character of George Dixon in the film *The Blue Lamp* (1950) and later resurrected in the television series *Dixon of Dock Green*.

The manpower problems of the Second World War had been met by calling on reserves, including police pensioners, 'Specials' and women. The war also brought into sharp focus the problems of coordination and efficiency. With no clear lines of demarcation to establish areas of responsibility and jurisdiction between various agencies the police often found themselves in conflict with the Air Raid Warden and the Home Guard – a situation the Home Office failed to resolve. Women first entered the police during the First World War via a number of competing organizations that grew out of various trends in the suffragette movement. The one that was acceptable to the authorities was the Voluntary Women's Patrols (VWP) which reflected the values of many women who volunteered for a job that one daily newspaper described as an occupation for 'gentlewomen'.

After the war many women police were axed in the public spending cuts. During the 1930s police forces could afford to be particularly choosy about recruits and most favoured the employment of men who, it was widely believed, could perform 'proper' policing tasks. As Louise Jackson has highlighted (2003), it was a persistent belief that women were only suited to welfare work within police forces. Despite this the Home Office did issue regulations in October 1931 to govern the employment of women police. This established a lower rate of pay and stipulated that only unmarried (or widowed) women between 22 and 35 could be so employed. The matter of employment and the nature of duties was left entirely at the discretion of Chief Constables. The Children and Young Persons Act 1933 required the attendance at court of a woman in cases involving children. While this opened the door a little wider it also established the nature of women police duties for the next forty years. With the notable exception of a few detectives in provincial forces such as Lancashire, women police were ascribed tasks that conformed to contemporary gender assumptions: cases involving women and children and being generally subservient to male officers by typing their reports.

The Second World War brought little change itself. However, the subsequent move towards professionalization resulted in a need to recruit more women after the war when their 'special' role, especially in relation to children, became more valued. In 1948 women were accepted into the Police Federation and the Home Office recognized the term 'police officer' rather than policeman or policewoman. Lifting the marriage ban in 1945, however, did little to attract women recruits and women police remained an unintegrated minority until the Sex Discrimination Act 1975 removed the formal basis for the bias against them.

Conclusion

A complex pattern of enforcement and discretion, change and permanence emerges when policing during the period 1750–1950 is considered. Certainly there were marked developments in the organization of policing in Britain over these two centuries, but it is an oversimplification to trace a line of 'progress' from the amateur patchwork of provision in 1750 to the recognizably 'modern' forces of the 1950s. Recent research has demonstrated that the 'old' police were remarkably effective in combating certain types of crime and that there was strong resistance to their replacement. Moreover, the difference in duties between 'old' and 'new' constables was (initially at least) not particularly marked. Equally, it might be argued that, despite changes in the organization and mechanisms of policing, the underlying 'purpose' of the police (to fight crime or to oppress the working class, depending on your point of view) has remained remarkably static. Certainly, the notion of a 'golden age' of consensual policing has now been discredited. Policing, even in the twentieth century, is defined by a mixture of compassion and repression, enforcement and tolerance. The mere existence of legislation means little on its own (unenforced legislation has scant social significance) and police officers have been, and continue to be, crucial in determining which aspects of the law get enforced rigorously and which social groups are the most closely policed.

Key questions

1. What were the principal differences between the 'old' and the New Police?

On one level, the differences between the older, more piecemeal systems of policing in operation up until 1829 (in London) and 1839/56 (in more provincial areas) seem easy to spot. It might be argued that the 'old' system of police was largely amateur in status. Constables were picked by their community to serve, and could be fined if they refused. They did not receive any professional training, and often their own judgement and character could shape the way they did the job. While professional law-enforcers (the so-called 'acting constables') did exist in many major towns, these were still often more involved with the recovery of private property than the maintenance of civil order. By contrast, the New Police have been depicted as uniformed professionals, received rudimentary training, had a strict set of instructions to follow and got involved in the 'policing' of a much wider range of issues.

However, while perhaps broadly true, this picture needs to be nuanced. For example, the 'old' police in some areas were actually quite good at controlling crime and criminals. Equally, the supposedly professional New Police didn't really have much training until the end of the nineteenth century and were often dismissed for drunkenness and discipline offences. Given that the differences between the two systems (at least in the early years of the New Police) are thus less than we might imagine, historians have posed other explanations for the introduction of the New Police. In particular, Marxist-influenced historians such as Robert Storch have argued that the New Police was introduced not so much because of the failure of the old system but because changing social and economic conditions meant that the 'ruling elite' came to demand a new standard of public order and decorum and sought a mechanism via which to impose this.

2. What factors can you identify which appear to contradict the idea of a 'golden age' of policing between 1870 and 1950?

Specific reading which would be useful in answering this question would include Chapter 7 of Emsley (1996), Chapter 9 of Weinberger (1995), Gatrell's essay 'Crime, authority and the policeman state' in Thompson (1990) and the relevant chapters of Geary (1985).

3. In what ways did the personal backgrounds of police officers shape the way they approached their profession?

Specific reading which would be useful in answering this question would include the surveys by Emsley and Clapson (1994, 2002) and Emsley (2000). Other sources of information on this question would include Shpayer-Makov (2002) and Lawrence (2003).

Note

1. For the seminal discussion of the concept of 'Whig' history, see Butterfield (1931).

Further reading

The references for this chapter can be found in the Bibliography at the back of the book. If you wish to do some further reading, you should investigate these first. However, below is a list of publications which could also be consulted.

Benewick, R. (1969) *Political Violence and Public Order*. London: Penguin.
Butterfield, H. (1931) *The Whig Interpretation of History*. London: Bell.
Emsley, C. (2000) 'The policeman as worker: a comparative survey *c*.1800–1940', *International Review of Social History*, 45, pp. 89–110.

Emsley, C. (2002) 'Street, beat and respectability: the culture and self-image of the late-Victorian and Edwardian urban policeman', in L. Knafla (ed.), *Policing and War in Europe. Criminal Justice History*, 16, pp. 107–32.

Foster, J. (1974) *Class Struggle and the Industrial Revolution: Early Industrial Capitalism in Three English towns*. London: Weidenfeld & Nicolson.

Gattrell, V. A. C. (1980) 'The decline of theft and violence in Victorian and Edwardian England', in V. A. C. Gatrell, Bruce Lenman and Geoffrey Parker (eds), *Crime and the Law. The Social History of Crime in Western Europe since 1500*. London: Europa, pp. 238–339.

Geary, R. (1985) *Policing Industrial Disputes: 1893 to 1985*. Cambridge: Cambridge University Press.

Goddard H. (1956) *Memoirs of a Bow Street Runner*. London: Museum Press.

Lawrence, P. (2003) ' "Scoundrels and scallywags, and some honest men ..." Memoirs and the self-image of French and English policemen, c.1870–1939' in B. Godfrey, C. Emsley and G. Dunstall (eds), *Comparative Histories of Crime*. Cullompton: Willan.

Palmer, S. H. (1988) *Police and Protest in England and Ireland, 1780-1850*. Cambridge: Cambridge University Press.

Philips, D. (1989) 'Good men to associate and bad men to conspire: associations for the prosecution of felons in England, 1760–1860', in D. Hay and F. Snyder (eds), *Policing and Prosecution in Britain 1750–1850*. Oxford: Clarendon Press, pp. 113–70.

3. The role of the 'victim'

Introduction

While, as detailed in the previous chapter, the New Police gradually developed into the default mechanism for enforcing the law and apprehending criminals, this process took a long time and was only partially complete by the 1850s. This chapter deals with the role of the victim in the criminal justice process – a role which was initially far more instrumental than it is today. Our contemporary view of the nature of crime usually places the victim in a *passive* role in relation to a criminal act. This is not to say that victims are marginalized or ignored in our current conceptions of crime, but rather that they are not seen to have a particularly proactive role to play in either the prosecution or detection of crime. It is true that, during the 1950s, liberal reformers such as Margery Fry (1951) argued that 'the injured individual [has] rather slipped out of the mind of the criminal court' and successfully campaigned for Criminal Injuries Compensation for the victims of violent crime. However, although this led to a growing interest in the needs of victims, such campaigns were very much based on the view that 'the suffering, and innocent victim of violence' (Rock 1990: 84) should receive redress via the professional criminal justice system. Equally, the rise of 'victimology' (the study of victims of crime) since the 1950s has certainly raised the profile of victims, but has also arguably not altered substantially perceptions of victims as passive actors. As Miers (1978: 15) notes, the very term 'victim' inevitably promotes an image of passivity, where the victim has 'traditionally been viewed as the "sufferer" in a simple "doer–sufferer" model of criminal interaction'.

In fact, victims have often played an active rather than passive role in the prevention, prosecution and detection of crime, even if that role has gradually been eroded by greater involvement of agents of the state. At the beginning of our period it was largely through individual or private actions that cases were prosecuted at all. The part played by private action was far greater than is generally believed. This chapter will begin therefore with a consideration of victims, the prosecution of crime and the changing face of the prosecutor. Before the police moved into this area of criminal justice the onus was on the victims to bring prosecutions. These could be expensive as well as difficult and we will examine the various ways by which private individuals were able to bring cases to court. Then in part two, the emotive subject of self-defence will be discussed. 'The Englishman's home is his castle' is not just a modern sentiment but is a long-established view. We will take a close look at how the use of 'reasonable force' has been variously interpreted and the underlying causes of any shifts in attitudes. Finally, there have always been measures that private individuals could take – and were often expected to take – to safeguard their own property and prevent crime. This *active* role became increasingly important as the government bureaucratic machinery became more efficient at counting crime statistics. Accordingly, the responsibility for crime prevention did not stop with the private individual but infiltrated 'normal' police activity. Nevertheless, the private sector (as we might label it) continued to implement its own crime prevention initiatives such as the employment of nightwatchmen.

Introductory reading

King, P. (2000) *Crime, Justice, and Discretion in England, 1740–1820*. Oxford: Oxford University Press, Chapters 2 and 3.

Philips, D. (1980) 'A new engine of power and authority: the institutionalisation of law-enforcement in England 1780–1830' in V. A. C. Gatrell, B. Lenman and G. Parker (eds), *Crime and the Law: A Social History of Crime in Early Modern Europe*. London: Europa, pp. 155–89.

Philips, D. (1989) 'Good men to associate and bad men to conspire: associations for the prosecution of felons in England 1750–1860,' in D. Hay and F. Snyder (eds), *Policing and Prosecution in Britain 1750–1850*. Oxford: Oxford University Press, pp. 113–70.

Zedner, L. (2002) 'Victims and crime', in M. Maguire, R. Morgan and R. Reiner (eds), *The Oxford Handbook of Criminology*. Oxford: Oxford University Press, Chapter 13.

'Victims' and the prosecution of crime

During the eighteenth century the state took a rather detached and piecemeal attitude towards the prosecution of crime. The matter will be dealt with in more detail in the following chapter but, broadly speaking and in keeping with the *laissez-faire* policies that dominated ideas concerning the role of government, the state was only involved in the prosecution of a limited number of offences.[1] These tended to be offences that directly impinged on the government's ability to run the country. Coinage offences, for example, could attract the attention of the Treasury Solicitor and occasionally resulted in prosecution of offenders. Forgery of paper money was also taken very seriously by government officials. Following the Forgery Act of 1729, there were about 120 statutes against forgery on the books by the 1830s (McGowan 1999: 107). As McGowan has shown, 'judges and the Crown' were 'the staunchest advocates of the death penalty for forgery', believing that the seriousness of the offence warranted the execution of the offender 'even in the face of the uneasiness of those who were victims of the crime' (1999: 140).

Similarly, the Attorney General would from time to time concern himself with the prosecution of cases of treason or sedition. Another type of case that presented a serious threat to the state was the mutiny of troops. The thought of soldiers – trained and armed – being beyond the control of the state was anathema to all shades of political opinion during the eighteenth century. The danger to society was obvious and the State acted accordingly. At the end of the seventeenth century a mutiny by the Royal Scots Regiment had caused the government of the day to rush through the Mutiny Act 1689 which for the first time empowered the army to try soldiers during peacetime.

But these were the exceptions rather than the rule. What bound all of these together was the seriousness of the threat that was presented to the running of government either through its finances (coinage offences), rebellion (treason and sedition) or armed insurgency (mutiny). Nevertheless, the government did not itself always directly pursue the prosecution of even these most serious offences. For example, in the late-eighteenth century magistrates were regularly urged to seek other means to fund the prosecution of sedition cases rather than relying on the Crown Law Officers to finance them (Emsley 2005: 183). The Bank of England, too, usually financed prosecutions for forgery privately and, indeed, built up a significant body of employees dedicated to this task (McGowan 2005). In the case of ordinary offences against persons or property that did not threaten the existence of the State the chances of government-funded or conducted prosecutions were minimal. In fact, until the Prosecution of Offences Act of 1879 there was no public prosecutor to take criminal cases to court, and even then only significant or important cases were taken forward. The New Police gradually assumed responsibility for the prosecution of most criminal cases but, as has been argued in the previous chapter, the adoption of new forms of policing was still not yet accomplished in many parts of the country by the mid-nineteenth century. This meant that, in the eighteenth century at least, a great many offences were probably dealt with entirely outside of the structures of the criminal justice system with which we are now familiar. Tolerance, 'rough music' (a form of public shaming ritual often associated with the punishment of henpecked husbands or adulterous couples) and community action were all much more common methods for dealing with minor issues than the constable and the courts.

Given the expense and difficulty that prosecution entailed, it is likely that the majority of offences committed early in the period under consideration were never brought to the attention of the courts and were dealt with in some other way. Minor offences would in all likelihood be ignored or even tolerated. These will not show up in criminal statistics and there is, therefore, no way of knowing the real extent to which crime was tolerated. However, some anecdotal evidence does exist that can give us a flavour of public opinion. There are a number of documented instances, for example, where prosecutors were attacked or pressurized in some way for their bringing of cases to court. Sometimes this was a reaction to severe sentencing by the court – especially if the death penalty had been inflicted – but was also motivated, so it seems, by a general community feeling that the case should not have been presented because the circumstances did not warrant it. Often this reflected the status of the offender. Children had a tendency to elicit sympathy, but stories have also survived of adult thieves being assisted by crowds. Clearly, *some* victims were expected to be tolerant of *some* offences. One factor which should perhaps be considered here is changing attitudes towards both property and violence. Levels of interpersonal violence which would never be accepted today used to be commonplace. As Emsley (2005: 10) notes, 'there is a general acknowledgement of an increasing intolerance and general decline of violent behaviour in Europe since the late medieval period'. Accordingly, much which would currently come within the purview of the criminal justice system was in earlier times simply ignored or settled privately between the individuals concerned.

If action was taken in relation to an offence, it was also common during the eighteenth and early nineteenth centuries for victims and communities to deal with offenders by *extra-judicial* means. In the first instance, it was often accepted that justice could be meted out by the victim themselves in regard to certain types of crime – particularly shoplifting and petty thievery. Wood (2003: 114) quotes a mid-nineteenth century boot seller who reported that when he caught young thieves taking boots or shoes he '[gave] them a stirruping [flogging] with whichever it is, and a kick and let them go'. Henry Mayhew, an early investigative journalist, also observed that 'sometimes when these boys are caught pilfering, they are severely beaten especially by the women, who are aided by the men, if the thief offers any formidable resistance' (Wood 2003: 114).

Communities, too, could act to mete out justice on behalf of the victim, although this was by no means always an act of altruism and often the targets of this action were outsiders or those seen as undesirable (Beattie 1986: 135). For example, a Jewish hawker was ducked in a horse pond at Huntingdon races in 1753 for trying to steal a ring from a young woman (Emsley 2005: 182). Of course there is no real way of knowing how many of these cases were genuine acts of meting out 'justice' and how many were simply aimed at misfits or minority groups and justified on some spurious grounds. Nevertheless, the important point here is that this was an accepted practice regardless of its authenticity. This practice appears to have occurred most often in the eighteenth century and the first half of the nineteenth century. Overall, as Wood (2003: 111) has argued, it was relatively common for order to be maintained

> through a distribution of violence legitimated by a 'customary' mentality that organized retributive, autonomous and disciplinary violence. From neighbourly 'rough music' to direct interpersonal assaults, customary violence marked and defended the boundaries of acceptable behaviour and enforced conformity to community standards (or individual interpretations of those standards).

In the nineteenth century, changes in the level of policing in Britain were part of a wider change in attitudes to violence. At the start of the century there was widespread acceptance that violence was an acceptable way of solving many problems – notably problems between working-class men and within working-class communities more generally. 'Fair fights' with seconds, rounds and the possibility of subsequent reconciliation were a common way for working men to settle disagreements (Wood 2003; Emsley 2005). People who broke the norms of the community – such as offenders against children – were often glad of the protection that the law offered them against the instant justice that their victims' neighbours were keen to mete out. The mid-nineteenth- century Edinburgh detective James McLevy wrote about the time that he unmasked a gang of women who were stealing clothes from children. When the area's mothers found out, the thieves needed police protection to prevent them from being stripped themselves and badly beaten (McLevy 1975: 204). But during the nineteenth century, more 'civilized' attitudes began to take hold, aided by the arrival for the first time of new police forces that could enforce a new standard of behaviour. The state began to take note of all violence in public places, with an eye on stopping it. In return, the new police and the court systems began to stake a claim that they could entirely protect the safety of the citizen. This claim, though, was not total: many police would rather look the other way than interfere in a 'fair fight' – or in any other fight if it looked like the participants and spectators were formidable enough to resist interference.

Thus a significant amount of crime (especially of the more minor type) was probably dealt with outside of the court system for much of the eighteenth and early nineteenth centuries. There was a gradual decline in *reported* occurrences of this type of extra-legal redress, which appears to coincide with the rise of a recognizable prosecution system. However, this does not necessarily imply a causative relationship. It might also be that newspapers – one of the best sources of evidence of this practice – gradually found it easier to glean their copy from the theatricals of the courtroom rather than more mundane human interactions in society itself. The practice did continue alongside the newly emerging professional prosecutors, but only the more sensational appears to have been newsworthy.

Moreover, even during the period 1750–1850, victims were instrumental in bringing cases to court. As Hay (1989: 24) has noted, private prosecution was the dominant mode in the eighteenth and nineteenth centuries. More than 80 per cent of all criminal cases were prosecuted by private individuals – usually the victim or somewhat less usually an agent acting on his or her behalf – rather than an agent of national or local government during this period (Hay 1983: 167). In Sheffield during the period 1859–62, out of 4,116 court cases of common assault, 3,303 individuals (80 per cent) had been summoned to court by victims under a private warrant rather than being arrested or summoned by the police. Victims thus played an extremely proactive role in the criminal justice process. In the first instance, of course, they were often involved in securing an arrest. With few police officers in many parts of the country, it was often down to victims themselves (particularly in rural areas) to arrange the apprehension of a felon, as the following extract from a theft trial at the Old Bailey in 1790 makes clear.

JOHN ASHWORTH and THOMAS WEBB were indicted for stealing, on the 23rd of December last, two live cocks, value 2 s. and three live hens, value 3 s. the property of Christopher Chapman

CHRISTOPHER CHAPMAN sworn

I live at Sudbury-green, a farmer; on December the 23rd, between five and six, I was alarmed with somebody getting into my yard, and taking my fowls; they roost in an out-house which was open; but the gate of the yard was shut; I found only one dead hen, and a dead turkey; one in the yard, the other in the outhouse: about an hour, or an hour and a quarter after, I went into the adjoining shed, where the cows eat; I found five more; I pursued from information; and going along, two people told me the two prisoners were at the Plow at Kelstone-green, about five miles from Sudbury; I found them about nine the same morning, and seven more of my fowls dead, and hung up for shew and sale, at the public house; they were in their feathers; they were my fowls of different colours; they were clipped in the wing.[2]

Clearly, victims of crime in eighteenth-century England could not afford to be passive if their cases were to be dealt with in or outside the courts. The preference for extra-judicial action was in no small part influenced by the anticipated cost of bringing a prosecution. For many this was prohibitive. However, one avenue of assistance with these costs for *some* victims was provided by the so-called 'Associations for the Prosecution of Felons', which had been established in most parts of the country from the 1760s (Gatrell, Lenman and Parker 1980: 179). These associations (which would assist fee-paying members with the costs of prosecution and sometimes finance them in full and/or pay a reward) made prosecution possible in many cases where previously it would have been impossible. By the early nineteenth century these associations were firmly established. However, they were formed through private rather than public initiative and as such only served a section of the community. The scope of these associations was, therefore limited. They only assisted their own members and had limited financial means at their disposal.

The origins of the Associations for the Prosecution of Felons can be located in informal agreements within communities collectively to contribute towards the costs of 'desirable prosecutions'. It is impossible to be certain of the earliest of these agreements – it is unlikely that records have survived if indeed they were made in the first place – but there is surviving evidence of one in South Yorkshire in 1737. On this occasion one hundred parishioners, including five women, agreed to contribute to the costs of a prosecution. By the 1790s these agreements were more usually formalized into associations with all the accompanying paraphernalia such as constitutions and rules. Most associations charged their members annual fees to ensure that the association continued and covered all its costs. Normally, the cost of a prosecution entailed hiring counsel to present the case in court and any witness expenses. If it had funded particularly expensive prosecutions then the premiums would have to be raised to recuperate the expenditure. Members, therefore, often saw premiums rise year on year and many associations folded when an insufficient number of members could afford to continue paying the annual fees. At least one association overcame this problem by charging a large joining fee and then smaller subsequent fees if that was necessary to balance the budget.[3] This way the association secured its money from the outset while members' enthusiasm was greater than their thrift.

Most associations remained relatively informal in so far as they were hardly permanent and were often formed in response to heightened concerns about crime. The associations were often as ephemeral as the feared crime waves that sparked their creation. Rather than representing a shift away from the private prosecution of offenders the formation of these associations actually reinforced – or consolidated – the practice by making the pre-existing system more workable – at least for its members.

But the associations did not limit themselves to expensive court action. First, offenders had to be apprehended and many associations paid rewards for the capture of the perpetrators of crime or the recovery of stolen goods. Some associations even organized local patrols or themselves conducted searches for stolen goods. But these were the minority and the most usual function in most associations was to pay for the advertising of rewards or the printing of handbills. This, of course, had the additional benefit of acting as a deterrent by advertising the fact that the association played such an active role. The impact of this effect cannot be measured but we might safely conclude that it was a cheap by-product of the association's activities.

The ideal association – that is the ones that appear to have functioned most effectively – consisted of between twenty and sixty members, preferably property-holders, from a small area (Philips 1989: 132). Clearly, the cost of belonging to an association was prohibitive for many. According to one historian, members came generally 'from among the middling property owners of a town or parish[es]' who were driven to take action 'by moments of acute anxiety about the level of crime' and concerns that 'crime was being encouraged by the uncertainty of punishment and the failure of victims to prosecute' (Beattie 1986: 48). However, claims that these associations amounted to some form of 'citizen self-policing' are missing the point (Palmer 1988: 148). Associations for the Prosecution of Felons were formed to protect the financial interests of their members. The citizens they were concerned about – and therefore wished to police – were not themselves but others. In fact, it is quite possible to interpret the formation of the associations as those with property protecting themselves against those without property. Even if we put aside any class-based explanation it is obvious that the associations were not formed for the benefit of the community as a whole but for a fee-paying section of it.

It could also be argued that there existed a hierarchy among associations with wealthier ones able to afford to prosecute more often than those that might have been strapped for cash from time to time. The impact of the associations on national prosecution rates was probably negligible at best – again suggesting that they operated in the interests of only a minor section of the community. Beattie (1986: 50) has suggested that they had 'no major effect', while in his study of Essex King has pointed out their tendency to follow rather than lead the indictment rate (in Hay and Snyder 1989: 202). While their impact as a deterrent – arguably their most significant function – will remain elusive, for the historian they do provide evidence that an important section of society were sufficiently disgruntled about the existing criminal justice system to invest time and money in organizing themselves against the threat of crime.

It is, of course, possible to view the formation of Associations for the Prosecution of Felons as an obstacle to the formation of the new police. In short, by doing one of the jobs we now associate with the police it removed or at least delayed pressure from the middle classes for the introduction of a new system. Other organizations, such as the Worsted Inspectorate discussed in Chapter 9, may also have had a similar effect (Godfrey 2002). As the upper classes could afford to prosecute in any case and the lower classes lacked influence, only pressure from the middle classes (many of whom were the entrepreneurs who were driving the British economy at this time) would have any impact on government policy. These members of the middle classes had little incentive to change the position – an argument best summed up by David Philips (1977: 133):

> Where property owners had an active Association for the Prosecution of Felons in existence their attitude is easy to understand. They paid their subscription to their association, which protected their property alone. Why, then, choose to pay [presumably much higher] rates for a police force to serve the whole country, which would spend much of its time policing other people's property?

Yet we should also consider the relationship between the associations and the police and point to the many instances when the police developed in parallel with the association, at least up to a point. In fact, there is some evidence to suggest that the new police benefited from the same movement that had spawned the associations for the Prosecution of Felons and that counties with most associations were more likely to adopt the new police if that was an option (Schubert 1981: 36). Where once fears about crime had motivated people to opt for the formation of an association so too could the same fears be expressed by opting to adopt the terms of the County Police Act 1839, but the choice was not limited to one or the other (Philips 1989: 150).

The associations often provided a stepping-stone towards establishing the police although it would be wholly incorrect to suggest that the police were grafted onto pre-existing associations. No doubt the police benefited from rewards offered by the associations, but a more significant legacy was the establishment of the principle of locally funded policing. After the passing of the County and Borough Police Act of 1856 it appears that the police increasingly shouldered the burden of prosecution, thereby eroding this particular role of the victim (Hay and Snyder 1989: 3–52). In addition, the growth of insurance companies eroded other roles of the associations such as the need to recover stolen goods and the offering and payment of rewards. However, conditions had also altered: the widening of summary prosecution had removed the enormous expense of indicting felons in many cases (Schubert 1981: 43). The situation remains blurred. There is no line of demarcation here – the moment of change cannot be pinpointed and is only visible when viewed across a long period of time. While the role of independent action on the part of victims in bringing prosecutions declined over the course of the nineteenth century and into the twentieth, it is important to realize that victims were instrumental to the operation of the criminal justice system for at least a half of the period under consideration here. Even later in the nineteenth century, with the police assuming responsibility for many prosecutions, the expansion of the summary courts (and hence the negation of the expense of a costly jury trial) meant that victims from lower down on the social scale increasingly used the law to mediate disputes. As Jennifer Davis (1984; Hay and Snyder 1989: 413) has shown, working-class prosecutors accounted for between a fifth and a quarter of all prosecutions for theft during the 1860s and 1870s.

Retribution, self-defence and other extra-judicial action

Clearly, then, victims have historically been quite proactive in the prosecution of crime and extra-judicial measures of redress have also often been employed by victims. Another area in which victims have traditionally been less than passive is in the measures which they might take to defend themselves against the perpetrators of crime, particularly in instances of burglary. Before the emergence of professional law enforcement through the police one might expect this to be the usual practice. Certainly, it has been argued that the 'right' of self-defence was implicit in the earliest laws of England and was eventually made explicit in the Bill of Rights of 1689 (Malcolm 2002: 4, 1996).[4] It is difficult to be certain how widespread significant incidents of self-defence have been. Evidence can only be obtained from court records which record only prosecuted cases and anecdotal or polemical sources such as newspapers. However, the issue of new government guidelines on the use of force against intruders by the Crown Prosecution Service and ACPO (the Association of Chief Police Officers) in 2005 shows that this issue remains contentious. The use of force to defend oneself or one's property is another area which challenges contemporary views of victims as passive actors in any criminal act.

The legal position on self-defence is surprisingly complex and has altered over the centuries. Like many things that are derived from common law, interpretations have varied over time. Broadly speaking, though, it has long been accepted in English law that a person can use *reasonable* force to protect himself or his property (legal language uses the term 'his' to signify both 'his' and 'her'). During the eighteenth century there was considerable debate over the rights and wrongs of self-defence causing Sir William Blackstone, author of one of the most widely read texts on English common law, to consider the problem.

> The law respects the passions of the human mind; and … makes it lawful in him to do himself that immediate justice, to which he is prompted by nature, and which no prudential motives are strong enough to restrain. It considers that the future process of law is by no means an adequate remedy for injuries accompanied with force. (Blackstone 1982: 3–4)

Blackstone appears to suggest that not only self-defence, but even retribution by victims of crime was acceptable provided they acted immediately. If violence was used against a law-abiding citizen, Blackstone proposed, it was perfectly understandable that this individual might not wish to wait for 'the future process of law' and might mete out violence in return immediately. This benign view of *extra-judicial* action by victims of crime can still be detected during the nineteenth century and, most importantly, it appears to have survived beyond the arrival of formal prosecution structures such as the new police.

During the nineteenth century, however, the widespread ownership of guns was an additional complicating factor and meant that increasingly self-defence was synonymous with shooting. Reasonable force, therefore, very often quickly became deadly force. For example, the following cases from the Sheffield area illustrate just how common these occurrences were. In August 1819, a resident at a warehouse fired a pistol at some burglars attempting to enter through a window – one was heard to cry out and fall to the ground. He was not apprehended. Another man 'shot through the thigh' in a similar attempt was convicted the following week. Burglars would often risk facing an armed house owner or at least a mechanical trap. Not always, though, did these have the intended results. In 1837 a spring trap killed its owner after he set it off by accident in his own workshop. In another case in 1841 the victim of a burglar found himself threatened by his own gun (Williams 1998: 278–9).

Public and press alike welcomed rather than condemned the use of weapons against criminals. Williams (1998) has studied the Sheffield press in detail. For example, when a 15-year-old girl in Brightside, Sheffield fought off burglars by shooting at them from the window with a horse pistol, the *Sheffield Independent* commented: 'If all men would act with the same gallantry this young woman did, only taking better aim, burglaries would be less frequent.' In 1839 the same newspaper welcomed the fact that three men had been 'armed and prepared' when they faced down a group of suspected robbers on the town's outskirts one night. In the early nineteenth century it was widely accepted that individuals had a duty to protect themselves. It could even be argued that there was an attitude that *force majeure* would prevail, and those who failed to secure their property properly deserved to lose it. An editorial in the *Times* of 1857 noted bluntly that:

> Self-preservation, if not the first instinct of nature, stands very high. Few would hesitate to destroy the highwayman or the burglar, even where property alone was in question. Indeed, in the matter of self-defence we make property part of self, and are all of the opinion [...] that life would not be worth living for without that proportion of wealth to which we have been accustomed.[5]

The perceived deterrent effect of deadly force was regarded as an essential element of crime prevention. This view was extended to public order and it was not unusual for such force to be threatened during riots – not by the rioters but by those seeking to protect their property and businesses. During the Sheffield election riot of 1832, a crowd attacked the house of lawyer Luke Palfreyman. Palfreyman and one of his clerks fired shots over the crowd's heads in response to their stones, and warned that if they advanced he would fire at them – an act described by the press as 'that defence which is lawful to every Englishmen in his own house'.

The use of 'deadly force' against burglars and other thieves appears to have fallen off after the middle of the century. It is quite possible that this reflects the impact of formalized systems to protect citizens and their property or to prosecute offenders. The most obvious development here was the emergence of police forces in many parts of the country as detailed in the previous chapter, and perhaps there no longer existed a need for private citizens to resort to such extreme measures to protect themselves. But as usual it is important to guard against drawing convenient conclusions from the patchy remnants of primary sources – much of it anecdotal. The apparent downward turn in the 'trend' might reflect nothing more than a difference in survival of the evidence. That in itself, though, might be significant because it could mean that newspapers were less enthusiastic in their reporting of such instances. If that is the case – and it remains a big 'if' – then this suggests that the use of deadly force against criminals had become less socially acceptable later in the nineteenth century, leaving us to ponder the reasons why this could be the case. One obvious argument is that the emergence of a 'proper' system to deal with crime rendered other systems 'improper'.

Whatever the reasons for the apparent decline in use of deadly force, attention turned towards the use of firearms towards the end of the nineteenth century. It was not so much that government was concerned about the 'right sort of people' being allowed to defend themselves and their property, but there developed an increased concern about the availability of firearms to just anyone. Much of this increased concern was linked to the rise of working-class movements such as the trades unions and the Labour Party. Fuelled by industrial unrest across Britain, many commentators were calling for the restriction of firearms. Initially there was public resistance. One letter to the *Times* on the subject of a gun tax suggested that it should only be imposed if a gun was used recreationally. If a man should 'in pure self-defence, be constrained to use the gun for destroying a mad dog on his premises, or the pistol for shooting a burglar in his house', then no fee should be imposed.[6] The comparison of burglars and mad dogs is instructive.

By the time fresh discussions took place in the 1880s, however (coincident with the rapid spread of cheap revolvers), the prevalent mood was changing somewhat. In contrast to the quotation above, a *Times* leader from 1885 claimed that 'an epidemic of revolvers and the violences attendant on the habit of carrying them has been ravaging the United Kingdom', and that 'peaceable subjects are seriously endangered in life and property by an immoderate toleration of the common use of concealed firearms, of which professional criminals and unruly spirits can always most readily avail themselves.'[7] These concerns continued into the early twentieth century. In a bizarre incident in 1912, members of the Territorial Army were relieved of their rifles when deployed at an industrial dispute in South Wales. The incident, which was reported to Parliament by the Labour MP for Merthyr

Tydfil, Keir Hardie, occurred when the owners of the colliery at the centre of the dispute convinced the army commander that his troops – some of whom were also colliers – could not be trusted with firearms. What motivated this action was clearly a concern that in certain circumstances the working classes could not be trusted with firearms – it was not the army's loyalty that was in question, having shot dead two protestors at an industrial dispute at nearby Llanelli only the previous year.

The outbreak of the First World War gave the government an opportunity to tighten control of society in the name of national security. This it did in the form of the Defence of the Realm Act 1914, which gave government sweeping powers to control the labour force, to requisition private property, to carry out surveillance of its own citizens and also to control the availability of firearms. It is debatable whether this was a conscious move on the part of government to legislate against the growing prewar fears about gun use or whether this part of the legislation would have been swept away after the end of hostilities had circumstances allowed. However, circumstances did not allow and the Bolshevik revolution in Russia in 1917 (followed by postwar revolutions in Germany, Austria and Hungary) meant that fears concerning an armed proletariat or demobilized army were heightened. The 'great fear' that swept Britain was probably out of proportion to the actual likelihood of a Marxist seizure of power, but the raising of the red flag over the town hall in Glasgow in 1919 and another armed rebellion in Ireland (this time successful) merely underlined the potential threat. These incidents and the police strike of 1919 gave an added impetus to the movement to limit and control firearms.

The usual fears of a postwar crime wave – a 'normal' response by governments fearful of desensitized former soldiers who are unable to secure work and unable to re-assimilate into society – combined with ever-increasing concerns about 'political crime' to ensure that gun control became a priority. The resulting Firearms Act 1920 effectively ended the unconditional 'right' of protestant British citizens to possess guns, although they could still be (and often were) acquired for specific purposes. In a bizarre incident in 1930, the Chief Constable of Buckinghamshire granted a permit to hold a revolver to Mark Trower of Taplow, but refused him a permit to purchase ammunition. Trower had suffered two attempts to break into his house and was convinced a revolver was necessary for self-defence. The Chief Constable argued (successfully) in court that Trower was not a suitable man to have a loaded revolver and that, anyway, most burglars would tackle a man even with a revolver.[8] Worse was to follow with the General Strike of 1926, which saw troops deployed on British streets alongside police to deal with a potential working-class revolt. But when the British Union of Fascists, led by Sir Oswald Mosley, took to the streets the prospect of open street war between them and British Communists resulted in a flurry of 'preventative' legislation. The Public Order Act of 1936 was specifically targeted at pacifying the streets, but a number of Firearms Acts (1934, 1936 and 1937) came in quick succession, each designed to tighten up gun control. In the context of warring factions on the streets and elsewhere, guidelines were necessary about the 'right' of self-defence and in 1937 the Home Secretary advised the police:

As a general rule applications to possess firearms for house or personal protection should be discouraged on the grounds that firearms cannot be regarded as a suitable means of protection and may be a source of danger. (Malcolm 2002: 157)

After the Second World War, when both fascism and communism were less of a public issue, similar concerns were again raised. An amnesty to recall the very firearms that had been issued to repel enemy troops should they land in Britain was the first step. But a new phenomenon emerged that forced the government to look again at deadly force and how it was often inflicted. Youth gangs had attracted media attention, supposedly terrorizing coastal resorts in particular. The Prevention of Crime Act 1953 outlawed offensive weapons, including objects not intended for offensive use but that might be used as such (a walking stick, for example). The implications for the 'right' to defend oneself were enormous and the ensuing debate a ferocious one. The government's adopted line – that preservation of the peace was principally a police responsibility – was voiced by the Attorney General in Parliament.

It is the duty of society to protect them [private citizens], and they should not have to do that [carry weapons] … the argument of self-defence is one to which perhaps we should not attach too much weight.

The legal definition of 'self-defence' remained but the interpretation of it was, by the end of our period, much different to the understanding that existed at the beginning. Moreover, legislation on firearms and other weapons had diminished the likelihood of deadly force in such cases, once again altering the perceived role of the victim in response to crime.

Victims and 'private' initiatives

Prosecution societies and armed self-defence both serve to dent the image of victims as passive actors in the sphere of criminal justice. However, there were also other means by which individuals, businesses, organizations or communities might defend themselves against crime, or ameliorate its effects once it had occurred. Most of these pre-date the police but many survived the arrival of formal policing. Again, these initiatives mostly reflected people's unwillingness to become victims of crime or at least to resist being merely quiescent victims. The employment of nightwatchmen, for example, was one way that businesses, associations or even private individuals could protect themselves against the criminal. Then there were a number of ways by which police officials could be encouraged to pay extra attention to a particular district or a particular crime. Paying for additional constables was one such method, offering financial incentives directly to police officers in the form of rewards was another. Predictably, these initiatives caused concerns about conflicts of interest or even outright corruption and eventually had to be supervised.

The payment by private individuals or institutions for the use of police officials in relation to a specific crime was an old practice, but one which survived the arrival of the new police forces. During the latter half of the eighteenth century, it was common for private individuals to offer rewards or engage thief-takers or police officials directly. Ruth Paley has shown that unofficial thief-takers, many of whom had never served as constables or watchmen, on occasion enticed beginners into crime simply in order to betray them for rewards (Hay and Snyder 1989: 301–40). Many thief-takers (who did not usually devote themselves to the task full time) were often associated with the lower classes and would, for example, also work as the landlords of seedy public houses. Nevertheless, the engagement of a known and respected thief-taker was one of the prerogatives of victims in the later eighteenth century. Recourse to a more respected official body was also open to victims during this period. A system of fixed parliamentary rewards were available for police officials who secured capital convictions, but organizations such as the Bow Street Runners, for example, were available to anyone who could afford the appropriate fee. John Townsend was one of the most famous of the Bow Street Runners. He was regularly engaged to appear at the Bank of England on Dividend Day, and fashionable people would place on their invitations the words 'Mr Townsend will attend', hiring him to protect their guests from pickpockets (Tobias 1972: 110). The practice continued until well into the nineteenth century. The Earl of Eustace, for example, employed a Bow Street Runner, George Ledbetter, to prevent an illegal prize-fight taking place on the extensive lands belonging to his father, the Duke of Grafton, around the village of Hanslope in Buckinghamshire. The fight between an Irishman called Simon Byrne and the Scottish champion, Alexander McKay, did go ahead on 2 June 1830, but on common land at nearby Salcey Green.

Even after the advent of the new police, the practice of retaining additional constables – serving policemen paid for by private individuals to watch private premises – was widespread among nineteenth-century police forces and enabled those who could afford it another opportunity to protect themselves further. According to Carolyn Steedman (1984: 45–6): 'In the 1860s and 1870s Additional Constables numbered up to 25% of the northern county and borough forces. They were usually appointed from the ranks of the local force (a plum for the long-serving, deserving man).' More often, though, the private payment for constables was a more mundane and localized affair. In nineteenth-century Sheffield, private individuals and corporations who rented the services of police officers included theatre owners, wine merchants and boiler-founders. About an eighth of the force was employed this way (Williams 1998: 188–91). The 'additional constable' was also specifically used to enforce industrial discipline. When in November 1865 R. T. Eadon, a saw and file manufacturer and member of the Watch Committee, learned that his works was under threat of reprisal from the trade society, he went to the Chief Constable '... and made an arrangement with him to send a policeman to stay from the time the wheel ceased to work until the next morning.' The system of additional constables, therefore, just like that which preceded it was a resource available only to those who could afford it.

Victims of crime also often offered rewards as a means of recovering stolen goods or for the apprehension of the offender. With the growth of mass printing, and hence provincial newspapers, from the 1750s, crime advertising (either in newspapers or on specially printed handbills) became very common. As the example given below (from the *Leeds Mercury*, 1784) shows, adverts were most typically related to crimes against property (Hay and Snyder 1989: 60).

Stray'd or Convey'd.

On Monday Night the 16ᵗʰ February instant out of a Farm Yard in Ledstone-Park.

A Black Teaming Gelding

Rising Six Years old, about 15 Hands high, a White Face, his Near Eye Blemished, a short Bob Tail, and three White Legs.
Whoever will bring the said Gelding to Mr. Edward Shirtliff, of Ledstone; Mr. William Simpson, of Newton; or Mr. John Jackson, of Fairburn, both near Ferrybridge, shall receive ONE GUINEA, and all reasonable Expences (sic).

Advertisements and rewards were placed by victims of crimes individually, but Associations for the Prosecution of Felons might also investigate this avenue of redress. Levels of success obviously varied, but John Styles' research indicates that, where a crime such as horse stealing was concerned, the practice of advertising a reward was 'an effective and successful instrument of detection, in the sense that it established itself as one of the most important means of bringing suspects to trial and conviction' (Hay and Snyder 1989: 86). Towards the end of the nineteenth century, the dissemination of information about thefts and other crimes became increasingly internalized within the official police service. Initially, however, financial incentives were open to everyone including the police provided it was approved by the Watch Committee. In Sheffield the official granting of rewards became increasingly common during the mid-century (Critchley 1967: 94). This enabled the Watch Committee to exercise subtle control over its officers and reward some while excluding others. For example, in 1865 one major subscription reward – divided among the 'deserving' by the Watch Committee – brought the year's total to £176, of which just £13 6s. went to ordinary constables. Rewards were not significant to more than a minority of policemen, but their discretionary nature again allowed the Watch Committee to exercise paternalistic favour and enabled certain victims to bring their case to prominence. The large-scale use of rewards had a potential drawback. It could weaken the police as an institution and induce the men to compete with each other. In Sheffield in 1858 Inspector Linley was censured for failing to submit proper expense claims for an investigation. His defence was that 'had he succeeded in obtaining any portion of the Reward [£50], he should have said nothing about such sums.' The police subcommittee concluded that one consequence of large rewards was that officers concerned 'withheld their information from the Head of the Police, from the Solicitor for the prosecution, and from each other'. Eventually, the privilege to accept

CONFIDENTIAL.
Police Information No. 2240.
Telephone Nos. 13—14.

Chief Constable's Office,
Blackpool,
13th June, 1932.

£100 REWARD

Stolen by means of housebreaking in this Borough between 7-40 p.m. and 10-10 p.m., Friday, 10th June, 1932. Entrance effected by forcing window at rear and climbing through.

BRACELET.
Lady's Gold Expanding Bracelet, diamond in centre surrounded by diamonds, with diamonds extending half way around the Bracelet. Valued £400.

RING.
Lady's Single Stone Diamond Ring, all platinum mounts, claw set, between 3 and 4 carat. Valued £450.

WRISTLET WATCH.
Lady's Platinum Wristlet Watch, about size of shilling, surrounded by 29 diamonds, attached to a Silver Bangle. No. of Watch 272655. Valued £100.

BROOCH.
Gold Bar Brooch with aquamarine in centre. Valued £5.

BROOCH.
Pearl Pear-shaped Brooch, filigree. Valued £5.

EAR-RINGS.
Pair of Ear-rings, pearl and aquamarine. Valued £5.

BROOCH. EAR-RINGS.
Gold Cameo Brooch, female head in pink and white, with Gold and Cameo Ear-rings to match. Valued £8.

FINGER WATCH.
Lady's Gold Ring with small oval-shaped watch in face, silver dial. Valued £12.

MESH BAG.
Gold Mesh Bag, 7ins. square, the clip set with black stone.

PENDANT CHAIN.
Antique Pendant, pear-shaped topaz drop, lemon coloured stone, rather large size, attached to silver chain, filigree pattern. Valued £25.

PENDANT.
Gold and Pearl Filigree Pendant. Valued £10.

A reward of £100 or pro rata of the value of property recovered is offered by Messrs. Marcus Fleeson & Co., 9, Albert Square, Manchester, Assessors, for information leading to the recovery of the above-described jewellery, and the apprehension of the offender.

Please cause enquiries to be made at Pawnbrokers and Jewellers with a view to tracing the property described herein and any information received kindly communicate with the undersigned, or to any Police Station.

H. E. DERHAM,
Chief Constable.

A police reward poster from 1932. Despite the predominance of the police in investigating offences, the posting of rewards (in this instance by the insurance company) remained common.
Source: European Centre for the Study of Policing Archive, The Open University.

rewards was removed from serving police officers – although many got around this by supplying the information through a third party. Nevertheless, it remained as an incentive to members of the public to assist investigations and victims often put up significant sums of money for recovery of goods or simply to raise the profile of their case.

There was also one other extra-judicial method of dealing with the aftermath of a crime available to victims which should perhaps be mentioned: the controversial 'compounding' of a felony – a private arrangement that often involved the restoration of stolen goods in return for not pressing charges, or the payment of some form of compensation. The practice was illegal, but there is very little record of it being prosecuted. 'Compounding' of even the worst crimes happened sometimes and not always was the practice truly extra-judicial. In 1837 it was reported in the *Sheffield Mercury* that a man who had assaulted, 'with intent to rape', 'a little girl' escaped conviction for this felony when the magistrates decided to 'exercise the discretion vested in them by the law; and they, therefore, ordered the prisoner to be discharged 'on paying the prosecutrix £4 costs'. Such arrangements were surprisingly common in Victorian England. Magistrates and judges could also make bargains with offenders brought before them. This might not always have been motivated by ideas of redress (as in the case above) but by those of redemption. Most notably, during the First World War men were often quite literally given a 'get out of jail' option if they enlisted in the armed forces. In one case a convicted housebreaker served with distinction on the Western Front and was awarded the Victoria Cross. This is an exceptional case, however, and most instances were far more mundane involving offenders pledging to leave the area. The problem, therefore, was 'decanted' into another parish or police district. Communities had dealt with persistent offenders or even undesirable types by this method for centuries and it was natural that the police would adopt similar tactics. Vagrants were often targeted and 'moved on', but how much further this practice extended is impossible to tell. Nevertheless, it was a cheap and highly effective method of dealing with crime and its perpetrators.

Throughout our period 'compounding' crime was a widespread practice that was hardly ever recorded. Unfortunately, it is not possible to estimate just how widespread was this type of case nor, therefore, to assess its importance. But we ignore it at our peril because it remains one of the most basic means by which a victim might deal with an offender. The rise in insurance during the late nineteenth and twentieth centuries has made it necessary for more people to report crime when in an earlier time they might not have bothered. The rise in *recorded* crime during the early twentieth century that partly resulted from this provides a glimpse of the possible extent to which crimes used to be dealt with by means such as 'compounding'. In fact 1923 had the highest annual 'crime rate' since records were first officially collated in 1876, but to what extent the apparent inflation in reported crime each year reflected not a rise in actual crime but the lessening impact of unreported crime – or compounding – will remain unclear.

Conclusion

Although many of the measures that were commonly adopted by victims of crime to protect themselves survived over the two centuries under discussion here, most had been adapted while others had disappeared altogether. There was no one single cause or turning point which provides the key to this process, but rather a culmination of numerous factors that impacted on the relationship between offender, offended and the criminal justice system. The emergence of the new police certainly had a great effect over the entire period. But this was no watershed and we cannot categorically say that because a formal policing and prosecuting structure had arrived so the prosecution associations, the need and or 'right' of citizens to defend themselves or other extra-judicial initiatives disappeared.

It is true that by about 1950 the police had assumed responsibility in areas that had previously been the domain of individual or collective private action. However, the process had taken almost a century in most cases and other factors had clearly played an important role. The police had accommodated the associations for the prosecution of felons – perhaps even thrived off them initially – but the widening role of the police, the introduction of cheaper summary trials and, most significantly, the growth of affordable insurance rendered the prosecution associations no longer necessary. Many existed only when there was a particular need and that need became less and less evident as the nineteenth century drew on.

Between 1750 and 1950 an evolving interpretation of what constituted 'reasonable force' in cases involving self-defence can also be traced. Responsibility, it seemed, had shifted from the 'individual' to a situation where the primary duty lay with society in general and the police in particular. It was not so much that the arrival of organized policing had caused this reinterpretation but that the police were on hand to accept responsibility at a time when government, fearing first of all the threat of political crime and later gang violence, felt obliged to act.

Many of the other private initiatives did survive, however. Nightwatchmen were still commonly employed during the 1950s to protect commercial premises. Later more of them would be placed in uniform and employed not directly by the business owner but by a security firm. Concerns about corrupt practices spelt the end for police accepting reward money, but these have remained available to the general public. As society has modernized and with the growth of accountability and a mass media so 'compounding' of crime – though never theoretically legal – has become socially unacceptable. But its practice undoubtedly continued albeit in a more subtle manner and there is much anecdotal evidence that police and local communities would waive prosecutions in return for the criminal leaving the area to become 'someone else's problem'.

Victims could (and did) play a role in the history of crime. That role was not necessarily a passive one; some could exert direct influence over responses to crime through prosecution associations or by individual action. For others the influence was more indirect by offering rewards or through preventative measures such as additional constables, nightwatchmen and so on. Nevertheless, the relationship between victims and criminals did alter in many ways between 1750 and 1950, but the evolution of this relationship owes as much to broad changes in society as to the expansion of the remit of the state.

Key questions

1. What role did the victim have in the prosecution of crime in the late-eighteenth century, and how did this change over time?

Initially, victims (those on whom a crime had been perpetrated) had a key role in the administration of justice. In an era before the 'New Police', for example, it was very often victims themselves who apprehended offenders, or paid for them to be tracked down. Victims, too, very often decided whether or not to press charges. The notion of the 'discretion' of a victim was important, as it enabled even those with little money to wield a measure of influence. It was not uncommon for those relatively low down on the social scale to press for a trial and then not appear. Although the case was then dismissed, the offender was put to the trouble of attending court, but the victim did not have any costs to pay. With few barristers during this period, victims would also often be called upon to present and gather evidence. Prosecution societies were often formed to help share the costs of a trial, but these were usually unavailable to those among the poor who arguably needed them the most.

This situation gradually changed throughout the course of the nineteenth century. With the advent of the 'New Police' more offenders were apprehended, and the police themselves were thus forced to take on a prosecution role. This was particularly true in towns and cities where instances of petty crime and minor offences – such as being drunk and disorderly – were rife. Police courts, however, also came to be a space within which the working classes could seek redress swiftly and cheaply. Pressure for a comprehensive system of public prosecution gradually grew, and a Director of Public Prosecutions was appointed in 1880. However, this officer handled only a tiny amount of very complex cases. The police continued to have the responsibility for the investigation and prosecution of most criminal offences until at least the 1960s.

2. Growing debates over the right of self-defence of victims in the nineteenth century in fact reflect declining tolerance of violence in society in general. Discuss.

There is relatively little written specifically on the right of self-defence. See Malcolm (2002), but be aware that this must be used with caution. See Williams (2004) for an instructive review. Malcolm (1996) is also useful, however, and can be used with more confidence. On the use of violence within English society more generally, you should consider Wood (2003, 2004), Emsley (2005) and Wiener (2004).

3. Account for the resurgence of interest in 'victims' of crime after 1950.

The criminological literature relating to this question is voluminous. Zedner (2002) provides a useful overview. Fry (1951) is a useful source and the work of Miers, editor of the *International Review of Victimology* (1978, 1990) will provide many further references.

Notes

1. Scotland differed from England in this regard, and followed the continental example of a Public Prosecutor. In England and Wales the *Common Law* tradition had prevailed over the legal reforms that had swept across Europe on the back of the Renaissance. The resulting introduction of *Roman Law* in most of continental Europe only really infiltrated Scotland which at that time enjoyed a closer relationship with France in particular (where many Scottish lawyers were trained). Some Roman Law *did* creep into the English system – in particular maritime law, which had to take account of the country's trading partners.
2. *Old Bailey Proceedings Online* (www.oldbaileyonline.org, 15 March 2005), January 1790, trial of John Ashworth and Thomas Webb (t17900113-18).
3. The Sheffield Association for the Prosecution of Felons charged £3 13s. for initial membership for personal and business premises and 6s. 10d. annually thereafter. The cost for personal premises only was considerably lower. *The Local Register and Chronological Account of Occurrences and Facts connected with the Town and Neighbourhood of Sheffield* (John Thomas, Sheffield, 1830), p. 143.
4. Malcolm's 2002 work addresses an interesting topic but should be used with caution as it does contain factual errors and its main premise is seriously flawed. For a review, see Williams (2004).
5. The *Times*, 28 January 1857, page 6, column b.
6. The *Times*, 27 April 1867, page 10, column b.
7. The *Times*, 26 January 1885, page 9, column e.
8. The *Times*, 19 November 1930, page 5, column f.

Further Reading

The references for this chapter can be found in the Bibliography at the back of the book. If you wish to do some further reading, you should investigate these first. However, below is a list of publications which could also be consulted.

Conley, C. (1986) 'Rape and justice in Victorian England', *Victorian Studies*, 29, 4, pp. 519–36.
Hay, D. (1975) 'Property, authority and the criminal law', in D. Hay *et al.*, *Albion's Fatal Tree: Crime and Society in Eighteenth-Century England*. London: Allen Lane.
Hay, D. (1983) 'Controlling the English prosecutor', *Osgoode Hall Law Journal*, 21, pp. 165–86.
Langbein, J. (2003) *The Origins of the Adversary Criminal Trial*. Oxford: Oxford University Press.
McGowan, R. (2005) 'The Bank of England and the policing of forgery 1797–1821', *Past and Present*, 186, pp. 81–116.

Wiener, M. (2004) *Men of Blood. Violence, Manliness and Criminal Justice in Victorian England*. Cambridge: Cambridge University Press.

Wood, J. C. (2004) *The Shadow of Our Refinement. Violence and Crime in Nineteenth-Century England*. New York: Routledge.

4. The law and the courts

Introduction

The period 1750–1950 witnessed far-reaching changes in trial procedures and court jurisdictions and in the administration of justice more generally. In the previous chapter, the gradual decline in the role of private citizens in bringing prosecutions to court was considered. In tandem with this, it is possible to trace the rise of the profession of barrister and an adversarial trial process. Significant change also occurred in the way in which trials were run, with increasing ceremony and more meticulous analysis of evidence becoming the norm. However, as with all historical study, the really interesting questions are not so much concerned with establishing *what* happened, but with *why* it occurred. A key question discussed below (and also touched upon in Chapter 9) is – in whose interests was the judicial system run at this time? Did 'the courts' serve everyone, or just a small, wealthy minority? The economist and philosopher Adam Smith asserted in 1766 that 'laws and government may be considered [...] in every case as a combination of the rich to oppress the poor, and preserve to themselves the inequality of goods', and many historians have subsequently agreed (Hay 1989: 344). There is, however, considerable debate about this issue, and recent research has returned a much more nuanced picture of the use of the criminal law. By the latter part of the nineteenth century, in any case, the role and appearance of the courts within English society had changed considerably. The class strife which had marked much of the early part of century was declining and the courts had arguably become much more accessible to previously marginalized groups such as women and the poor. However, even into the twentieth century, the criminal law and the courts were on occasion operating in a manner suggestive of what, for want of a better term, might be called 'class bias'.

This chapter is divided into three sections. The first provides a broad, largely factual, overview of some of the main changes which occurred in the administration of justice during the period 1750–1950. The ways in which the courts operated altered considerably during these two centuries, and a firm grasp of major milestones and trends is necessary. The second section considers some of the debates which historians have conducted over the exact role of the court system during the period c.1750–c.1850. It considers how accessible the legal infrastructure actually was at this time, and whether it primarily served the interests of a small, privileged elite. The final part of the chapter will consider the further development of the criminal justice system during the period 1850–1950. Did the image of the courts as primarily the preserve of a privileged elite change significantly during this period?

Introductory reading

Davis, J. (1984) 'A poor man's system of justice? The London police courts in the second half of the nineteenth century', *Historical Journal*, 27, 2, pp. 309–35.
Emsley, C. (2005) *Crime and Society in England, 1750–1900* (3rd edn). Harlow: Longman, chapters 3 and 8.
Hay, D. (1975) 'Property, authority and the criminal law', in D. Hay *et al.* (eds), *Albion's Fatal Tree. Crime and Society in Eighteenth-Century England*. London: Allen Lane, pp. 17–63.
King, P. (2000) *Crime, Justice, and Discretion in England 1740–1820*. Oxford: Oxford University Press, pp. 353–73.
Langbein, J. (1983) 'Albion's fatal flaws', *Past and Present*, 98–101, pp. 96–120.
Wiener, M. J. (1990) *Reconstructing the Criminal. Culture, Law and Policy in England, 1830–1914*. Cambridge: Cambridge University Press, chapters 2 and 7.

An overview of the court system, 1750–1950

It is obviously impossible in reality to separate 'the law' (the official, codified rules of society) from the operation of the court system which enforced and interpreted it. Clearly, if the courts did not enforce certain aspects of the law, such legislation was effectively null and void. When the law *per se* is considered, particularly during the first half of our period, 1750–1850, it can appear a rigid, imposing apparatus of power. However, recent work on the court system appears to show that implementation of the law was actually much more variable and fluid than historians had previously assumed.

It is important, first of all, to realize the extent to which the criminal justice system and the administration of punishment changed in the two centuries preceding 1950. The professionalized, bureaucratic courts which we know today were a distant dream in the latter half of the eighteenth century. The lawyer (and later clergyman) Martin Madan complained in 1785 that the practice of hearing cases in the afternoon following a lengthy lunch break meant that drunkenness was 'frequently apparent' and that 'the heat of the court, joined to the fumes of the liquor [...] laid many an *honest juryman* into a calm and profound sleep' (Emsley, 2005: 201). Similarly, consider the recollection of a 20-year-old student who had gone to observe the Oxford Assize court c.1800. Even the Assizes, which tried the most serious criminal cases, were not as solemn as one might expect. On finding that he 'could not get a tolerable place', the student recorded that he jumped from two men's shoulders and leaped upon the heads of several men and then scrambled into the prisoner's place where the judge said I must not stay, so one of the counsellors desired me not to make a noise, and he would let me have his place, which was immediately under the prisoners and opposite the judge. (King 2000: 253)

Clearly, courts in the eighteenth century were not the havens of procedure and uniformity they were to become by 1950, and trials could be quite turbulent affairs. However, this informality and seeming disorder may also have been partly due to the fact that there was no real 'legal profession' as we would now understand the term. Hence the participation of the general public in the legal process was arguably more wide-ranging than it is today. As detailed in the previous chapter, for instance, more than 80 per cent of criminal prosecutions in the 1790s were brought by the victims themselves (Emsley 2005: 183). In other words, the state rarely prosecuted offences – if you had been the victim of a theft or a mugging, it was up to you to bring charges. Moreover, while solicitors did exist, they were not often employed in criminal cases, and there was generally no professional representation in court. Trials thus consisted primarily of a face-to-face confrontation between plaintiff and accused, mediated by the judge and the jury (who at this stage were still allowed to ask questions), and could be very short. Trials themselves, particularly those involving magistrates sitting in petty sessions, could take place in a number of venues, from the parlour of the county gentry to a private room off the local pub. Thus, as Peter King notes, far from reflecting solely the majesty of the law, 'many assize proceedings may perhaps more fruitfully be seen as "participatory theatre"' (King 2000: 255). By the 1950s, of course, following a long period of bureaucratization and rationalization over the course of the nineteenth century, most of this had changed. The judiciary was fully professional (although magistrates were still voluntary), trials took place in purpose-built premises and were conducted by specialist personnel, the state customarily prosecuted criminal offences and legal assistance was available to all under the Legal Aid and Legal Advice Act of 1949.

Given these broad changes, it might be tempting to read the history of the courts as a gradual change from a chaotic and biased system to the more orderly, representative arrangement we know today. However, it is important to avoid simplistic notions of 'progress' when studying history, and many of the developments in the criminal justice system alluded to above were hotly contested at the time, as can be seen if we consider the operation of the courts in more detail.

Obviously, the further back in time one peers, the more basic the 'official' structures of justice. Rural medieval and early-modern communities had a number of ways of resolving disputes without recourse to law and the courts. Community sanctions (such as *charivari*, for example) could be applied, or mediation by a local person of authority (such as a member of the clergy or a representative from the nobility) could be sought. However, the gradual expansion of the state during the sixteenth and seventeenth centuries meant that the 'rule of law' was becoming increasingly dominant within English society. This was, however, by no means a uniform system. Indeed, a variety of courts were in still in existence in England during the mid-eighteenth century. Ecclesiastical courts, which had once been extremely powerful, still retained vestiges of authority. They could theoretically try certain offences against morality and retained their authority over divorce until the mid-nineteenth century. Military courts were influential, too, particularly during times of war when they exercised virtually sole jurisdiction over large groups of enlisted men. Aside from these, however, the main courts throughout the period in question were the magistrates' courts, the quarter sessions and the assize courts. In magistrates' courts, one magistrate sitting in 'petty sessions' decided cases alone, and these usually handled the bulk of minor crime. The quarter sessions and assizes tried more serious offences where a jury was present.

Over the course of the eighteenth century, the number of offences which could be heard 'summarily' (by one magistrate sitting alone in 'petty sessions') had increased significantly to embrace the majority of thefts and also minor crimes such as poaching. As noted already, most prosecutions, both criminal and civil, were privately brought. The state had very little role in bringing cases to court, except in a few limited instances, like that of treason. In practice, these two developments meant that, firstly, the magistrates' courts were the busiest element of the criminal justice system and that, secondly, the plaintiff bringing the case to court could often decide him/herself whether to opt for a summary trial (which was likely to be quite quick) or press for a trial by jury (where the sentences could be stiffer but which would inevitably take much longer). In addition, as Peter King has noted, it also meant that the boundaries between criminal and civil cases were 'extremely blurred', as legislation usually allowed plaintiffs to opt for either (2000: 8).

More serious trials took place in the higher courts – the quarter sessions and the assizes. Outside of London, quarter sessions only took place four times a year (hence the name) and assizes usually only twice. Bail was rarely granted in such cases and hence the accused was often in gaol for several months *prior* to the trial itself. There is an interesting modern parallel here, with 60 per cent of the defendants remanded into custody awaiting trial never actually receiving a prison sentence in the end. Further, the significant delays between the apprehension of the accused and the administration of justice also added to the costs of justice for the victim/plaintiff. After bringing a case, the plaintiff would have to travel to attend the court (which was usually held in the county town) and pay to stay for several days while waiting for his case to reach the top of the list (no timetable was drawn up). Those prosecuting might also have to pay the expenses of any witnesses they wished to appear. A consultant before the 1819 Select Committee on Criminal Laws testified that numerous cases seemed to be going unprosecuted due to 'the considerable sacrifice of time, the additional cost, nay the *heavy* load of expense, the tiresomeness of attendance, and keeping witnesses together' (Emsley 2005: 192). Such concerns eventually resulted in Robert Peel's 1826 Criminal Justice Act which, among other things, provided for the paying of expenses for some witnesses as well as prosecutors.

Some reformers also concluded in the wake of the 1826 Criminal Justice Act that a system of public prosecutions, as was in fact in operation in Scotland

and parts of continental Europe at the time, would be preferable to this private system. However, this took a long time to introduce. Successive bills failed in the House of Commons in the 1830s, the 1850s and the 1870s, partly due to vested interest on the part of solicitors, partly due to fears of cost and partly because of concerns over the erosion of individual liberties. While a director of public prosecutions was appointed in 1879, this post was mostly advisory for almost thirty years. However, as Emsley notes, until recently, 'the increasing role of the police as prosecutors from the middle of the nineteenth century has been largely ignored by historians' (Emsley 2005: 195). This is despite the considerable impact which the introduction of police prosecutors had on crime (particularly violent crime) statistics. There is a noticeable decline in prosecutions whenever the police – rather than individuals with summonses – were the route to trial.

So, in the mid- to late-nineteenth century, most defendants faced a police prosecutor and a single magistrate (or as many who bothered to turn up that day) in provincial police courts. In London, the situation was slightly different. There stipendiary magistrates (professional lawyers who were paid a salary), again sitting in so-called 'police courts', dealt with the large number of petty cases heard in the capital. By 1850 these courts were dealing with over 100,000 cases a year in London alone. As will be discussed in the third section below, they also acted as advice centres and places where the neighbourhood disputes of the poor could be settled swiftly and cheaply (Davis 1984).

The development of the legal system over the course of the nineteenth century is thus a complex one, but by the First World War the courts as we know them today were largely in operation. Of course, there were changes to the system even in the twentieth century, particularly in relation to magistrates' courts. An Act of 1908, for example, known as the 'children's charter', established specialized juvenile courts. Following the Children and Young Persons Act of 1933 magistrates with special qualifications were henceforth selected for this work. The Sex Disqualification (Removal) Act of 1919 ensured that women were able to become magistrates for the first time. The quarter sessions had lost their administrative function in 1888, when the passing of the Local Government Act empowered county councils to take charge of matters such as the upkeep of the roads. However, both the assizes and quarter sessions continued in roughly the same form until 1971, when the Courts Act replaced them with Crown Courts run by central government.

Clearly then, radical changes took place in both the administration of justice and the dispensation of punishment in the period 1750–1950. On the one hand, there was a trend towards increasing uniformity and professionalization. Yet, on the other, there was no real state prosecution or profession of 'barrister' until relatively late in the nineteenth century (Rock 2004). While the Prisoner's Counsel Act of 1836 had recognized the right of a defendant in a felony case to legal representation (and also allowed defence counsel to address the jury for the first time), many lawyers in fact doubted its efficacy in the criminal courts and the public remained sceptical until quite late in the century. Moreover, despite the retrospective pride often taken in the English 'trial by jury' system, the Jervis Acts of 1848 had massively expanded the jurisdiction of the summary courts, and meant that magistrates sitting alone were dealing with twenty times the number of cases dealt with by all the other criminal courts combined (Emsley 2005: 210). In fact, even trials in the Old Bailey, the foremost criminal court, could be hasty affairs. In 1833 it was calculated that the average trial took under nine minutes with a trial of several hours being noteworthy (Beattie, 1986: 376).

Thus, as with the New Police discussed in Chapter 2, it is too simplistic to view the changes which took place over this period as merely 'progress' or 'professionalization'. Certainly, as Emsley asserts, 'the relaxed, relatively informal magistrates' tribunals of the eighteenth century had little place in the increasingly urbanized England of the nineteenth century with its emphasis on decorum and bureaucratic formality', but change was slow and often contradictory, and the reasons driving it were far from simple (Emsley 2005: 205). Moreover, as already noted, it is not enough for the historian simply to *narrate* these developments, and it is too simplistic to attribute them merely to 'progress'. *Why* did these changes occur? What *significance* did they hold for those involved in reform? Such 'historiographical' questions will be the subject of the sections which follow.

The Old Central Criminal Court at the Old Bailey. The Sword of Justice can be seen suspended above the seat of the Judge.
Source: *The Police Journal*, Vol. IV, 1931.

Historians, law and the courts between 1750 and 1850

There has been considerable debate among historians concerning the evolution of the criminal law and its enforcement in the courts during the period 1750–1850. At a first glance, much legislation passed in the late eighteenth and early nineteenth century appears overly concentrated on property crime and less concerned about violent crime. The so-called 'Bloody Code' (a series of over 200 statutes via which the death penalty could be applied to relatively minor theft offences) has often been cited as evidence that the criminal law was primarily a mechanism via which class power was maintained. In a fairly typical instance from 1796, for example, a 15-year-old boy from a poor family was sentenced to death for pick-pocketing a leather notebook worth two shillings. His situation was characteristic of many thousands of other petty pilferers and thieves who faced capital punishments. By contrast to this ferocious response to a case of petty theft, John Beattie (and many others) have noted that 'there was clearly a high tolerance of violent behaviour in eighteenth-century society' (Beattie 1986: 75). What appear to us as quite shocking instances of violence were often virtually ignored by legislators and the courts. The Old Bailey sessions papers detail quite a number of instances where backstreet fights (often with hundreds of spectators) ended in the death of one participant. In one such case from 1803, the guilty defendant was briefly imprisoned and fined just six shillings.

However, Emsley has argued that in fact the 'Bloody Code' of the late-eighteenth century has been somewhat misread by some historians of crime. While it was undoubtedly a harsh and noteworthy set of statutes (over 200 by 1820), there were many overlapping areas covered by separate laws. 'Destroying Westminster Bridge' was one statute, and 'Destroying Fulham Bridge' (to all intents and purposes the same offence) was another. There were 20 separate statutes, for example, protecting trees, hollies, thorns and other types of plants from theft. Thus the sheer number of capital statutes, which might initially appear to indicate an extreme disciplinary code, has to be approached with caution. Moreover, as Emsley notes, there were 'real and heated' debates in Parliament over many aspects of the Bloody Code, and it is certainly not the case that it was an unmitigated attempt to discipline the poorer classes. On occasion, legislation introduced to protect the property of the rich had a hard time passing through the House of Commons (Emsley 2005: 15). Gatrell, moreover, claims that most of those hanged were convicted under 'straightforward' statutes which had been capital for centuries and that pardons were the end result in over 90 per cent of cases by 1820 (1994: 7).

The Bloody Code was gradually dismantled from around 1820 onwards. Martin Wiener has argued persuasively that legal history must be more broadly located within its cultural context, and attributed the dismantling of the Bloody Code to changing Victorian perceptions of offenders, which dictated a rationalization of the criminal law. This idea is covered in greater depth in Chapter 7 but, essentially, Wiener argues that crime came to be seen in the early Victorian period not as an expression of poverty or social circumstances but as the result of 'a fundamental character defect', one which stemmed from 'a refusal or an inability to deny wayward impulses or to make proper calculations of long-run self-interest' (1990: 46). In other words, criminals were simply those who could not control their primitive urges. Thus Victorian reformers aimed to replace the unsystematic and flexible 'Bloody Code' with 'a more defined and impersonal, and thus more predictable, criminal law'. As he notes, the twin aims of 'deterrence and popular character building' dictated that 'the sanctions of the criminal law should be clear, consistent and certain' (Wiener 1990: 61).

However, as Wiener has also noted elsewhere, research among historians has tended to concentrate far more on the criminal law's *administration* than on changes in the law itself (1999). Most debates about the law during this period have addressed not simply the evolution of statutes and laws *per se*, but the wider context of their administration, focusing on the judges, juries and courts which applied the law. A great deal of attention has been applied to the trial process, particular during the period 1750–1820. More specifically, two models have been debated – a 'consensus' model of the law as a system whereby the accepted norms of a society are expressed and enforced, and a 'conflict' model in which the law is viewed as, essentially, an apparatus which operates in the interests of and for the maintenance of a dominant class. Consensus models of the law were often implicit within the work of early historians of crime and the law, such as Sir Leon Radzinowicz, author of the five-volume *A History of the English Criminal Law and Its Administration from 1750* (begun in 1948). The unproblematic use of the theme of 'progress' meant that the administration of justice was dealt with 'as a self-contained and self-explicable sphere whose history can be best understood by working back from later twentieth-century professional perspectives' (Wiener 1987: 85). Conflict models of the law, often initially associated with the work of Marxist historians, viewed the law as primarily constructed to oppress the poor and the working class, and as a mechanism by which the sanctity of the private property of the rich was ensured. More recent research has sought to mediate these two stark positions, and a more nuanced picture of the use of the courts has emerged. These debates are perhaps best illustrated by reference to some key texts.

As noted, early works of criminal justice history such as Radzinowicz's *History of the English Criminal Law* took a somewhat one-dimensional approach to the subject. To understand this, it is important to understand the context in which books such as this were written. In 1948, when the first volume of Radzinowicz's series appeared, it was practically the first book ever published in the field of British criminal justice history. It appeared at a time when pride in British institutions was at a peak. After all, British democracy in the aftermath of the Second World War stood in stark contrast to the revolutions and dictatorships in evidence throughout much of Europe. As Wiener notes:

> At such a moment, the outlines of the nation's criminal justice history seemed quite clear: a gradual and more or less continuous advance out of a 'medieval' world of disorder and cruelty to the present era, in which serious crime had been largely conquered and criminal justice [... had been] made both humane and efficient. (Wiener 1987: 94)

Such complacent approaches to the history of crime and the law remained popular until the early 1970s, when they began to be challenged by a new generation of Marxist historians (Iggers 1997: 78–94). In relation to the courts, Douglas Hay's now well-known essay 'Property, authority and the criminal law' appeared in an edited collection entitled *Albion's Fatal Tree* (1975). This was a bold statement of the working of the courts and the law during the latter half of the eighteenth century, based on a 'conflict' model. Hay argued that the criminal law of the time was constructed by elite groups to serve their own interests and that, as such, it was primarily concerned with protecting the property of the rich. The harsh use of the gallows combined with *discretion* (the possibility of mercy and a reprieve) gave magistrates and judges (all of whom were drawn from the ruling classes) a tool by which to inspire awe and deference in an age before a regular police force. Hay quoted men like the Oxford Professor of Law William Blackstone, who claimed in 1793 that 'the execution of a needy decrepit assassin is a poor satisfaction for the murder of a nobleman in the bloom of his youth, and full enjoyment of his friends, his honours, and his fortune' (Hay 1975: 19). Clearly, argued Hay, all men were *not* equal before the law in this age.

He then further focused on three particular aspects of the work of the courts – the *majesty* of the law, the notion of *justice* and the prerogative of *mercy*. The ceremonial *majesty* of the law, typified by the solemn wearing of a black cap when the death sentence was pronounced or the pure white gloves worn after a 'maiden assizes' (one in which no death sentences had been passed), inspired deference and awe in the lower classes. Combined with this, the criminal law seemed to offer *justice*. It appeared impartial, an appearance sustained by the occasional execution of a minor member of the nobility. In fact, the weight of the law pressed down harder on the poor than on any other group, but this seeming impartiality helped to secure its acceptance. Finally, argued Hay, the prerogative of *mercy* on the part of those bringing the prosecution (by only pressing minor charges, or by dropping the charges altogether) meant that, 'in short, it was in the hands of the gentlemen who went to law to evoke gratitude as well as fear in the maintenance of deference' (1975: 41). Thus, as E. P. Thompson noted in developing Hay's thesis, while it was not the case that the ruling classes could simply do as they pleased (they too were bound by the law which they had constructed to an extent), certainly 'the law did mediate existent class relations to the advantage of the rulers' (1975: 264).

However, Langbein (1983) critiqued Hay's essay from a conservative perspective. He argued that, in fact, while many of the 'accused' appearing in court were drawn from the lower classes, most of the 'victims' pressing charges were not that much better off. Anyone studying the Old Bailey sources, Langbein claimed, 'will conclude that the victims seldom come from the propertied élite' (1983: 101). Moreover, in numerous instances, sentences of death were commuted or lowered not by the judge but by the jury, which was often drawn from men of the more 'middling sort'. Far from the elite bulwark that Hay claimed them to be, Langbein quotes Martin Madan, who worried in 1785 that petty jurors at assizes were usually 'low and ignorant country people' (Langbein 1983: 107). Thus, overall, Langbein maintained that 'the whole of the criminal justice system, especially the prosecutorial system, was principally designed to protect the people, overwhelmingly non-elite, who suffered from crime' (1983: 105). Clearly, this was a much more 'consensual' view of the law than that constructed by Hay.

John Beattie's *Crime and the Courts* contributed significantly to moving this complex debate forward. He looked at assizes and quarter sessions cases (as opposed to very big state trials or magistrates' petty sessions), concentrating on those of Surrey and Sussex. Beattie agreed with Hay that the preponderance of offences against property in the courts was striking, and noted that violence which did not cause death was rarely the subject of successful prosecution. However, he went on to argue convincingly that the criminal law was by no means simply a tool fashioned to maintain the power of the propertied classes. Gentlemen, in fact, were the smallest group of prosecutors in his sample, while 14–18 per cent of prosecutions were initiated by labourers or servants. The criminal law was used by all classes but did not, of course, treat all with equality.

These debates continued, in one form or another, for some time. It is important to realize, as Peter King noted:

> The development of an increasingly subtle and detailed picture of how the administration of the criminal justice system worked has not [...] always led to greater agreement among historians about who controlled the law [...] or about the extent to which the law [...] underpinned and legitimized the rule of the eighteenth-century elite. (King 2000: 3)

That said, King does provide a near definitive (or at least highly convincing) statement on the matter. He adopted a pluralistic view of the criminal law of the period, proposing neither a wholly consensual or an entirely conflict driven model, and questioning the very idea that 'the law' can be considered as a unified concept. Rather, he argued, 'the law held different meanings for different people and its pluralistic nature meant that each individual or social group might have a range of often contradictory experiences of legal institutions' (2000: 3).

More specifically, King asserted initially that the law *was* applied unequally within late eighteenth-century society. Wealthy individuals who purloined money or property (either by weights and measures fraud or tax evasion) were rarely branded as criminals, but rather usually faced a *civil* case. By contrast, those among the poorer classes accused of theft were routinely dealt with via the *criminal* law, with all the stigma this held. However, it is important, he argued, to move beyond this assumption of inequality to a more nuanced picture. Historical evidence shows that a substantial number of labourers brought prosecutions to the courts, thus using the law for their own protection. Only 5–10 per cent of prosecutions involved the gentry or professional classes as victims/plaintiffs (2000: 3). Moreover, members of the lower classes bringing cases to court often used *discretion* themselves, by initiating a prosecution but not actually turning up for the trial. The case was then dismissed, but they had the satisfaction of knowing that the accused had suffered a lengthy period of pre-trial imprisonment. Thus as King argued, 'the decisions that pulled the levers of fear and mercy were not taken by propertied men alone' (2000: 358).

Petty jurors of the 'middling sort', King claimed, also played an important part in the trial process. Primarily shopkeepers and prosperous artisans, they acquitted or reduced the charges against nearly half of all indicted property offenders. Thus, the 'theatre of the law' did not always function as elite groups wished. While undoubtedly disadvantaged in the courts, the lower classes still used the law to their own ends, bringing cases themselves, exercising discretion and (on occasion) making their presence felt in noisy courtroom protests. The concept of discretion thus tempers straightforward class views of the operation of the criminal justice system during the period 1750–1850.

Of course, this debate is just one among many you may encounter in studying the courts and the development of the criminal justice system. Most discussions, however, start from the assumption that the law favoured some groups in society more than others, and then argue about the precise extent of this bias and the timing of its erosion. Most historians would probably agree that by 1850 the application of the law was more consensual than it was in 1750. However, did that continue in the following century?

Historians, law and the courts between 1850 and 1950

The first half of the nineteenth century had witnessed a huge increase in the use of the courts. Gatrell and Hadden claim that while around 4,500 men and women had been prosecuted in assizes and quarter sessions in 1805, this figure had risen to over 30,000 by 1842 (1972: 293–3). The expansion of the jurisdiction of the summary courts via statutes such as the Criminal Justice Act of 1855 meant that the lower courts (arguably more accessible to the ordinary member of the public) also witnessed a great rise in business. By 1857, justices sitting in petty sessions had to cope with over twenty times the total number of cases dealt with by all other courts combined (Emsley 2005: 210). Partly, this development can be seen as a reflection of the increased expansion of the state into everyday life throughout English society. As the jurist J. F. Stephen noted in 1863, 'the administration of criminal justice is the commonest, the most striking, and the most interesting shape, in which the sovereign power of the state manifests itself to the great bulk of its subjects' (Gatrell 1990: 239). Thus again the question arises – in whose interests did this growing use of the courts operate? The extent to which different groups within society were able to access and use the legal system has already been debated in the second section above. Current thinking emphasizes the way in which the law and the courts, while expressive of an elite perspective, were also used artfully by a broad cross-section of individuals to obtain what they felt to be 'justice'. This mixture of partiality and even-handedness is also in evidence later in the century in, for example, London's police courts. The rapid growth of London at the end of the eighteenth century had led to calls for stipendiary (salaried) magistrates. In 1792 a system of paid magistrates for London was set up. Initially, these officials sat in police offices and even had certain investigative powers. The posts were further reformed in the 1820s and 1830s, and after 1839 lost their police functions and became attached to the newly established Metropolitan Police Courts (Davis 1984, 1989). By mid-century there were

Bow Street Police Court.
Source: A. Griffiths (1898) *Mysteries of Police and Crime*. London: Cassell.

13 such courts with 26 magistrates dispensing rapid justice on all manner of small misdemeanours. By 1855 the courts were handling around 100,000 cases per annum (Davis 1984: 312). If an individual was arrested on a minor matter (including offences such as being drunk and disorderly, petty theft and vagrancy), they were likely to be held in the cells overnight and to appear before the police court magistrate the following morning. The police courts handled a vast range of business and, as Davis notes, 'at mid-century, the stipendiary magistrate probably wielded more unsupervised power then any other paid functionary of the legal system' (1984: 311). Police court magistrates were highly paid (deliberately so, to avoid attracting merely rejects from the bar) and were often both socially and professionally prominent. How then did they deal with those who came before them, who were overwhelmingly (but not entirely) drawn from the working class?

According to Davis and others, stipendiary magistrates often went beyond a strict enforcement of the law. They also distributed financial relief to destitute supplicants, used their 'enormous' discretion to arbitrate disputes between the poor and 'offered a wide range of individual advice to their predominantly working-class clientele' (1984: 309). In the words of a witness to the 1837 Select Committee on Metropolitan Police Offices the police courts came to be seen as 'a poor man's system of justice'. The police and the propertied classes certainly used the police courts to prosecute members of the lower classes, but they were not solely an apparatus of social discipline. A fifth of all larceny charges heard by the police courts were brought by working-class prosecutors. Although most assault charges were presented by the police, it was also relatively common for residents of working-class neighbourhoods to bring assault charges, or for women to seek redress for violence perpetrated on them by their husbands. Overall, the police courts have been represented by historians as an arena in which family and neighbourhood disputes could be arbitrated and free legal advice received.

However, while many justices were no doubt sympathetic towards their clientele, part of the rationale behind the police courts (as Davis makes clear) was to win working-class support for the law. The Metropolitan Police were, during the latter part of the century, still immensely unpopular with the working class. An explicit motivation behind the setting up of the police courts was 'not merely to suppress law breaking but also to win lower-class acceptance of the law and, thus, implicitly of the social order' (Davis 1984: 315). Certain types of cases, particularly those which might be seen as challenging to the existing social order (such as complaints of police brutality and mistreatment while in custody), generally received an unsympathetic hearing. Thus, as during the earlier period under discussion in the second section above, it is clear that the law and the courts were not entirely consensual, nor yet entirely a mechanism of social control, but rather an admixture of both fairness and support for the existing social order.

The role of the criminal justice system in supporting the existing status quo (both social and political) is quite evident during the period 1850–1950, albeit not perhaps as clearly as a century before, and is worth exploring in rather more detail. Arguably, there was a marked decline in 'class strife' by the end of the nineteenth century and recorded crime rates dropped year on year between 1850 and 1900. This is not to say that there were not moments of real public concern over the threat of disorder. During the mid-1880s, for example, following a severe economic depression, unemployed workers had taken to sleeping in large numbers in Trafalgar Square. A series of mass demonstrations were clumsily handled by the police who vastly underestimated the manpower required for the job, and prolonged rioting broke out. A thick fog descended on London and for several days looting and disorder swept the West End (Stedman Jones 1971). However, in general, historians believe that the bulk of the working class was gradually co-opted into mainstream society during the latter half of the nineteenth century. By the end of the period, only the 'residuum' (a derogatory term for the poorest, roughest and most unproductive element of the working class) was feared.

However, these social changes do not mean that the 'class' bias in the use of the law and the courts necessarily disappeared. The growth of general consent to the rule of law and the gradual acceptance of the role of the police and the courts by the majority of the population did not end the suppression of certain forms of public dissent. It is possible to argue that the law and the courts were, until well into the twentieth century, still a vehicle for the suppression of dissatisfaction with the status quo, particularly on the part of the working class and the political left (which were often virtually synonymous). As Gatrell notes:

> The construction of consent through more or less concealed forms of coercion remained an option with which the liberal state could no more dispense than could the totalitarian. For it was an inevitable corollary of

consent-building that *dissent* should come to be invested in the liberal state with new, increasing and peculiar significance. (Gatrell, 1990: 265)

The judiciary, and magistrates in particular, had a role in the suppression of political unrest and the maintenance of public order throughout the nineteenth century. In the first half of the century, especially before the establishment of the New Police, magistrates and troops combined to suppress disorder. If a disturbance (or potential disturbance) was brought to the attention of a magistrate, it was generally his responsibility to decide how to handle the matter. Under common law a 'riot' (sometimes involving only two or three people) was a minor matter, punishable only by prison or a fine. In such circumstances the magistrate might just ask the local sheriff or constable to deal with the situation. However, if a more serious disturbance seemed to be on the horizon, the magistrate could 'read the Riot Act' (or rather, a small section of it) – as detailed below:

> Our Sovereign Lord the King chargeth and commandeth all Persons, being assembled, immediately to disperse themselves, and peaceably to depart to their Habitations, or to their lawful Business, upon the Pains contained in the Act made in the first year of King *George*, for preventing Tumults and riotous Assemblies – God Save the King

Proclamation of the Riot Act 1715

Once the Riot Act had been read out at the scene in a loud voice, the offence of 'riot' became a felony, punishable by death. Thus any individuals who failed to leave the area within an hour could be subdued by force (as opposed to the 'reasonable means' which applied to the offence as a misdemeanour). In the case of a major disturbance, the magistrate was likely either to seek assistance from troops or to enrol special constables (or 'specials') – local men of property sworn in for a limited period to help keep the peace.

Once the New Police had been established, magistrates often requested their assistance rather than resort to the use of troops or special constables. Obviously, between 1829 and about 1839, the Metropolitan Police were the sole 'new' police force. As such, their assistance was often requested by local magistrates who feared unrest. Between 1830 and 1838 a total of 2,246 officers from London were sent to the provinces to quell rioting (Vogler 1991: 97). These forays were generally successful. Aided by the new inventions of the telegraph and (particularly) the railway, officers were now able to move around the country swiftly in response to the threat of disturbance, often arriving in hours rather than days. The fact that London was the hub of the new rail network bolstered this process. In some cases police squads sent to the provinces worked alongside the military and cooperated successfully with them.

During the early part of the twentieth century, the responsibility of magistrates to quell public dissent was gradually shifted to Chief Constables and to central government. Vogler argues that the direct intervention by the Home Secretary (Winston Churchill) at the Tonypandy strike disturbances in

1910 was crucial in this regard (Vogler 1991). However, the judiciary remained a core element in the suppression of political and labour unrest until well into the twentieth century. Fears over the rising influence of the political left and the possibilities for public disorder that might ensue led to the passing of several statutes (including the Emergency Powers Act of 1920 and the Public Order Act of 1936) which were enforced via the courts. The case of *Duncan* v. *Jones*, for example (actually just prior to the passing of the Public Order Act) concerned the power of the police to stop meetings even where no obstruction or disorder was apparent. The police case was upheld by the High Court. As Barbara Weinberger notes, 'in other words, the police were granted the right to ban any political meeting in the street, where previously they had only been able to intervene if an immediate breach of the peace was threatened' (Weinberger 1995: 174). Thus it is possible to argue that one of the principal activities of magistrates, the courts and the law throughout this period was the maintenance of the status quo in the face of demands for the reordering of society from below.

Once again, then, it is apparent that the law and the courts (although they had changed considerably from the 1750s) were not necessarily the wholly consensual system we might like to imagine. Changes in the role of women within society, and in relation to the law and the courts in particular, serve to underline this further. Perceptions of women as criminals and the role of women as offenders are discussed in Chapters 7 and 8. However, what about the involvement of women in the criminal justice system from the other side, as prosecutors, witnesses – even as magistrates and judges? To what extent did the courts consider and satisfy the needs of women? A brief consideration of the issue of domestic violence can perhaps illustrate the now familiar picture of use of the courts by a group within society, but only within a set of constraints not always particularly favourable to or understanding of the needs of that group.

During the seventeenth and eighteenth centuries, the physical chastisement of women by their husbands was generally accepted by the courts. However, by the mid-nineteenth century, this was becoming less and less publicly acceptable. By the start of the twentieth century, notions of 'reasonable chastisement' had all but disappeared. This changing tolerance of violence against women was mirrored by legislative changes. The Matrimonial Causes Act of 1878 gave magistrates the power to order separations and insist that husbands paid a weekly sum for the maintenance of their wife and children. The Summary Jurisdiction (Married Women) Act of 1895 allowed women to make the decision to separate from their husbands themselves. As Shani D'Cruze notes, 'this legislation meant that the magistrates' courts became a more frequent resort of women subject to violence by their husbands, and magistrates took on the role of both "marriage menders", and overseers of separations' (D'Cruze 1998: 11). Given this, it is tempting to see here gradual 'progress' and the evolution of a more civilized vision of society. However, on closer inspection the picture is, perhaps not unexpectedly, more complex than that.

On the one hand, it is undeniable that the courts increasingly sought to protect women from violence, and to stiffen the sentences given to those who transgressed. Martin Wiener has dissected the case of George Hall, tried in 1864 for shooting his new bride Sarah (Wiener 1999). After courting for 3½ years George married Sarah (with whom he had sung for years in a church choir) on Christmas Day 1863. Shortly afterwards, Sarah left the marital home. Her parents brought her back and she stayed a few more weeks before leaving again – almost certainly because of her infatuation with a young Irishman with whom she had been sleeping all along. George purchased a set of pistols, called on Sarah and took her for a walk, shot her in the head and turned himself in. The fact that Hall was convicted of murder despite 'enormous popular sympathy' does indicate the fact that 'judges and other officials were attempting to place violence against wives – regardless of provocation, and despite the lowliness of social position of the perpetrator and victim – beyond the pale of acceptability' (Wiener 1999: 186). However, the scale of the appeals for clemency attached to Hall's case (and his eventual reprieve) perhaps demonstrate that there was still a discrepancy between juries and the public who often advocated leniency, and the judges and officials determined to make a stand on this issue.

Moreover, even in the final quarter of the nineteenth century, if a wife was seen to have 'aggravated' the situation, via nagging, taunts, insults or wilful behaviour, then the verdict of the law could still appear harsh. D'Cruze notes that 'magistrates used the courts to discipline the perceived "rough" elements, particularly among working-class men given to drunkenness and violence. Women whose sexuality was seen to be lax could also receive the opprobrium of the court' (1998: 4). Adverse assumptions about the evidence of women in such cases remained common among the judiciary. A handbook on sentencing published by Edward Cox in 1877 argued that:

> In the vast majority of these cases the suffering angel of the sensation 'leader' [newspaper article] is found to be rather an angel of the fallen class, who has made her husband's home an earthly hell, who spends his earning in drink, pawns his furniture, starves her children, provides for him no meals, lashes him with her tongue when sober and with her fists when drunk, and if he tries to restrain her fits of passion, resists with a fierceness and a strength for which he is no match. (Tomes 1978: 339)

Thus, while women gradually (and increasingly) grew to use the law and the courts to protect themselves from violence and to seek redress, even at the start of the twentieth century the protection afforded by the courts only really reflected changing conceptions of what *men* thought was acceptable. It is an obvious point, but one worth making, that women were not actually involved in the courts as representatives of the state until very late in the period. Judicial appointments were only opened to women in 1919 (coincident with granting of the franchise). The first female magistrates were appointed in 1919 and the first female barrister in 1922. However, it was not until 1945 that the first female judge (Sybil Campbell) was appointed. Obviously there is a limit to how 'consensual' a system which excluded approximately half of the population from direct participation could ever have been.

Conclusion

Clearly, 'the law and the courts' is too big a topic to discuss comprehensively in a single chapter. However, a number of issues have hopefully been clarified somewhat. While changing significantly in appearance and usage over the period 1750–1950, the law and the courts can essentially be viewed as arenas where competing social demands are exercised. As Wiener has argued, '"Courts" have been regarded as a single thing – the "courts" did this or that. Yet, before they produced verdicts and rulings, courts were settings for events – arenas where competing narratives were in play, sites of contestation where values and beliefs were not only declared but shaped' (Wiener 1999: 469/70). A wide range of debates have been conducted by historians researching the courts. Many of them, however, have focused on the extent to which the law and the courts acted more in the interests of some groups within society than others. As Gatrell notes: 'The question of how poorer people regarded the law and its enforcers – the question of consent itself – is central to all assessments of the legitimacy of the state. It is a question on which opinions divide' (Gatrell 1990: 281). Historians have sought to show how poorer members of society (and other groups such as women, trade unionists and those on the political left) sought to use the law, often in ways which confounded the intentions of those shaping legislation. It is clear that the law and the courts were not entirely consensual, nor yet entirely a mechanism of social control, but rather an admixture of both fairness and support for the existing social order. It would be hard to argue that law did not become any more consensual during the period 1750–1950, but it perhaps did not change as quickly or as completely as might initially be imagined.

Key questions

1. To what extent did the law and the courts reflect the needs of the whole of English society during the period 1750–1950?

This is a vast period of time, and any answer must take account of the significant changes which took place in the administration of justice during these two centuries. Broadly speaking, there was a shift from a lively, contested, amateur court system where prosecution was usually initiated by the aggrieved party (at their own expense) to a more professional, orderly system where the police were responsible for bringing most cases to court with the aid of full-time lawyers and judges. It is tempting to view the development of the modern court system as 'progress' and to make glib assumptions as to the extent to which courts gradually came to work more efficiently and to serve all members of English society equally. There is some basic truth in this portrait, but it needs to be nuanced considerably. In the first instance, there is much historical evidence to suggest that, if not solely a vehicle for elite repression of the masses, the law and the courts in the period to 1850 by no means represented all members of society equally. Women were often absent from the courts, and the poorer classes often found that the system did not work to their advantage. Violent crime was often sidelined by legislators in favour of a concentration on property crime. That said, recent research by King and others into the use of *discretion* has strengthened the notion that all but the poorest were able to use the law to further their aims, albeit often not in the ways those in authority intended. In the period after 1850, while it might be argued that London's police courts did function as a 'poor man's system of justice', the role of the law and the courts in maintaining the social and economic status quo (often by marginalizing the needs and demands of women, trade unionists and those on the political left) should not be underestimated.

2. Assess the ways in which women participated in the courts during the period 1850–1950.

There is a growing literature which addresses issues of gender in relation to crime and the law, considering women as both offenders and active participants in the criminal justice process. See initially the pioneering work by Walkowitz (1980), Zedner (1991) and D'Cruze (1998). From a criminological perspective see Carlen (1985) and Heidensohn (2002). For focused articles see Feeley and Little (1991) and D'Cruze (1999).

3. 'During the period 1780–1820, the courts were primarily a mechanism via which property rights were maintained.' Do you agree?

There is a tightly focused body of historical work which addresses this period. See Hay (1975), Langbein (1983) and Thompson (1975) in the first instance. This early work has been enriched by Beattie (1986), Brewer and Styles (1980) and, most recently, by King (2000). Other work touching on the topic includes McGowan (1983) and Rock (2004).

Further reading

The references for this chapter can be found in the Bibliography at the back of the book. If you wish to do some further reading, you should investigate these first. However, below is a list of publications which could also be consulted.

Brewer, J. and Styles, J. (eds) (1980) *An Ungovernable People. The English and Their Law in the Seventeenth and Eighteenth Centuries*. London: Hutchinson.
Cairns, D. (1998) *Advocacy and the Making of the Adversarial Criminal Trial 1800–1865*. Oxford, Clarendon Press.
Carlen, P. (1985) *Criminal Women*. Cambridge: Polity.
D'Cruze, S. (1999) 'Sex, violence and local courts. Working-class respectability in a mid-nineteenth-century Lancashire town', *British Journal of Criminology*, 39, 1, pp. 39–55.
Davis, J. (1989) 'Prosecutions and their context. The use of the criminal law in later nineteenth-century London', in D. Hay and F. Snyder (eds), *Policing and Prosecution in Britain, 1750–1850*. Oxford: Oxford University Press.

Feeley, M. and Little, D. (1991) 'The vanishing female: The decline of women in the criminal process, 1687–1912', *Law and Society Review*, 25, pp. 719–57.

Hay, D. (1984) 'The criminal prosecution in England and its historians', *Modern Law Review*, 47, pp. 1–29.

Heidensohn, F. (2002) 'Gender and crime', in M. Maguire, R. Morgan and R. Reiner (eds), *The Oxford Handbook of Criminology*. Oxford: Oxford University Press, pp. 491–535.

Iggers, G. (1997) *Historiography in the Twentieth Century*. Hanover, NH and London: Weslyan University Press.

McGowan, R. (1983) 'The image of justice and reform of the criminal law in early nineteenth-century England', *Buffalo Law Review*, 23, pp. 89–125.

May, A. (2003) *The Bar and the Old Bailey – 1750–1850*. Chapel Hill, NC: University of North Carolina Press.

Zedner, L. (1991) *Women, Crime and Custody in Victorian England*. Oxford: Oxford University Press.

5. Punishment, 1750–1950

Introduction

The contrast between the punishments dispensed by the courts in 1750 and 1950 is, if anything, even starker than the changes in the judicial system outlined in the previous chapter. In the late eighteenth century, execution or transportation (initially to America and then to Australia) were the norm for all serious (and many more minor) offences. Prisons were used primarily to detain offenders before and after trial, and to imprison debtors who could not pay their fines. Executions were public, and regularly drew crowds numbering in their thousands. While it is true that many of those condemned to death received reprieves, many thousands did not (Gatrell 1994: 7). Even young teenagers were, on occasion, executed. While more serious non-fatal mutilations (such as the burning of the hands for thieves) were declining by c.1750, whipping (in public, too, for men until c.1830) remained 'a common punishment for petty offences' (Emsley 2005: 254). The offender, male or female, was 'stripped to the waist and flogged along a public street'. As late as 1820 men convicted of treason could have their heads cut off and held up to the crowd. By 1950, however, this system of bodily punishment had been largely replaced by the almost exclusive use of the prison in serious criminal cases. While the death penalty was not finally abolished until 1969 (with the last person hanged in 1964), transportation had ended in the 1860s along with public executions, and the prison had long been the primary punishment inflicted by the courts. While discussions about the purpose of prisons had been raised by books such as John Howard's 1777 treatise *The State of the Prisons in England and Wales* it was during the nineteenth century, and particularly during the relatively short period c.1830–c.1880, that the prison rose to prominence. This change, and indeed almost all of the changes outlined above, have been the subject of heated debate among historians. Does the rise of the prison indicate a growth of 'humanitarianism', or just a switch to a different (but similarly severe) method of discipline? Was there a relationship between changing modes of punishment and the rise of industrial society and (later) the welfare state? When precisely did the 'rise of the prison' occur? Some of these debates will be explored in the second and third sections below. First of all, however, we need a clearer idea of how and when all these changes occurred.

FLOGGING GAROTTERS AT LEEDS

The Police Illustrated News of 18 December 1869 reported on the new legislation which allowed the flogging of those convicted of robbery. The cat o'nine tails (nine pieces of thin leather with three knots in each strand) was used here to inflict what was hoped would be a deterrent to violent offenders.

Introductory reading

Emsley, C. (2005) *Crime and Society in England, 1750–1900* (3rd edn). Harlow: Longman, Chapter 10.

Garland, D. (1985) *Punishment and Welfare. A History of Penal Strategies*. London: Gower, Chapter 2.

Gatrell, V. A. C. (1994) *The Hanging Tree: Execution and the English People, 1780–1868*. Oxford: Clarendon, pp. 1–25.

Ignatieff, M. (1978) *A Just Measure of Pain. The Penitentiary in the Industrial Revolution, 1750–1850*, London: Macmillan, chapter 1, 'Pentonville'

McGowan, R. (1987) 'The body and punishment in eighteenth-century England', *Journal of Social History*, 59, December, pp. 651–79.

Changing patterns of punishment, 1750–1950

The period 1750–1950 witnessed a profound shift in the forms of punishment most commonly dispensed by the courts. Essentially, there was a gradual but comprehensive change from 'punishments of the body' (corporal punishment, including the death penalty, and transportation overseas) as the primary sanction for serious offences to incarceration. These two centuries also witnessed significant fluctuations in the aims and social meanings of punishment. Clearly, the death penalty was a purely *retributive* punishment, at least for the individual on the receiving end (it was, however, supposed to deter others). Prisons, by contrast, were (and indeed are) at least partly associated with a belief in *reformative* punishment, although the expression of this changed over time. Training in the virtue of work and frequent visits by the clergy featured heavily in early Victorian regimes, while the period *c*.1865–1895 was marked by the return of harsh prison conditions imbued with a significant deterrent intent. After 1895 the pendulum swung the other way again and the early twentieth century witnessed the rise of what David Garland has termed a 'penal-welfare complex'. The prison was arguably *decentred* from punitive policy in the early part of the twentieth century, and became 'one institution among many in an extended grid of penal sanctions' (Garland 1985a: 23). Britain in fact closed 15 out of 26 local prisons between 1914 and 1930, and the daily average prison population remained between 9,000 and 13,000 throughout the interwar period, roughly half that at the start of the century (Emsley 2005: 21).[1] The rise of penal welfarism is considered in more detail in the third section below but, as stressed in previous chapters, it is important not to see the historical development of the prison and the end of punishments of the body as a smooth continuum of 'progress'. The changing nature of punishment (and the causes behind these changes) have been the subject of many debates among historians. Before considering these debates, however, it is important first to map out the main trends in punishment. Three interlinked and overlapping forms of punishment must be considered – the death penalty, transportation and the prison.

Capital punishment (the death sentence) was still an active penalty for many offences, not just murder, until at least 1830. As discussed in the previous chapter, it was once common for historians to point towards the eighteenth-century Bloody Code (a long series of capital statutes, many of which applied to relatively minor offences) and to assume that punishment in the period was inevitably harsh and unfair. After all, capital offences in the 'Bloody Code' included 'being in the company of gypsies for one month', 'vagrancy for soldiers and sailors' and 'strong evidence of malice in children aged 7–14 years of age'. However, while there were certainly a lot of executions in the period 1750–1850, many for quite minor offences, the code itself has often been misinterpreted. While voluminous, many of its statutes overlap considerably, merely outlawing the same offence in different areas of the country, for example. Moreover, by the end of the Napoleonic Wars, around 90 per cent of those condemned to death were receiving pardons or having their sentence commuted to transportation. Juries appear to have been increasingly unwilling to convict on an array of more minor capital charges. As Emsley notes, many in authority began to worry that this tendency was 'making the judicial system appear an unsustainable lottery' (Emsley 2005: 258).

However, while there was increasing debate about the efficacy of the death penalty as a deterrent, there is another side to this picture of gradual decline in usage. Gatrell, among others, has noted that there was actually an overall

'Capital punishments around the world' – a selection of forms of capital punishment used around the world.
Source: Police Illustrated News, 29 June, 1872.

rise in executions during the early part of the nineteenth century, claiming that

> as many were hanged in London in the 1820s as in the 1790s, and twice as many hanged in London in the thirty years 1801–30 as hanged in the fifty years 1701–50. How easily has this extraordinary fact been forgotten – that the noose was at its most active on the very eve of capital law repeal. (Gatrell 1994: 7)

The picture towards the end of the eighteenth century and the start of the nineteenth is thus a complex one. On the one hand, the 'Bloody Code' was still enforced to some extent. On the other hand, actual executions did not match sentences and calls for change were growing. Reform itself was slow in arriving, however. It was only between 1832 and 1934 that Parliament abolished the death penalty for shoplifting goods worth five shillings or less, returning from transportation, letter-stealing and sacrilege. It was not until 1861 that the number of capital crimes was reduced to just four: murder, treason, arson in royal dockyards and piracy with violence. Moreover, attitudes towards the death penalty, even in the mid-nineteenth century, can seem quite alien to us today. Consider, for example, the following report from the *Times* in 1831 on the execution of John Any Bird Bell.

Report from *The Times*, 2 August, 1831, page 4, col. a

Execution of John Any Bird Bell, For Murder

MAIDSTONE, Aug. 1. – The execution of this wretched youth, who was convicted at our assizes, on Friday last, of the murder of the boy Taylor in a wood near Rochester, took place over the Turnkey's lodge, in the front of the county gaol. The tender age of the culprit, for he was not yet 14, and the circumstances under which the atrocious crime was perpetrated, drew together an immense concourse of people to witness the sad spectacle. [...] by half past 7 o'clock, at least 10,000 persons had congregated near the gaol. [...]
   At half past 11 o'clock, the solemn peals of the prison bell announced the preparations for the execution. After the operation of the pinioning, &c had been completed, the culprit, attended by the chaplain, &c., walked steadily to the platform. When he appeared there, he gazed steadily around him, but his eye did not quail, nor was his cheek blanched. After the rope was adjusted around his neck, he exclaimed in a firm and loud tone of voice, 'Lord have mercy upon us. Lord Have mercy upon us. All the people before me take warning by me!' [...] At the appointed signal, the bolt was withdrawn, and in a minute or two the wretched malefactor ceased to exist.

The execution of John Bell was actually the last of a boy that age. However, it is revealing on a number of counts. Firstly, the reporting of the conduct of the condemned is interesting. This was a significant feature in newspaper accounts of executions, and was often (as here) worded to support the legitimacy of the punishment. Executions were carried out in public due to the perceived 'example' they set, and for the condemned to ask for mercy (and preferably repent) seen as a good thing. Secondly, it reveals the extent to which public executions did draw very large crowds. Executions continued in public until 1868, providing a popular 'thrill' for thousands in a way which seems abhorrent to us now. Martin Wiener argues that the 'thrill' seemingly gained by crowds and the fears of the authorities that onlookers were failing to draw the correct message from executions (but were rather being corrupted by them) were both important factors in the ending of public executions (Wiener 1990).
   The novelist Charles Dickens attended the execution in 1849 of the notorious husband and wife murderers Mr and Mrs George Manning (even hiring a room with a good view of the gallows for ten guineas). He later described vividly the disorderly crowd and noted (perhaps somewhat hypocritically for he too had come to watch) that

a sight so inconceivably awful as the wickedness and levity of the immense crowd collected [...] could be imagined by no man [...] The horrors of the gibbet and of the crime which brought the wretched murderers to it faded in my mind before the atrocious bearing, looks, and language of the assembled spectators. When I came upon the scene at midnight, the *shrillness* of the cries and howls that were raised from time to time, denoting that they came from a concourse of boys and girls already assembled in the best places, made my blood run cold. (Wiener 1990: 97)

Dickens's fear and distaste of the mob are readily apparent. Thus, as Gatrell notes, 'if there was any single reason why executions were hidden behind prison walls from 1868 onwards it was because the crowd's sardonic commentaries could no longer be borne. Too often that despised crowd denounced justice as murderous in itself' (Gatrell 1994: viii). The gradual decline of capital punishment was thus a far from straightforward story. While no longer, by the 1860s, the default punishment for a wide range of crimes, change had been slow in arriving and was not always prompted by the motives which might be expected.

The punishment of transportation shows a similar boom and decline over roughly the same period. Transportation – the removal overseas of offenders not warranting the death penalty but deserving of something more than whipping and a discharge – began following the Transportation Act of 1718. Initially convicts were sent to America, for periods of 7 or 14 years, or for life. Transportation to America was stopped by the outbreak of the War of Independence and the British government looked for another destination. Australia had been claimed as a British territory in 1770 and hence in 1787 the first 778 convicts set sail for Botany Bay in Australia. Convicts sentenced to transportation were initially held on 'hulks' – disused warships. Harsh conditions prevailed even here, and death rates prior to transportation were high. The voyage to Australia was routinely at least six months, and many more died *en route* – locked below decks. On arrival, convicts lived in barracks and were sent out to work for local farmers. As in England, their sentence could be reduced by the granting of a 'ticket of leave' for good behaviour.

As with the death penalty, transportation, which had declined following the American War of Independence, increased during the early part of the nineteenth century. By the 1830s around 5,000 prisoners per annum were being forcibly removed to Australia (Hughes 1987). Between 1787 and 1857 around 160,000 convicts were transported to Australia, the vast majority of them male. Transportees could be as young as 10 or as old as 80, and political prisoners were also transported. Emsley notes that from the beginning of the 1820s to the mid-1830s, 'about one-third of all those convicted at assizes or quarter sessions were either sentenced, or had a death sentence commuted, to transportation' (Emsley 2005: 275). By the mid-nineteenth century, however, public opinion began to turn against the use of transportation as a punishment. Not only were there doubts as to its deterrent efficacy (particularly given that most convicts chose to remain in Australia after the end of the sentence), the system also gradually came under increasing pressure from colonial groups unhappy at the use of their locale for the dumping of dangerous offenders. Both types of views were aired in front of the Select Committee on Transportation which met between 1837 and 1838 (chaired by Sir William Molesworth) and, following prolonged debate, transportation was abolished as a judicial sentence in 1857.

Thus there was a gradual decline in the use of both transportation and the death penalty during the first half of the nineteenth century. Both came gradually to be replaced by the sanction of the prison. Here too, however, developments were by no means sudden. As touched upon above, concerns over the ineffectiveness of the death penalty had been discussed since the English publication of Cesare Beccaria's *Dei Delitti e delle Pene* (On Crimes and Punishments) in 1767. Beccaria had argued that punishment should be more rational and that, rather than relying mainly on the death penalty, it would be more sensible to deprive offenders of their liberty and put them to work. Continuing this debate, the reform advocate John Howard published his treatise *The State of the Prisons in England and Wales* in 1777. Drawing on a study of a number of local prisons, where he had 'beheld scenes of calamity', this text condemned the existing use of prisons in England (largely for the pre-trial detention of offenders) and contributed to arguments that punishment should be both more humane and more consistent (Howard 1929: xix).

Certainly then, by the nineteenth century, there was a growing interest in the prison as an effective deterrent alternative to the death penalty. It is by no means certain, however, that this reform movement was solely (or even primarily) motivated by humanitarian concerns. Partly, perhaps, it grew out of fears that the huge crowds attending executions were not drawing the

Fleet Prison – a debtors' prison – in 1808. Inmates were forced to pay for their own upkeep.
Source: European Centre for the Study of Policing Archive, The Open University.

appropriate lessons from the spectacle and partly it was prompted by a growing desire for a more *effective* and *uniform* system of punishment. Regardless of intent, however, there was a swathe of prison building in the early part of the nineteenth century, and a concomitant decline in the numbers of those being sentenced to death. Construction work on Millbank prison began in 1812 and it was the largest in Europe when it opened in 1816. Pentonville, with its innovative 'separate system' of solitary confinement, was opened in 1842. By the 1830s it was rare for the death sentence to be applied for anything except murder and by the 1850s, imprisonment had become the norm for almost all serious crimes. During the 1860s, over 90 per cent of those convicted of indictable offences went to prison (Wiener 1990: 308). Thus, as Emsley notes:

> If controversy continued to remain about sentencing policy a significant change had taken place. In the space of 100 years a custodial sentence had become virtually the only punishment that the courts could award; fines continued to be imposed for many petty offences, but with the proviso that failure to pay would lead to imprisonment. (Emsley 2005: 287)

As noted above, early prison regimes had a clear reformative intent, based on the understanding that habits of good behaviour could be learnt, principally via strict discipline, hard work and silence. This interest in reform was, however, largely abandoned in the period 1865–1895, for reasons which are debated below. Conditions during this period were such that it has been described as 'the most deterrent period in the history of the modern prison' (Brown 2003: 83). There was a clear increase in the intensity of the punishment of penal servitude (imprisonment with hard labour). Each day was a monotonous and lonely repetition of the one before. Florence Maybrick, for instance, convicted in 1899 of the poisoning her husband with arsenic, spoke of 'the voiceless solitude, the hopeless monotony, the long vista of tomorrow, tomorrow, tomorrow' (Brown 2003: 17). Towards the end of the century, however, the pendulum swung the other way again. A series of social surveys by investigators such as Charles Booth revealed the extent of social deprivation in England, and a succession of economic crises in London meant that:

> By the 1890s it was becoming apparent to all but the most reactionary sections of the bourgeoisie that any adequate solution to the social problem would involve large-scale intervention in the shape of welfare provision, housing improvements, medical care and unemployment relief. (Garland 1985: 56)

This, coupled with a general recognition of the failure of the prison as a disciplinary institution, meant a refocusing of punishment. Prison was still the default sanction, but was bolstered by an array of welfare and medical interventions by the interwar period. The first decade of the twentieth century, for example, saw the rise of the probation service. The origins of probation go back to the nineteenth century practice whereby members of the clergy would agree to take responsibility for young offenders in order to prevent them entering the prison system. However, closely allied to the growth of the discipline of psychology, this charitable system gained official status in 1907 following the Probation of Offenders Act, which enabled courts to assist and advise offenders via specially appointed probation officers. Like the Prison Service, the Probation Service developed locally within regional law enforcement structures like local councils. In this, as in many other new agencies, control and reform were gradually linked to welfare and rehabilitation (Vanstone 2004).

Clearly then, radical changes took place in the dispensation of punishment in the period 1750–1950. However, as already noted, it is not enough for the historian simply to *narrate* these developments, and it is too simplistic to attribute them merely to 'progress'. *Why* did these changes occur? What *significance* did they hold for those involved in reform? Such 'historiographical' questions will be the subject of the sections which follow.

Historians, sociologists and the rise of the prison

There has been a multiplicity of debates among historians, sociologists and criminologists about the changing nature of punishment in the period 1750–1950. Many, however, have the same starting point – how can we account for the sudden dismantling of a system of capital and corporal punishment (executions, whippings and the 'Bloody Code') and its replacement with the prison as the main viable penal sanction? As we have already seen, this change was (in historical terms) rapid. Gatrell notes than 'there has been no greater nor more sudden revolution in English penal history than this retreat from hanging in the 1830s' (Gatrell 1994: 10). It was also very complete. In less than 100 years, a largely novel system of punishment supplanted one which had been in place for centuries. Why was this?

Older, traditional views of this shift (typified by the work of historical criminologists like Sir Leon Radzinowicz) focused on the idea of 'progress', this time in relation to the growth of 'humanitarian' ideas and the spread of liberalism. For Radzinowicz, the 'march of penal progress' was seen as the result of far-sighted policy-makers implementing steadily more rational and effective forms of punishment in response to increasing levels of crime (which eventually declined at the end of the nineteenth century, thus demonstrating the effectiveness of their choices) (Wiener 1987). Certainly, considerations of 'humanitarianism' need to be taken into account when the retreat from the death penalty is analysed. Beccaria and Howard have already been considered above and other philanthropist reformers, such as Sir Samuel Romilly, campaigned vociferously for the end of the 'Bloody Code' from the start of the nineteenth century. However, this 'humanitarian progress' argument cannot simply be taken at face value. As Randall McGowan has noted, Radzinowicz's depiction of a battle between far-sighted reformers and blinkered reactionaries is too simplistic (McGowan 1983). Wider social and political factors have customarily been ignored by proponents of the 'progress' argument but need, equally, to be taken into account.

Consider, for example, the ending of public executions in 1868. In Radzinowicz's eyes, this might be seen as a triumph of human sensibility over irrational barbarism. In fact, both the political climate of the time and changes in broader social sensibilities need to be considered. Fear of the huge, unruly crowds attending executions troubled many in 'polite society' and certainly contributed to the debate. This is not, strictly speaking, a 'humanitarian' concern. Equally, Gatrell notes that it is likely that the liberal government only agreed to the ending of public executions in 1868 in order to outflank the abolitionist camp. In other words, by agreeing to conduct executions in private, the government actually guaranteed that prisoners *could* still be executed. Again, this is hardly a 'humanitarian' motive. Thus older views of changes in punishment find it hard to account for the specific 'timing' of the shift to the prison which, as we have seen, happened quickly, primarily between *c*.1820 and *c*.1870.

Leaving 'humanitarian' concerns to one side, there have been a number of attempts to provide explanations of 'punishment' which, by reference to deeper, structural 'causes', can better account for the specific timing of the rise of the prison. Most notable among these are the work of the Marxist scholars Georg Rusche and Otto Kirchheimer in the 1930s, and the ideas of Michel Foucault and Michael Ignatieff in the 1970s (Rusche and Kirchheimer 1968; Foucault 1991; Ignatieff 1978). All these accounts primarily try to link changes in punishment during the nineteenth century to the Industrial Revolution and

The Old Scaffold at Newgate Prison where numerous executions were carried out. *Source: The Police Journal*, Vol. IV, 1931.

the development of modern, capitalist society. Rusche and Kirchheimer argued that there was a relationship between certain forms of punishment and certain 'modes of production'. They claimed that there was little point studying nineteenth-century penal theory, or the intentions and work of humanitarian reforms, because it was the underlying *economic structure* of society which held the key to the rise of the prison. There is not space to outline these ideas at length, but basically the Marxist approach to punishment held that 'every system of production tends to discover punishments which correspond to its productive relationships' (Rusche and Kirchheimer 1968: 5). The agricultural, medieval economy favoured capital punishment because there was plenty of available labour, and hence some could be wastefully executed as 'examples'. However, during periods of labour shortage, such as the seventeenth century, the labour of convicts could not be wasted and was instead exploited in 'houses of correction'. Such views can easily be criticized as 'reductionist'. In other words, Marxist analyses tend to reduce complex changes to a single driving factor – the economy. Hence they are unlikely to be particularly subtle and are usually no more convincing than the 'progress' view already considered.

However, the works of Foucault (and, to some extent, of Ignatieff), while taking a similar 'structural' approach to the history of punishment (seeking the *underlying* causes of change), were in some ways far more ingenious. Foucault's work in particular is hard to summarize, but his central concern is perhaps with 'power'. Where Rusche and Kirchheimer related punishment to economic production, Foucault linked it to forms of government. He began *Discipline and Punish* with a contrast between a state execution for attempted regicide (killing of the King) in France in 1757 and daily life in prison 80 years later. The plan for the execution specified that:

> On a scaffold that will be erected there, the flesh will be torn from his breasts, arms, thighs and calves with red-hot pincers, his right hand, holding the knife with which he committed the said parricide, burnt with sulphur [...] and then his body drawn and quartered by four horses and his limbs and body consumed by fire [...] and his ashes thrown to the winds. (Foucault 1991: 3)

By contrast, the prison rules from 1838 are a model of uniformity and order. It was decreed that:

> The prisoners' day will begin at six in the morning [...] They will work for nine hours a day throughout the year. Two hours a day will be devoted to instruction [...]. At the first drum-roll, the prisoners must rise and dress in silence [...]. At the second drum-roll, they must be dressed and make their beds. (Foucault 1991: 6)

Foucault believed that the huge contrast between these two forms of punishment could be explained by a consideration of changing forms of government. The harsh public execution was linked to the early-modern absolutist monarchy. The king personally had 'absolute' power over his subjects in all matters, and demonstrated this 'ownership' by punishments effected visibly on their bodies. In the new, increasingly democratic nation-states of the nineteenth century, the individual was the 'property' of society as a whole, and hence punishments were designed not to damage individuals, but to set them to productive work, to reform them, to make them more 'useful' to society.

Foucault also considered a wide range of institutions in addition to the prison, including hospitals, workhouses and army barracks. He regarded all of these as 'mechanisms of control', where new types of 'bureaucratic' discipline were vested. Whereas power in pre-industrial societies was largely individual and hence variable (in other words, it was vested in the *person* of the king or his representatives), power in industrial society resided more in *institutions*. The complexities of modern capitalist society meant that it could not function adequately by relying on the authority of individuals, who could, after all, die or change the way they did things. Rather, power in the nineteenth century rested not with specific individuals but with specific institutions and their abstract knowledge. One prison governor could be replaced by another, who would fulfil the post in the same manner because the 'system' would remain the same. As he expressed it:

> The power in the hierarchized surveillance of the disciplines is not possessed as a thing, or transferred as a property; it functions like a piece of machinery […] it is the apparatus as a whole that produces 'power' […] the disciplinary principle […] constantly supervises the very individuals who are entrusted with the task of supervising. (Foucault 1991: 177)

Hence, for Foucault, the key to an understanding of the prison was primarily a consideration of the changing nature of politics and society in the nineteenth century. Many of his ideas are hard to grasp, especially when described so briefly. The bibliography at the end of this chapter gives some indications as to further reading.

However, Foucault can be criticized on a number of counts. Specifically, historians such as Peter Spierenburg have condemned his lack of historical method. Foucault did not work from archives, by looking at original documents. Rather, he constructed his theory primarily from printed texts. Spierenburg (1991), attempting to assess the changing nature of punishment by a consideration of a wide range of archival sources, dates the rise of the prison much earlier than Foucault, claiming that he [Foucault] merely provides an 'ideal type' which does not stand up to scrutiny. It has also been observed that while Foucault *describes* the transformation in punishment rather well, he does not really provide any convincing *explanation* of it.

However, once explanations of punishment based on the economy, on politics and on notions of 'progress' have been considered but found flawed, what else remains? Some historians stress the need to consider broader social and cultural trends as a way of illuminating changes in punishment. David Garland has pointed to the work of Emile Durkheim (one of the founders of modern sociology) as giving useful insights to any historical criminologist (Garland 1990: 47–83). In his 1925 work *L'Education Morale*, Durkheim was one of the first to consider the moral and social-psychological roots of punishment. He was especially interested in what he termed the 'collective conscience'. In other words, rather than focus on the administrative and managerial aspects of punishment, Durkheim was more interested in its functional role within society, and concluded that it acted to produce solidarity. A re-reading of Durkheim's work can thus help the modern criminologist to understand the importance of the symbolic and emotive roots of punishment, and the wider social context of changing methods of punishment.

One historian who has placed particular emphasis on this wider social context is Martin Wiener. Wiener explicitly rejects explanations of changes in the law and punishment based on what he calls 'internalism' and 'pragmatism'. In other words, nothing is gained (in his view) from writing legal history from an 'internal' standpoint – relating it primarily to the legislation which preceded it and that which came after. Equally, an approach based on 'pragmatism' – the assumption that changes in punishment were primarily the result of short-term pressures – reveals little. Rather, he argues, it is vital to take a broad, *cultural* approach to the history of punishment. Wiener focuses primarily on changing Victorian notions of the body and of the individual in an attempt to account for both the rise of the prison and increasing dissatisfaction with it by the end of the nineteenth century. He claims that in the early Victorian period there was a decline in the religious view of crime as 'sin', and a rise in the notion that it was caused by a deficiency of character, by a crack in the thin veneer of civilization which covered man's primitive and selfish desires. Once this idea had arisen, public executions (which were seen to inflame the baser instincts of the watching crowd) and a discretionary justice system (which was sometimes severe and sometimes lenient) had to be replaced. Instead, there was a need to inculcate responsibility and forward planning in individuals, and hence the use of the 'Bloody Code' gradually declined and its place was taken by the rise of a reformist prison agenda based on solitude and hard work. The following quotation by the Radical MP Charles Pearson (made in 1857) illustrates the way in which criminality was now believed to stem from wayward desires rather than logical calculation. Base instincts could, it was felt, be quashed via a combination of repression and rewards.

Labour should be made to feed the appetite, or the appetite should be made to enforce the labour. Nine times out of ten the irregular indulgence of appetite will be found either the proximate or the remote cause both of the commission of crime and the suffering of punishment amongst our prison population. Appetite has been to the criminal outside of the prison both a tempter and a traitor; within the walls it should be made his teacher or his tormentor [...] the right hand of industry, long neglected and despised by the idle criminal, will then be taken into his confidence as the only friend that can save him in the hour of distress [...] [It] shall be the instrument of his restoration to freedom, not by being put forth by fits and starts of exciting activity, but by constant and continuous exertion, cancelling hour by hour the sentence under which he is confined. (Wiener 1990: 120)

It can easily be seen from even this brief survey that a wide range of explanations have been advanced to account for the decline of capital punishment and the rise of the prison. Politics, the economy and prevalent trends of social thought have all been cited as key factors driving major shifts in punishment which occurred during the nineteenth century. While complex, you can follow up any (or all) of these debates by doing some further reading. Details of the most relevant works can be found in the bibliography at the end of the chapter. However, it is important to bear in mind Garland's point that punishment often puzzles us primarily because we have 'tried to convert a deeply social issue into a technical task for specialist institutions' (Garland 1990: 1). Explanations of punishment which focus exclusively on one particular factor are unlikely to prove convincing. What is necessary is 'a multidimensional interpretative approach' which combines study of a number of different factors (Garland 1990: 2).

Debates over punishment and welfare, 1850–1950

The decline of hanging and transportation, the end of corporal punishments such as flogging and the rise of the prison have been quite well researched in recent decades. Discussions continue among historians, but it seems unlikely that any major new interpretations will be advanced. However, while the prison was to remain the pre-eminent punishment within English society between *c*.1850 and 1950, it was by no means unchanging. While the period 1850–1950 witnessed no change in punishment quite so dramatic as the initial rise of the prison, there were big differences between the harsh penal regime of the late-Victorian period and the combination of welfare, punishment and reform which were the norm by 1950. Consider, for example, the case of 15-year-old Edward Andrews, who committed suicide in Birmingham borough prison in 1854. The governor at the prison routinely kept petty offenders in solitary confinement where they had to turn a hand crank weighted at thirty pounds pressure ten thousand times every ten hours. Should they refuse (as Andrews did) they were soaked with cold water, put into a straitjacket and fed only on bread and water. After two months of this treatment, Andrews eventually hanged himself in his cell. The prison schoolmaster was the last to see him alive

> going up the steps to his cell; had the straitjacket last Sunday morning two hours. It made shrivelled marks on his arm and body. A bucket of water stood by him in case of exhaustion. He stood with cold, red, bare feet soaked in water. He looked very deathly and reeled with weakness. Had been sent regularly to the crank except when confined in the jacket [...] Food, usually bread and water. (Ignatieff 1978: 208)

Yet, by the early part of the twentieth century, a very different approach was taken to young offenders. By the interwar period it is likely that a young offender such as Andrews would either have received a short spell in a specialist reformatory Borstal, or would have been assigned a probation officer

81

to work with him and his parents in an effort to foster more positive social mores. As a Fabian tract from 1912 noted:

> The parents quite as much as the children are 'put on probation': Working through the family and the home, the system gives the unfortunate a strong friend from the outside who can provide education and training and employment. (Garland 1985a: 240)

Clearly then, while prison remained the primary sanction for most offences, very big changes in the administration of (and social attitudes towards) punishment took place during the period c.1850–1950, the causes of which have also been debated by historians and criminologists alike.

The historical criminologist David Garland has provided one of the most convincing investigations of the rise of what he terms our modern 'penal-welfare complex' (1985a). In *Punishment and Welfare* he noted the striking differences between late Victorian penal policy (typified by the widespread use of harsh sentences of penal servitude) and the softer, more nuanced approach to punishment of the twentieth century (characterized by probation and aftercare, institutions with a reformist agenda and the rise of specialist detention centres for problematic cases such as persistent drunks and the 'feeble-minded'), and sought to consider how this change came about.

The centralized and harsh late-Victorian penal system (1865–95) was characterized by what the historians Beatrice and Sydney Webb once called 'the fetish of uniformity'. As Garland notes:

> The primary concern was with the production of a disciplined and orderly regime, a regime which enforced an intense form of obedience through a number of uniformly distributed conditions and procedures. (Garland 1985a: 12)

Such an approach to the use of the prison was very much based on what Garland calls 'classical criminology' – the idea that 'all individuals are free, equal, rational and responsible' and that criminals, therefore, had made a rational choice to commit crime based on a desire for short-term gain. Given such a view of criminality, the Victorians believed that prison should give offenders their just deserts in the form of a proportional measure of retribution. Thus, arguably, *retribution* and *deterrence* were the keystones of penal policy.

All this changed rapidly around the turn of the century. Garland dates the formation of our modern system of penal punishment to the period between the Gladstone Committee Report of 1895 (which recommended modifications to the existing prison system) and the outbreak of the First World War in 1914. During this relatively short period, the range of sanctions available to the criminal court almost doubled. For example, the 1907 Probation of Offenders Act introduced probation orders, thereby establishing 'a non-custodial, supervisory sanction for both juveniles and adults which was to be used in cases where the character of the offender or the nature of the offence made "punishment" inexpedient' (Garland 1985a: 19). Similarly, the Prevention of

Crime Act of 1908 introduced Borstal training provision for young offenders and also dealt with 'habitual offenders'. Preventive forms of detention, such as detention in an inebriate reformatory, were also introduced. The Mental Deficiency Act of 1913, for example, gave the courts the authority to detain in a specialist institution for the mentally defective anyone found guilty of a criminal offence and who met the rather loose definition of 'mentally defective'. In addition, supervised fines were introduced through the Criminal Justice Supervision Act of 1914. Thus the prison quite quickly became just one of a range of interventions aimed at modifying behaviour not sanctioned by society.

Garland cites a number of factors in an effort to explain why this happened and, in particular, why this happened so suddenly. The end of the nineteenth century was a period of rapid change and, arguably, crisis in England. Economic and political structures underwent transformation as the liberal, *laissez-faire* capitalism of the mid-Victorian period gave way to monopoly capitalism and cyclical depressions between 1873 and 1896 led to calls for state intervention in the economic sphere. There was also a growing awareness of the persistence of poverty. The social investigator Charles Booth published his seventeen-volume *Life and Labour of the People* in London between 1889 and 1903, with detailed colour-coded maps showing the extent of poverty in the capital. By the 1890s, therefore, many members of the middle and upper classes had come to believe that any solution to 'the social question' would have to involve state intervention on an unprecedented scale. This awareness coincided with a general recognition of the failure of the prison as a disciplinary institution and 'a remarkable public outburst which severely criticised the penal system, its institutions, principles and authorities' (Garland 1985a: 64). This period of turmoil was resolved, according to Garland, by the piecemeal development of the 'welfare state' and the 'welfare sanction'.

In England, the involvement of non-governmental agencies (including both the philanthropic organizations set up by the middle classes and the mutual assistance schemes set up by workers themselves) remained crucial to welfare provision at the turn of the century. However, while a mix of state/private agencies continued to administer welfare, state provision gradually rose to the fore. Britain introduced the first compulsory unemployment insurance scheme in 1911, pensions were administered by the government from their introduction in 1908, and local authorities were empowered to build and manage council housing. By 1939, 12 per cent of housing stock was owned by the government (Hohenberg and Lees 1985: 314). According to Garland, this 'welfare state' (together with the expanding franchise) gave the working classes a 'stake' in English society which they never previously had. Acceptable social behaviour – working hard, acting in a orderly manner, maintaining allegiance to the existing social structure – was reinforced and ensured by the positive rewards of the welfare state.

In tandem with this, however, a new range of penal practices and institutions was assembled (as outlined above). These new sanctions served as a 'back-up mechanism' for the small minority of obdurate deviants and recidivists. Garland divides the new policies and procedures into three sectors. The *normalizing* sector included initiatives such as probation and the aftercare of offenders. This shallow end of penality was intended to 'normalize' minor misbehaviours and to correct offenders within society. The *correctional* sector (which included new institutions such as Borstals and reformatory schools, described in Chapter 8) was institutionally based, but still correctional in intent via training and education. Finally, the *segregative* sector (including the prison, but also new state reformatories for the mentally deficient) was intended to provide for long-term removal from society of its most troublesome elements. The development of this new range of sanctions was sponsored by the newly emerging discipline of criminology.

Criminology as a discipline aimed to *individualize* the criminal. By contrast with prior thinking, which aimed to treat all offenders as equal, rational beings before the law, criminologists sought to explain what predisposed specific individuals towards criminality. As Garland notes:

> Perhaps the major implication of the criminological programme was th[e] social-engineering capability which it claimed to offer. Criminology would replace the ineffectual niceties of legal punishment by practical technologies involving diagnostic, preventive and curative instruments and institutions. (Garland 1985a: 106)

By shifting attention away from specific *criminal acts* (which might be explained by environmental factors such as poverty) to criminals themselves, and by claiming a competence beyond the legal sphere (for example by analysing vagrants, the 'feeble-minded' and inebriates as *potential* criminals), criminology was thus conceivably another mechanism which enabled the continued association of the poor with crime.

Thus the 'penal-welfare complex' with which we are familiar today evolved as an amalgam of a diverse range of social trends and forces, including the birth of criminology itself. Despite its changed role, however, the prison remained the dominant mode of punishment until 1950 and beyond. Moreover, it is also important (as ever) to guard against interpretations of change in the sphere of punishment which focus solely on 'progress', 'humanitarianism' or 'welfare'. It is a mistake to look back at punishment in the first half of the twentieth century and see *only* the genesis of our present system. It is clear (as Garland and others acknowledge) that there were a number of competing interests and programmes at work during the period. Many of the ideas being discussed may appear strange to us now, and even those elements which were eventually successful were clearly not based solely on compassion and consideration but were in fact simply different, more subtle mechanisms of power and control. Two examples can perhaps serve to illustrate this.

Traditional histories of the probation service, for instance, tend to depict its development as the history of a 'moral good' driven by 'humanitarian concern' (Vanstone 2004: 34). However, another case could be made. It might be argued that the early twentieth century was marked in England by an expanding franchise, by a growth in the power of organized labour and by a better educated and more vocal working class. Hence, it became increasingly less easy for social elites to adopt openly repressive policies towards the poor (as had arguably been the case in the nineteenth century). Thus new initiatives such as probation helped to enable the continued regulation of the poor. As Vanstone notes:

> Each attempt to control the behaviour of others requires 'experts' who have a key role in moulding the problems to be dealt with and regulated, and who constitute the connection between government and the 'sites' where behaviour is processed and responded to. (Vanstone 2004: 38)

The development of the probation service was strongly influenced by the development of eugenic thought. Indeed, eugenics was (as Garland and others argue) a crucial factor in the development of the penal-welfare complex, even if the project was ultimately unsuccessful. Ideas of 'degeneration' – the notion that the health (both mental and physical) of the English 'race' was declining due to the unhealthy conditions of modern, urban life – had permeated the last decades of the nineteenth century. Such ideas remained persistent well into the twentieth century, where concerns were often focused on the degenerate physical and moral condition of the urban poor. Charles Masterman, for example, writing in the wake of the shock revelation of the poor health of the urban working class during recruitment of soldiers for the Boer War, described the characteristic physical type of a town dweller as 'Stunted, narrow-chested, easily wearied; yet voluble, excitable, with little ballast, stamina, or endurance – seeking stimulus in drink' (Masterman 1901: 8).

This theme of actual *physical* difference declined as the century progressed but was replaced by a focus on the poor standard of mental health of the lowest segment of the population and on the social problems (alcoholism, vagrancy, petty criminality) seen to be associated with this. The Report of the Women's Group on Public Welfare, from as late as 1943, identified a putative 'submerged tenth' – a strata of 'problem families' at the bottom end of the social spectrum – 'always at the edge of pauperism and crime, riddled with mental and physical defects, in and out of the courts for child neglect' (Macnicol 1987: 297). Eugenicist organizations developed throughout Europe which proposed radical solutions to these perceived problems. Those set up in Nazi Germany are perhaps the most well-known but England, too, had a thriving Eugenics Society (Dikötter 1998; Stone 2001). The English Eugenics Society proposed a range of options for problem groups within society, including permanent removal from society in specialist institutions. Some, such as Anthony Ludovici, went further, proposing involuntary sterilization. He argued that reformers had to 'do what no society hitherto has ventured to do, i.e., they must determine by law beforehand who is and who is not to be sacrificed', believing that 'where they [governments] take over the whole burden, as they do in this country, of indigent lunatics and other degenerates, they have the right to exercise all the means at their disposal for preventing degenerates from being born' (Stone 2001: 401). Ludovici was no mere crank. His books were discussed favourably in *Eugenics Review* and, indeed, the views of the Eugenics Society more generally informed government reports and scientific publications.

In the end, England escaped the sterilization legislation which was implemented upon the mentally unwell (associated with social problems such as alcoholism, vagrancy and petty criminality) in many other European countries (Dikötter 1998). During the 1920s and 1930s, however, this was by no means a foregone conclusion. Thus these examples serve perhaps to show that the development of our modern penal-welfare complex, as with the rise of the prison before it, should not be read simply as a function of the growth of compassionate approaches to individuals and to punishment. While it is true that punishment in the first half of the twentieth century developed a greater understanding of (and focus on) the diversity of individual experiences and needs, it remained very much grounded in control via the prison and the new adjuncts of medicine and scientific knowledge.

Conclusion

Significant changes occurred in the way punishment was both conceived of and administered between 1750 and 1950. Firstly, there was a rapid decline in the use of capital and corporal punishment, although it must be remembered that the death penalty lingered for a long time. Moreover, even at the time of its abolition in 1964 (by a temporary act, made permanent ten years later) a majority of the public remained in favour. Secondly, the nineteenth century witnessed the ending of transportation, the removal of convicts to lands which were, at the time, immeasurably far away and required a sea voyage of many months to reach. Finally, this period witnessed the rise and entrenchment of the prison. Debates continue over the precise chronology, but it is impossible to dispute the fact that between 1800 and 1850 the prison became *the* default sanction for all but the most serious of crimes. As noted, the reasons behind these changes are complex. One thing is certain, however. Any convincing explanation of punishment needs to consider the interplay of a wide range of social, cultural, economic and political factors.

Key questions

1. What, if anything, appears to have changed during the nineteenth century in terms of the main punishments for criminal offenders and *why* do you think these changes might have taken place?

In Britain, as in the rest of Europe, there was a shift in the way punishment was administered, primarily between about 1800 and about 1840. At first, the main punishment for almost all felonies (serious offences) was death. The majority of offenders who were sentenced to death were not executed but reprieved, to face transportation for life as a secondary substitute punishment. Prisons were largely holding cells in which those accused of crime waited before their trials could commence or those newly convicted waited to be transported. Few prison sentences of more than two years were ever given. Gradually, however, the death penalty was abandoned, except for the crime of murder, to which it applied until the 1960s. Transportation, too, came to an end around the middle of the century. Instead, new prisons were built and a prison sentence came to be the default punishment for most felonies and many misdemeanours.

The reasons behind the ending of transportation are relatively straightforward. Throughout the first half of the nineteenth century Australian lobby groups, unhappy with the dumping of convicts on their doorstep, sought to put pressure on the British government to end transportation. This pressure, coupled with public suspicions that transportation was not an unpleasant enough experience to deter crime, led to its abolition as a judicial sentence in 1857. The gradual decline in the use of capital punishment is a more complex phenomenon, however, and is intrinsically bound up with the rise of the prison. Certainly, it might be argued that the ending of *public* executions (in 1868) was due to fears that the watching crowds were deriving vicarious excitement (rather than moral instruction) from the spectacle. However, executions had declined massively as a judicial sanction significantly prior to the 1860s, and it would appear that this decline had more to do with the growing enthusiasm for the sanction of the prison than with 'humanitarianism' or 'progress'. Explanations for the rise of the prison are varied. Certainly, the desire of reformers such as John Howard for a more humane form of punishment must not be discounted. However, as Foucault has argued most strongly, the rise of the prison in the nineteenth century did not necessarily lead to a diminution of punishment, but rather to a new type of agony and one more fitted to an industrial society.

2. Was transportation more than simply a punishment? Answer with reference to either Britain and/or the colonies in the eighteenth and nineteenth centuries.

The history of transportation has now been quite well researched. A good overview is provided by Hughes (1987). Emsley (2005) also provides some information regarding transportation. More specialist literature includes Neal (1987), Duffield and Bradley (1997), Nicholas (1988) and Shaw (1966). The experiences of female transportees are considered specifically in Daniels (1998) and Oxley (1997).

3. Assess Garland's contention that a 'penal-welfare complex' had arisen in England by the early twentieth century.

The obvious starting point in answering this question is the work of Garland himself (1985a, 1985b, 1990). In addition, useful information can be found in Wiener (1985) and Vanstone (2004). The significance of eugenic thought in England is covered by Stone (2001) and Dikötter (1998). Debates concerning a putative underclass during the first half of the twentieth century can be found within Macnicol (1987), Morris (1994) and Welshman (2005).

Note

1. This downward trend has, of course, been massively reversed in recent decades. Numbers rose from 45,817 incarcerated in England and Wales in 1992 to 75,324 in mid-2004 (Emsley 2005: 15).

Further reading

The references for this chapter can be found in the Bibliography at the back of the book. If you wish to do some further reading, you should investigate these first. However, below is a list of publications which could also be consulted.

Forsythe, W. J. (1990) *Penal Discipline, Reformatory Projects and the English Prison Commission, 1895–1949*. Exeter: Exeter University Press.

Forsythe, B. (1991) 'Centralisation and autonomy: the experience of English prisons 1820–1877', *Journal of Historical Sociology*, 4, pp. 317–45.

Garland, D. (1985) 'The criminal and his science. A critical account of the formation of criminology at the end of the nineteenth century', *British Journal of Criminology*, 25, 2, pp. 109–37.

Hay, D. (1975) 'Property, authority and the criminal law', in D. Hay, P. Linebaugh, J. Rule *et al.*, *Albion's Fatal Tree. Crime and Society in Eighteenth-Century England*. London: Allen Lane, pp. 17–63.

Hirst, J. (1995) 'The Australian experience: the convict colony', in N. Morris and D. Rothman (eds), *The Oxford History of the Prison*. Oxford: Oxford University Press.

Ignatieff, M. (1983) 'State, civil society and total institutions: a critique of recent social histories of punishment', in S. Cohen and A. Scull (eds), *Social Control and the State. Historical and Comparative Essays*. Oxford: Martin Robertson.

King, P. (2000) *Crime, Justice and Discretion in England, 1740–1820*. Oxford: Oxford University Press.

Langbein, J. (1983) 'Albion's fatal flaws', *Past and Present*, 98–101, pp. 96–120.

McConville, S. (1981) *A History of English Prison Administration Volume I, 1750–1887*. London: Routledge & Kegan Paul.

McConville, S. (1995) *English Local Prisons 1760–1900: Next Only To Death*. London: Routledge.

McGowan, R. (1994) 'Power and humanity, or Foucault among the historians', in C. Jones and R. Porter (eds), *Reassessing Foucault*. London: Routledge.

Morris, N. and Rothman, D. (eds) (1995) *The Oxford History of the Prison*. Oxford: Oxford University Press.

Spierenburg, P. (1984) *The Spectacle of Suffering: Executions and the Evolution of Repression*. Cambridge: Cambridge University Press.

Thompson, E. P. (1975) *Whigs and Hunters: The Origins of the Black Act*. London: Allen Lane.

Weiss, R. P. (1987) 'Humanitarianism, labour exploitation, or social control? A critical survey of theory and research on the origin and development of prisons', *Social History*, 12, 3, pp. 331–50.

Part 2 Crime and Criminals

6. The measurement and meaning of violence

Introduction

Some of the most important and interesting questions that we can ask about ourselves involve 'violence'. How violent are we as a society, and how do we compare with other countries? Is violent crime rising or falling? Is aggression against others innate – a natural emotion – or an effective and convenient means of communicating power and authority over others? Who can use legitimate violence – the police, the state? Does violence have 'rules', as some suggest? Why does the media concentrate on some forms of violence such as football hooliganism, but tend to downplay police violence or violence against minority ethnic groups? The list does not stop there, but this chapter will approach the broader questions to do with violence and its control in the nineteenth and twentieth centuries.

The first question we will discuss is 'when was violence?' because all of the above questions are, in part, historical ones. The media and older generations of society constantly tell us that violent crime and public disorder are now much higher than they were some (usually undefined) time ago. We are also familiar with historical reconstructions of Victorian streets where murderers lurk around every murky fog-laden London street corner. Neither myths of a putative 'golden age' in the 'peaceable kingdom' nor media depictions (past and present) of ever-escalating social violence seem entirely convincing or particularly analytical. This chapter will take a more rigorous approach – firstly taking the statistics of violent crime from 1857 (when annual statistical measures started) through to 1950, asking when the figures rose or fell. Then it will question the reliability of those statistics – and what alternatives there are to governmental statistics.

After discussing whether the level of violence in society has changed, it will discuss whether the 'meaning' of violence has also changed. Despite queries about the accuracy of the statistics of murder and assault, the changing amounts of prosecuted violence are often used to suggest that societal attitudes have also shifted considerably since the Victorian period. This chapter will explore what these changes might be and how they were brought about, and will offer a critical view of the apparent decline and subsequent rise in violence over the last hundred years.

Introductory reading

Emsley, C. (2005) *Crime and Society in England, 1750-1900* (3rd edn). Harlow: Pearson Longman, pp. 21–56.

Gatrell, V. A. C. (1980) 'The decline of theft and violence in Victorian and Edwardian England', in V. Gatrell, B. Lenman and G. Parker (eds), *Crime and the Law: The Social History of Crime in Western Europe since 1500*. London: Europa, pp. 238–337.

Levi, M. and Maguire, M. (2002) 'Violent crime', in M. Maguire, R. Morgan and R. Reiner (eds), *The Oxford Handbook of Criminology* (3rd edn). Oxford: Oxford University Press, pp. 795–843.

Measuring levels of violence

Even the most unambiguous of violent offences – murder – is not simple to measure, and the importance of that most decisive of acts seems to change over time. For most people 'murder' is simply the unlawful killing of one person by another and is not layered with ambiguities, as are offences like theft and other types of property crime. Murder is often termed 'the ultimate crime', and depriving a person of their life is, in every society for many hundreds of years, viewed as the most serious offence. It always attracts the heaviest penalties given out by the courts and is always reported in the popular press. Has that always been the case – does 'murder' have a universal and unchanging value – or is it historically contingent – does murder have a historical 'meaning'? For example, did a murder committed in 1750 when people were accustomed to a high rate of infant mortality, deadly epidemics like cholera sweeping the cities, and thousands of husbands and lovers perishing in wars across Europe and the empire, *mean* the same as one committed two hundred years later? Why do some murders seem to be timeless in their impact, attracting a greater level of speculation and public interest than others? Is it the vulnerability of the victims (as was the case with the murder of James Bulger in 1993), the 'contrariness' of the circumstances (as with murderesses like Myra Hindley) or simply the extraordinary level of brutality involved. An appropriate example might be the Whitechapel murders of 1888. The murders by 'Jack the Ripper' are the most famous set of murders in history.

> JACK THE RIPPER! Few names in history are as instantly as recognizable. Fewer still evoke such vivid images: noisome courts and alleys, hansom cabs and gaslights, swirling fog, prostitutes decked out in the tawdriest of finery, the shrill cries of newsboys – 'Whitechapel! Another 'orrible murder! Mutilation!' – and silent, cruel death, personified in the cape-shrouded figure of a faceless prowler of the night, armed with a knife and carrying a black Gladstone bag.

The book that the above quote comes from (Sugden 1995) is but one of the hundreds of pseudo-academic essays written by amateur sleuths on the true identity of 'Jack'. In addition, hundreds more fictional representations of the crimes, a handful of feature films (both serious and comic) and (at least) one journal dedicated to 'Ripperology' exist. All of this 'Ripperology' is based on a series of relatively small reports in newspapers over three months in 1888. Indeed, those press reports compromise almost all of the remaining evidence that we can look at in connection with these murders.

It is not surprising that the murders of 1888 collectively became a cultural phenomenon which has become emblematic of Victorian society. Both Walkovitz (1992) and Leps (1992) have described how stories woven around the Whitechapel murders both contributed to and were located within existing anxieties. 'Jack the Ripper' and his work personified sexual danger and fears about sexual freedom, the dangers that lurked in the working-class districts and the physical and moral degeneration of the species. He was also the embodiment of fictional gothic terrors that were current in the popular imagination – the similarities between Jack the Ripper and Dracula are unmistakable. The huge amount of both accurate and wildly inaccurate information about the murders published both at the time and later encouraged speculation in a way that made the story seem 'bigger' than it was and allowed myths and stories to grow up around it. Coming at a time when the English people seemed very anxious about the way the world was moving, Jack the Ripper was newsworthy in a number of ways.

First, he committed his crimes in London, the national capital, and symbol of the British Empire. Events in London 'mattered' in a way that provincial capitals or towns did not, not even murders as brutal and bloody as Jack's ripping up of bodies. In Shropshire, for example, at about the same time, the parents of a small child murdered and beheaded their daughter, and the mother wrapped the head in brown paper and threw the parcel in the village pond while the father remained behind to burn the body on the family hearth. The local newspapers reported the case in great and gruesome detail but the *Times* afforded it a small report tucked away on an inside page. In the same region and in the same month, an elderly couple were brutally slain in their home and a mother and child were kicked to death so violently that their faces were unrecognizable. Neither case was reported in any of the national newspapers. However, the Whitechapel murders struck at the image of Britain, and so they were regarded as being of national importance. Second, the true identity of Jack the Ripper remains unknown to this day. A faceless man can always have identities superimposed upon him – the degenerate East End criminal, the Jewish ritualist, the respectable man turned sexual deviant (all of which were suggested at the time); a member of the Royal family, or a woman (both of which have subsequently been suggested) – all stoked up the story and kept it playing in the public eye. At least it did while the media agenda chimed with contemporary concerns. While anxieties about the moral and physical decline of urban areas were high enough in 1888 to propel a few gruesome murders into a world-renowned phenomena, by 1891 the news agenda and public concern had moved on. For example, while the Whitechapel murder described below reached the provincial press, it did not create a media sensation. Yet how might this report have been received if it had been published a few years earlier?

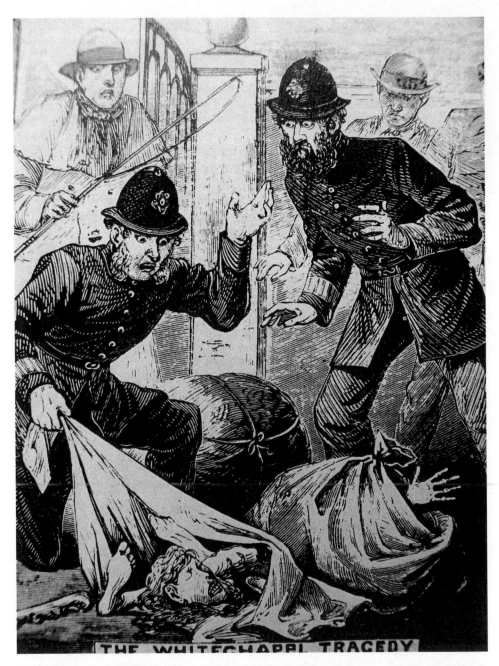

THE WHITECHAPEL TRAGEDY

At first glance this Whitechapel murder has all the familiarity of a Jack the Ripper report. However, this illustration dates from *The Police Illustrated News* from 18 October 1875, not from 1888. It serves as a reminder that horrific murders in the East End of London were not uncommon in the nineteenth century.

The deceased woman has been identified as an unfortunate known as 'Carrotty Nell' and is well-known in the neighbourhood of Tower Hill [she was a local prostitute] ... The medical examination, so far as it has gone, bears out the view that this is a Jack the Ripper murder. The cuts on the throat are not as clean as on previous occasions, but the direction is the same ... all the heads of Scotland Yard have visited the scene, and the consensus of opinion is that PC 240 H was within ten seconds of catching the Whitechapel fiend red-handed at his bloody work. A remarkable feature was the finding of two bonnets, and it is surmised that the murderer was disguised as a woman. In an interview one of the detectives said 'this is the narrowest escape Jack has ever had'. (*Staffordshire Advertiser*, 14 February, 1891)

In any case, what do these isolated cases really tell us about homicide in the Victorian period? Instead of picking out one (admittedly interesting) example, should we not look at the typical or general picture? What about the statistics of homicide? How many murders were committed in this period? Was a murder an extraordinary or a common feature of everyday life?

When criminal statistics for all offences prosecuted at magistrates' and quarter sessions' courts began to be collected nationally and published annually from 1857, it became possible to chart changes in prosecutions for violence until the present day. For example, Clive Emsley (2005: 41–2) notes that:

Homicide is the most dramatic crime of violence, and it is generally acknowledged that, for a variety of reasons, it is probably among the most frequently reported offences. The statistics of homicide are therefore probably closer to the real level of the offence ... While people were concerned about homicide throughout the eighteenth and nineteenth centuries, it was never a statistically significant offence ... In Victorian England the homicide rate reached 2 per 100,000 of the population only once, in 1865; generally it hovered around 1.5 per 100,000 falling to rarely more than 1 per 100,000 at the end of the 1880s and declining still further with the new century. In round figures this means that between 1857 and 1890 there were rarely more than 400 homicides reported to the police each year, and during the 1890s the average was below 350.

Figure 6.1 shows homicide rates in England and Wales, 1856–1914, per 10,000 population, and is compiled from the annually published judicial statistics. In the Victorian period then, and despite the stories of Jack the Ripper, murder was not common, and society was not as violent as it is often portrayed. At least that is what the statistics suggest, and they have supporters among the criminological community. For example, Ted Gurr (1981: 266–7; 298–9) stated:

The incidence of serious crime has traced an irregular downward trend for a much longer period of time, in some places for a century or more. When the historical and contemporary evidence are joined together, they depict a distended U-shaped curve...From the perspective of the

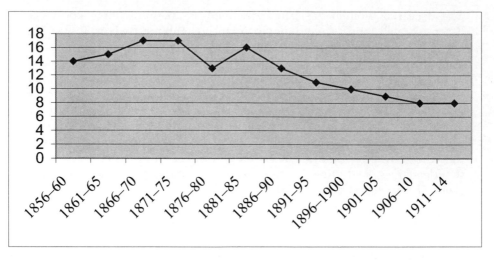

Figure 6.1 Homicide rate in England and Wales, 1856–1914 (per 10,000 population). *Source*: Gatrell, 1980.

social and cultural historian, the distribution of these offences [homicide and assault] across time, space, and social groups is of particular interest because of what it tells us about interpersonal aggression and the complex of social attitudes towards it. And from a methodological viewpoint, when dealing with data on homicide in particular we can be more confident that trends reflect real changes in social behaviour rather than changes in the practices of criminal justice systems. There is some discernible correspondence between trends in some kinds of official data on crimes against persons and real changes in the incidence of interpersonal violence in society. The validity of many of the criticisms of crime statistics is accepted. It is clear, for example, that the reported incidence of many kinds of offences can be affected by changing degrees of public concern and by changes in the level and foci of police activity. But I contend that it is possible to overcome these limitations of official data by focusing on the most serious offences and by obtaining converging or parallel evidence on trends in different types of offences and from different jurisdictions.

However, the easy reliance on statistics of major violence (particularly murder) has recently been criticized by Howard Taylor (1998b). As the following extract makes clear, the basis for his challenge is that murder investigations and trials were too expensive for authorities to finance them out of their budgets, and that consequently they contrived to reduce the number of officially recorded murders:

In the first half of the nineteenth century, Parliament passed a series of measures to encourage prosecutors. Between 1805 and 1842 the number of trials in higher courts rose seven-fold, while the population increased only by half. Yet, after this, growth ceased and the statistics remained remarkably constant until about 1925 ... This was also true for the statistics of murder which for the period 1880 to 1966 kept to a cumulative average of 150 a year, again within a range of 20 per cent either side of the average ... The traditional literature has sought to explain this largely by arguing that there occurred an 'English miracle' when crime diminished as the population rose ... Instead, when the new police forces were created in the period after 1829, there was political pressure for them to reduce the number and cost of prosecutions ... it was an open secret that most murders and suspicious deaths went uninvestigated.

Certainly there were some 'strange' decisions taken by the authorities when presented with a dead body. John Archer (1999: 171–90) summarizes some cases found by Carolyn Conley:

This concerned a corpse found on Ramsgate beach in 1859. Both the magistrate and the coroner felt it was that of a foreigner and hence not worth the taxpayers' expense of an investigation. The verdict of suicide passed by the coroner's jury seems strange given that the corpse had stab wounds in its back. It would appear that just a few weeks later another body was found naked at the foot of some cliffs at Ramsgate. In this case the German had been staying at a local hotel where a porter recalled him with a heavily bandaged left hand. This led some to argue that his death was suicide, and that 'in a fit of frenzy, (he) first chopped off his hand and then stabbed himself in the heart'. In this state, it was claimed, he then threw himself off the cliff.

However Archer (1999) goes on to debate whether this was common practice, and whether the homicide rate was really severely depleted by administrators and politicians 'cooking the books'. There is clearly an argument over whether the number of homicides in the nineteenth century is accurate, and it may be that administrative and political influences combined to reduce the number of murders that were reported, investigated and prosecuted. But what does that say for today's figures? These show that, although there have been rises, notably after the Second World War, rates of homicide in the twentieth century were fairly stable (see Figure 6.2). Despite more people reporting victimization, the vast increase in crime reportage, and higher levels of policing and surveillance in society, rates of murder seem to have been predictable and relatively low. Although there were 186 murders committed in 1970 and 1,045 in 2002 (according to Home Office statistics), given the rise in population, murders are still very infrequent in this country (as Figure 6.2 shows).

Changes in the meaning of violence?

As Levi and Maguire state (2002:797), views about offending behaviour (even murder) are shaped by a wide variety of individual, social, and cultural influences. Because social conditions change over time we know that historical

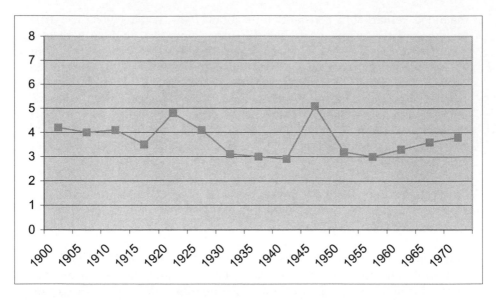

Figure 6.2 Homicides in England and Wales, 1900–70, per 10,000 population.
Source: Published annual judicial statistics, 1857–1970.

shifts may also change the way murder is viewed. For example, during peacetime society is concerned at rises in the homicide rate, but is willing to tolerate the wholesale killing of thousands of 'enemies' during wartime. If we included all deaths in wartime in the murder rate, then it would look very different. In the nineteenth century we can see longer-term and slower shifts in public opinion (and for the eighteenth century see King 1996). For example, the murder of newly born children by desperate young women (infanticide) was usually punished by hanging in the early part of the nineteenth century. However, by the mid-century, juries were increasingly becoming sympathetic to the plight of women (usually servants who had become pregnant by their employers) charged with infanticide, and were reluctant to bring in guilty verdicts. The authorities responded by reducing the charge to 'concealment of birth' and that was not a capital crime. Indeed, the 'Bloody Code' of over 200 capital offences was gradually whittled down to just hanging for murder (eventually abolished in 1857) as public opinion came to regard judicial murder to be intolerable. But the numbers of assaults, domestic attacks, street fights and drunken brawls dwarfs the number of murders committed each year. Can a study of minor violence tell us more about violence in society?

Contemporary opinion formers in the newspapers, pamphlets and parliamentary speech believed that society was becoming more violent in the early- to mid-nineteenth century. Judicial or criminal statistics confirmed a rise in prosecutions between 1857 and 1880. In his well-known 1980 study, Vic Gatrell stated that the growth of industrial and urban-based capitalism in nineteenth-century England had fostered criminal acts through the impact of social alienation, the anonymity of urban dwelling and the opportunities the city provided for crossing the invitational threshold to crime. Although he also believed that industrial prosperity, for those in work, mitigated the

The infanticide of a two-month old child by her mother in Hull resulted in a conviction for wilful murder, although the report in *The Police Illustrated News*, 24 May 1873, made it clear that the mother was in a depressed state and clearly suffering from mental illness at the time. Had this event taken place twenty or thirty years later, the mother might well have been locked in an asylum rather than being at the mercy of the criminal courts.

conditions that fostered crime, his view is that industrialization created the preconditions for a general rise in crime. After 1880 the statistics of violence began to decline rapidly, falling away to all-time lows. In 1875 the number of people convicted of common assault in England was 38,331; this rose to 39,837 in 1885 but had fallen to 26,976 by 1900 (in 2001 there were about 600,000 offences against the person).

The downward trend in assault statistics (England and Wales, 1856–1914, per 10,000 population) shown in Figure 6.3 continued until the 1920s when violent crime, as with all crime, began to rise again. This can be seen in Figure 6.4 which shows the situation from 1900 to 1970. You can also trace this rise in crime from 1900 (for offences of violence and for property offences) and compare them with the figures for many countries contained in Archer and Gartner (1984).

Although a *statistical reality*, some have questioned whether the 1880–1920 statistics mirror an actual *real* fall in offending. For example, Howard Taylor has used the criminal statistics, as well as the census statistics, to show that economic expediencies shaped government statistics to a large degree, and that the fall in rates of violent crime were heavily affected by Treasury policy.

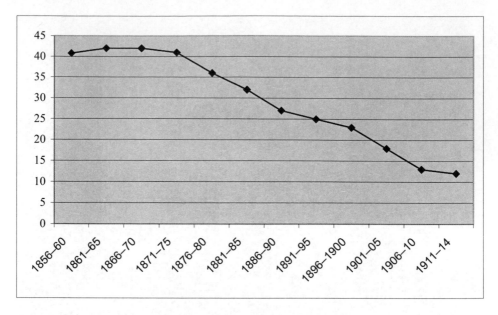

Figure 6.3 Prosecutions for common assault, 1856–1914.
Source: Published annual judicial statistics, 1857–1915.

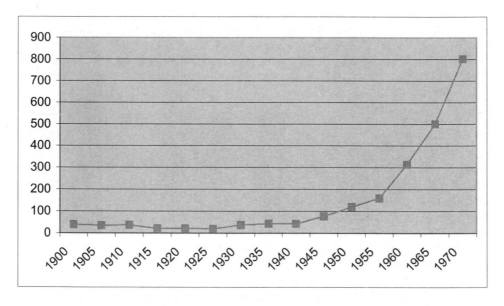

Figure 6.4 Prosecutions for common assault, 1900–70.
Source: Published annual judicial statistics, and Home Office Research Unit figures.

For Taylor there are two key events. First, in the early part of the nineteenth century the local county authorities began to take the burdensome costs of prosecution off the shoulders of individual crime victims, and then immediately petitioned for help from central government to pay the costs that rising numbers of prosecutions brought. From the mid-century onwards there was a constant battle between county and national authorities to, firstly, cover the costs of prosecuting wrongdoers, and, secondly, to keep the prosecution costs to their bare minimum. Although he does not state it explicitly, for Taylor, the movement of most indictable offences to petty sessions in the 1840s and 1850s may well have been a Treasury inspired way of reducing trial costs. Taylor also points to the New Police whose formation in 1829, he reminds us, was supposed, not to increase, but to reduce the number of prosecutions by their deterrent impact. Indeed, that was a crucial argument employed in their favour by police advocates such as Pitt and Chadwick – that fewer prosecutions meant fewer costly trials, and fewer convictions meant less pressure on the prison budget. For the Treasury, preventative policing would have the twin benefits of cutting crime and lowering budgets. It has always been thought that the New Police were anxious to demonstrate their worth by arresting as many offenders as possible. However, it seems that the New Police walked a thin line – too few arrests demonstrated inactivity, but too many proved they lacked deterrent impact. Chief constables themselves were probably adept at massaging figures either to show their effectiveness or in order to increase police establishment or win other resources from the County authorities.

Certainly it is the case that as soon as police officers overtook the magistrate as the most approachable official agency for victims to report crimes, the crime rates for violence fell. One reason may have been because the police viewed time spent in court as a waste of time: it took men from the streets and left the 'thieving magpies' without street scarecrows to warn them away. Moreover, it was having a deleterious effect on police budgets. Prosecutions were useful propaganda tools – magistrates could make homilies in the press about how crime did not pay; the punishments meted out may also have deterred potential offenders – but too many prosecutions could have an unfortunate effect: they reduced police staffing at street level and therefore helped negate preventative policing. The amount of physical punishments, cautions and admonishments, all meted out on the streets by the police, may have far outnumbered the times police actively sought the prosecution of offenders. It seems that Weaver might have been right to state that: 'It is worth noting again those complications with the data that stem from peculiarities by individuals to prosecution with the aid of the police. This fact could mean everything in terms of how we come to understand an apparent decline in the assault rate.' Indeed, Weaver goes on to suggest a number of factors that may have affected crime trends (1995: 188–225).

For any violent incident to end in the conviction of an offender, or even their appearance in court, it had to pass through a number of processes – a victim willing to report it, police action taken to apprehend the accused and a court case where all the injured parties turned up (many prosecutors agreed to settle minor cases of violence before trial started – particularly in cases of domestic violence where husbands and wives were reconciled before trial). If we also look at some police reports of the day, we can see that the difficulties of finding and apprehending people accused of violence also might have caused a shortfall between real and reported levels of crime. Consider, for example, the following extracts:

(The victim said) I was in Rose Barn Lane with master's child in a perambulator when a woman followed her and asked her for some money. she told her that she had got none. the woman then took her by the arms from behind. put her hand into the pocket and took out her purse (there was nothing in it) and would not let her go, or give up the purse, before a soldier and another woman came and made her let the girl go. the servant describes the woman as about from 30 to 40 years of age, medium build dressed in an old black dress, black jacket and black hat. (Exeter City Police, Occurrence Books, 1889 Report of 25 October 1889).

Mary Anne Lofters aged 12 years residing in apartments on the 1st floor landing at 8 Mary Archer St complained of a man coming up to her mother's room where she and her little brother and sister were, and said he came there to kill her mother and the children – the mother was then coming up the stairs – and on hearing the children crying met a man coming down, and in passing her he caught her around the waist and put his hand under her clothes. She said you villain what are you doing of. He then ran down the street, shortly afterwards he returned again. the mother then caught hold of him so he pushed her down and ran away, a stick was picked up and brought to the station house, supposed to belong to the man as the children stated he had a stick when in the room. Description of him; short, dark, moustache, and black hat. (Exeter City Police, Occurrence Books, 1889 Report of 4 August 1889)

The descriptions of offenders in the two cases from Exeter were broad and must have matched hundreds of similarly dressed people. At least with property crime, the police had a chance to catch the offender with the stolen goods, thereby providing some linkage between the accused and the crime. With cases of violence, the police officer could only arrest the suspect if they had actually witnessed the assault, otherwise they could only arrest the suspect for a breach of the peace (in which case the incident would never be recorded as an assault) or advise the victim to bring the offender to court on a summons.

Between the eighteenth and twentieth centuries the criminal justice system underwent immense changes. The public uniformed police services introduced from 1829 impacted both upon the surveillance of the streets and the ease of reporting crimes to a person 'in authority', and also on the collection of evidence. The proficiency of the police investigating the case and the quality of the physical evidence became ever more important, particularly with property cases, as the following extract shows:

There were a number of fingerprints on the fanlight. I immediately got particulars of the stolen cheque and stopped it, and also sent particulars to the Police Station and full particulars of the robbery and stolen cheque was at once circulated by Supt. Dymond. I then took out the fanlight and carefully packed it, and it was sent with full particulars of the robbery to Scotland Yard to see whether the prints and he concurred with me that they were useless for identification. I then made enquiries at the prison as to the character of prisoners recently liberated and also made all possible enquiry in the neighbourhood. The constables on duty during the night in the vicinity was also interviewed but no person of a suspicious nature was seen loitering. Public Houses, Refreshment Houses and Common Lodging Houses were also worked. I may add that robberies of this character are the most difficult for the police to investigate as it was only cash stolen with the exception of the cheque. In my opinion had 'Mr Manley' notified the police at once when he discovered the robbery some valuable clues may have been obtained in the shape of the fingerprints, but should the robbery have been committed by a thief who has been previously convicted. I have reason to think that the prints on the fanlight may yet be of some assistance. (Exeter City Police Felony Report Book, 10 March 1908)

Forensic evidence offered some hope in property cases, but again, with prosecutions for violence, the circumstances were different. With violent crime in particular, it was often the credibility of the victim and their witnesses pitched against the credibility of the accused which determined whether a conviction was achieved. In court, the police usually prosecuted the case until lawyers were introduced to put the evidence to the defendant, as discussed in Chapters 3 and 4. Only in the nineteenth-century was the defendant legally represented – and only then by the relatively few that could afford their services. The 'character' (as well as gender and class) of the defendant, and to some extent the complainant, has long played a part in the prosecution process, and it is easy to see how class and gender might have played a part in determining the outcome of trials for assault and threatening behaviour. If a working man assaulted a social superior, he was more likely to be convicted than for an incident between social equals. How much validity would a Victorian magistrate give, for example, to the word of a prostitute complaining about an assault committed by a client – conversely, would a magistrate doubt the word of a police constable who said he had been assaulted while arresting a drunk man?

Many have critiqued the reliability of criminal statistics for these reasons. Moreover, Godfrey has pointed to the problem of identifying changes in public attitudes towards violence from statistical measures. He suggests that, since a vast number of violent acts were not reported or prosecuted, it is not possible to say with certainty that violence fell in the 1880–1920 period, and that the 'U-curve' might be flattened out to produce more of a continuous level of violence per population across the nineteenth and twentieth centuries. Godfrey cites the vast number of unprosecuted acts of violence which are revealed in oral history interviews (Godfrey 2003):

You see that's why so many went to back-street abortionists, you see they went to ... two of my friends died through that. One, er ... oh he were a pig were her husband, er ... Dolly W[1]... Ooh she looked shocking. I said 'Ooh Dolly, what's the matter with you?' She says 'I'm haemorrhaging ... I've got to go straight away, see to the kids, I've got to go to hospital'. Well she'd had – they were all boys she had. Ooh he were a pig was Jess W, her husband, he used to beat her up. Anyway they took her to Scafforth Road Hospital, and it were her cousin as it happened, she says, 'You know our Dolly, she's dead'. (Female interviewee, born 1904, Bradford Central Library, tape A0098/03)

Abortion was illegal in the nineteenth and early twentieth centuries. That might explain why Dolly, the unfortunate woman remembered by this interviewee, felt she had to run the risk of a backstreet abortionist. These were usually local women who were reputed to have medical or folk knowledge of these matters, but who often caused the death of their 'patients'. We have at least two crimes reported here – the domestic violence committed by Dolly's husband and the illegal abortion (in effect an unlawful homicide of the child and the manslaughter of the mother). However, the interviewee confirms that there was never a complaint made to the authorities, the police took no action and the offences never reached the attention of the statistical compilers at the Home Office. Were these isolated cases? If so, that would contradict everything we know about domestic abuse in this period, where thousands of spousal assaults remained unreported. What about violent acts carried out by the police, such as this one taken from an Australian oral history interview?

We used to have to scatter from the police. If the police come we'd run – that's why they called Baby Face. He'd run that fast, he'd catch you and give you a knock up the behind and tell you to get home. That's when they had the 21 Gang ... The Dirty Dozen, they were a bad mob. They [the police] lined the Mad Digger up on the Iron Cave Bridge at the wool store that got burned down two or three years ago. There's a little walkway in there and one or two of them was talking outside and when the Mad Digger came up ... it might have taken them 18 months or two years, but they caught him there on his own and he was in hospital for six months ... they beat him up.

The police fairly regularly used physical violence to control difficult situations or to informally punish people they felt deserved a beating rather than arrest. These cases of violence rarely appeared in the statistics of violence. We could go on and list a huge number of incidences recorded in people's memories but not reported to the police. Are these valid? Do people remember events of sixty or seventy years hence accurately enough for historians to give them credence? What about the bias of the interviewee, the mixing up of two stories into one tale, the 'invention' and embellishment of stories told to an interviewer? These are issues which have tested and intrigued oral historians, and you should consider the 'weight' of oral evidence against contemporary statistics because, given the vast scale of under-reporting of cases of minor (and some not so minor) assaults, there must be some considerable doubt as to whether crime statistics really give us an accurate picture of the amount of violence in society. However, it is true that there are other sources – such as contemporary diaries and biographies – that suggest that there has been a decline in violence from the mid-nineteenth century until around the 1920s. Let us assume that, although the fall in violence was probably not as dramatic as the statistics record, there was a gradual reduction in the amount of casual violence experienced by 'ordinary' people around the turn of the century. If we do accept that the fall was real, then how can we explain it?

Sensitivity to violence and the civilizing process

Although from different viewpoints, Gatrell (1990) and Critchley (1970) agree that the introduction of public policing (which some maintain was intended to maintain public order rather than prosecute crime) ensured a greater surveillance of the streets and meant that violent offenders were dissuaded from committing offences – this is a similar argument to those that justify CCTV (closed circuit television). As police services became more efficient, the impact of their efforts became more noticeable, hence the fall in prosecutions after the 1870s. However, by the 1920s, Gatrell (1990: 293) asserts, the deterrent impact was reduced:

> If for half a century before 1914 policemen were in the ascendant, the argument might therefore go, twentieth-century law-breakers were better able to exploit the social camouflages, opportunities, techniques and forms of mobility which the modern environment has massively multiplied. Policing became more difficult, accordingly: 'success' was less easily registered; crime rates began to climb.

Wiener (1998: 230) believes that the courts and legislators may have added to the mid to late nineteenth-century 'police dividend' by targeting male aggression. He states, specifically that, 'in virtually all times and places, violent behaviour has been highly gendered, far more characteristic of males than of females.' In the eighteenth century and before, traditional values of aggression and competitiveness were deeply rooted in the male identity. When these values caused excessive violence or challenged public or social order, the authorities stepped in to enforce control and this naturally resulted in large numbers of men being indicted for homicide and other forms of violence. Martin Wiener argues that, in the nineteenth century, legislators and moral entrepreneurs accelerated and mobilized the civilizing influences that Norbert Elias (1978/2000) and others have described into a concerted assault on male aggression. The decapitalization of offences for various categories of property offences (for which women were mainly prosecuted), and the increasing intolerance of the public towards violence in public and (increasingly) private spaces (such as the armed forces, the workplace and the domestic household) caused three effects. First, the law acted mainly against men (who held positions of power in the military, the workplace and the home). Second, men suffered relatively harsh penalties because of the type of violent offences they committed, or, as D'Cruze (1998 and 1999) stated, 'public court hearings undertook surveillance of disorderly working-class masculinity, principally by adjudicating what were acceptable boundaries of conduct' and imposing suitable punishments accordingly. Lastly, because more and more men were flowing through the courts, there was a 'masculinization' of the social perception of 'the criminal' (Wiener 1998: 197–231).

The edited collection in which Wiener's 1998 essay appears and Pieter Spierenburg's introductory chapter to it both draw out another reason for high rates of male violence – the connections between masculinity, honour and violence. As Spierenburg (1998: 2) writes:

> For one thing, in societies with pronounced notions of honor and shame, a person's reputation often depends on physical bravery and a forceful response to insults. Second, notions of honor and shame are characteristically gendered. In almost every society, male honor is considered to be quite different from female honor. Men may take pride in attacking fellow men, whether they use this force to protect women or for other reasons. Passivity, in violent and peaceful situations, is a cardinal feminine virtue.

Honour contests and the preservation of status could explain many of the street fights, drunken brawls and spousal assaults which characterize much of male violence in the nineteenth century. Similarly, police campaigns against these types of offences and against masculine aggression may, over time, have both caused a drop in prosecutions and caused a change in attitudes towards violence.

It is the change in attitudes towards violence that we turn to now. The last theory we will consider is that civilizing processes gradually inculcated modes of self-control, and that masculine rituals of aggression were replaced with internal control of emotions such as anger. The major proponent of this theory, Norbert Elias, suggested that when the state had established itself as the legitimate source of power and lawful authority over a territory (a nation) and had become stable (as happened in Europe in the late seventeenth and early eighteenth centuries), the citizens of that state developed manners and sets of practices which assisted in the formation of a capitalistic economy. People had to interact socially with neighbours, strangers and foreign traders. In doing so, they adopted common understandings of how to behave and less aggressive ways of settling disputes – usually bringing in state agencies such as the police or taking civil action in the courts. Over time, societal norms became internalized. As Pratt comments (2002: 5):

> As these internalised controls on an individual's behaviour became more automatic and pervasive ... they eventually helped to produce the ideal of the fully rational, reflective and responsible citizen of the civilised world in the nineteenth and twentieth centuries: one who would be sickened by the sight of suffering and, with their own emotions under

control, one who respected the authority of the state to resolve disputes on their behalf.

This would indeed help to explain the fall in recorded crime in the 1880–1920 period. It might also explain current sensitivities towards violence. For example, media reporting of crime, as the earlier reports of the Whitechapel murders showed, could be very short and confined itself to the briefest details of the offence, the victim and the defendant. These two reports from the 1850s (reprinted in their entirety) both reveal an indifference to serious violence and the consequences for the victims and their families, and also a reserved style of reporting which has now largely disappeared from broadsheet and tabloid newspapers:

Manslaughter by a Lad – George Best, a lad of 11 years of age pleaded guilty to a charge of killing and slaying George Davis, another lad, on 4th July, at the township of Wolverhampton. It seems that death had ensued in consequence of the prisoner striking the deceased with a constable's staff. His LORDSHIP, in sentencing the prisoner to a week's imprisonment, trusted that he would never be guilty of a mischievous act again, seeing the disgrace he had brought upon himself, and the unhappiness upon his family.

Manslaughter at Wolverhampton – John Fletcher, 44, was charged with the manslaughter of Thomas Lowe, at the borough of Wolverhampton, on the 9th of April. The prisoner, who pleaded guilty, was sentenced to two months' imprisonment.

Compare the newspaper report of 'The Murder by Boys in Liverpool' from 1895 with the reporting of the murder of James Bulger nearly a century later:[2]

At the Liverpool Police Court on Monday, the boys named Samuel Crawford, aged nine, and Robert Shearon, aged eight, were brought up on remand and charged with causing the death of another boy named David Dawson Becks, aged eight, on 7th inst. by drowning him in some water in the foundations of an unfinished building in Victoria St. A Coroner's jury had already found a verdict of 'Wilful Murder' against the boys as they had confessed to the crime. The evidence given before the Coroner was repeated and the boys were committed on the capital charge by the Magistrates. (*Crewe and Nantwich Chronicle*, 11 September 1895)

Statistically our chances of being the victims of violent crime, or of our children being abducted and murdered by a stranger, are remote. Yet these statistics are unlikely to make us feel any easier. And our fears should not be dismissed therefore as irrational. Those who dismiss them fail to take into account other factors which are as important to our perceptions of our safety as are the Home Office figures ... James Bulger's death appals not least because it exposes once again our society's growing indifference and our own increasing isolation. He trusted a stranger and now he is dead. It is a death for our time. (Melanie Phillips and Martin Kettle, *Guardian*, 16 February 1993)

Jon Venables and Robert Thompson, both aged 11, became the youngest convicted murderers in Britain for almost 250 years when a jury at Preston crown court found them guilty yesterday of abducting and murdering two-year-old James Bulger. They were sentenced to be detained at Her Majesty's pleasure and were expected to be kept locked up for at least 20 years. Mr Justice Morland described the abduction and murder of James on the railway track at Walton, Merseyside, as a cunning and wicked act of 'unparalleled evil and barbarity' ... Outside the court, a crowd of about 200 people had gathered by 6.20 pm when separate police vans drove Thompson and Venables away. There were shouts of 'kill them' and 'hang them' but no violence. (Edward Pilkington, *Guardian*, Thursday, 25 November 1993)

Of course, we should not assume that the different style of news reporting reflects a heightened sensitivity to violence, or that there was not a growing interest in sensationalist reporting from the mid-nineteenth century onwards (see Archer and Jones 2003; Sindall 1990). Modern media comment on violent crime may seem disproportionate to the amount of actual violent offending, and to portray the details of violent offences in vivid and exaggerated style (see Soothill and Walby 1991; Jewkes 2004). However, this may reflect a prurient pleasure on the part of tabloid readers rather than being evidence of the lack of tolerance towards violence.

Conclusion

It is clear that there is a variety of views on violence. This chapter has challenged the validity of statistics to accurately measure violence in society, suggesting that they can only be a rough estimation of the amount of prosecuted violence and that there is a large amount of daily violence that never reaches the courts. It has not, however, tried to suggest that (whatever you think of statistics) the civilizing effects of social processes of education, commerce, trust and manners have not curbed the amount of violence in daily life. We are left with a range of views as to which processes had the most impact. The attack on male violence by the courts, the increased capability of the State to survey and control its problem populations and the change in public sensibilities towards inappropriate aggression may all have played a part.

It may be that you feel that all of these explanations for the *fin-de-siècle* decline in violence can stand independently, and that statistics of assault and murder represent a useful but partial view of violence. In order to test your opinions you must question whether the statistics reflect a real decline in offending, then you must assess the evidence for each of the theories described in this chapter – what kinds of evidence are there for a change in sensibilities? Would trial reports in newspapers offer sufficient evidence, for example? How about oral evidence, can that be trusted? And can arguments for civilizing processes which indicate that such processes depressed levels of violence also explain the rise in violent crime after 1920? In other words, is society de-civilizing, and what does that term really mean? The following tutorial questions should help you to focus your thoughts.

Key questions

1. Summarize the views of Howard Taylor and V. A. C. Gatrell in relation to criminal statistics and say which you find the more convincing argument.

This is a very important discussion. You will find that many of the articles you find referenced in this book will support the argument they present with statistics. Few now believe that crime statistics completely match real incidence (as the Positivist school of criminology asserts). Gatrell's view lies within the majority opinion that if the various forces that control fluctuations in prosecution policy/practice can be accounted for, then the statistics can be useful. In other words, if we can identify changes in legislation, police campaigns that 'target' particular crimes, practices which inhibit or encourage prosecution, judicial biases in favour of prosecution and so on, then we can strip these away to reveal a rate of real incidence of offending behaviour. This is obviously very difficult. Obtaining relevant evidence of policing campaigns is hard enough, but second-guessing the mind of victims – what makes a nineteenth-century victim report one crime but not another – is almost impossible. Many have turned to national aggregated statistics that 'smooth out' some of these difficulties. If the police are very active in Manchester, they are balanced by less active police in Cheshire, goes the theory. Certainly longitudinal runs of national statistics over decades can illuminate apparent trends in crime, and these can be compared and contrasted with other countries (although cross-national comparisons bring their own problems). Taylor's view that the statistics of violence (especially murder) were substantially manipulated because of financial pressures is a radical departure from this consensus and there is some evidence to support his view. But there is not as much evidence as one would expect if this is the massive conspiracy perpetrated on the Victorian public. There should be a mass of Home Office, police and coroners' documents stating how suspicious deaths could be labelled 'accidental' (or other reasons why they should not be investigated) and in time these might appear, but until then his views are unsubstantiated. Without further work on this subject, most researchers will stick with the 'partial' reliability of statistical measures.

2. How do we 'know' about violent crime? How useful are newspapers and oral interviews as historical sources?

In answering this question, a good place to start is Sindall (1990) for a discussion of how newspapers helped to develop a panic over 'garrotting' in the mid-nineteenth century; also see Godfrey (2003a) for a discussion of oral sources of historical evidence.

3. Evaluate the theories which try to explain the decline in violence in the 1880–1920 period – including the increase in control by the police and the idea that violence reduced under the 'civilizing offensive'.

Here you could start by looking at John Pratt's introduction to *Punishment and Civilization* (2002); Spierenburg's (2000) article, and then go on to read Eisner (2001) and Wood 2003.

Notes

1. Although the name of the interviewee is known, the authors have chosen to delete the surname. If you wish to know more about the ethical complexities both of oral history and when using secondary analysis in oral history, see Godfrey and Richardson (2003).
2. Archer and Jones (2003: 21) found another very similar case of children murdering a child in 1855.

Further reading

The references for this chapter can be found in the Bibliography at the back of the book. If you wish to do some further reading, you should investigate these first. However, below is a list of publications which could also be consulted.

Bauman, Z. (1989) *Modernity and the Holocaust*. Cambridge: Polity Press.

Curtis, L. P. (2001) *Jack the Ripper and the London Press*. New Haven, CT and London: Yale University Press.

Eisner, M. (2001) 'Modernization, self-control and lethal violence – the long-term dynamics of European homicide rates in theoretical perspective', *British Journal of Criminology*, 41, pp. 618–38.

Girling, E., Loader, I. and Sparks, R. (2000) *Crime and Social Change in Middle England. Questions of Order in an English Town*. London: Routledge.

Godfrey, B. and Richardson, J. (2004) 'Loss, collective memory and transcripted oral histories', *International Journal of Social Research Methodology*, 7, 2, p. 143–55.

Jackson, J. (2000) *Child Sexual Abuse in Victorian England*. London: Routledge.

King, P. (2003) 'Moral panics and violent street crime 1750–2000: a comparative perspective', in B. Godfrey, C. Emsley, and G. Dunstall (eds), *Comparative Crime Histories*. Cullompton: Willan Publishing.

Monkonnen, E. (2001) *Murder in New York City*. Berkeley, CA: University of California Press.

Pratt, J. (1997) *Governing the Dangerous*. Annandale, NSW: Federation Press.

Spierenburg, P. (1996) 'Long-term trends in homicide: theoretical reflections and Dutch evidence, fifteenth to twentieth centuries', in E. Johnson and E. Monkkonen (eds), *The Civilization of Crime: Violence in Town and Country since the Middle Ages*. Chicago, IL: University of Illinois Press, pp. 63–108.

Williams, C. (2000) 'Counting crimes or counting people: some implications of mid-nineteenth-century British police returns', *Crime, Society and Histories*, 5, 2, pp. 77–93.

Wood, J. C. (2003) 'Self-policing and the policing of the self: violence, protection and the civilizing bargain in Britain', *Crime, History and Societies*, 7, 1, pp. 109–128.

Wood, J.C. (2004) *Violence and Crime in Nineteenth-Century England: The Shadow of Our Refinement*. New York: Routledge.

7. Changing perceptions of crime and criminals

Introduction

Perceptions of both crime and criminals changed significantly during the two centuries 1750–1950. At the start of the period, crime was often perceived to be a 'moral' issue, and criminals were commonly seen as those simply too greedy or lazy to control their most base desires. While the poor were often associated with crime, the role of poverty in engendering crime often went unacknowledged. By the turn of the twentieth century, however, this view of crime as a 'choice' taken by rational individuals had declined. Instead, early criminologists, psychologists and social commentators had shifted towards the view that crime was often the product of either inbuilt hereditary deficiencies or the exhausting and degrading urban environment in which much of the population now lived. Perceptions of criminals themselves also changed considerably. Certainly, fears of an alienated, 'professional' class of criminals can be traced throughout the period 1750–1950, but these were perhaps at their peak during the 1850s and 1860s. During the nineteenth century, society's views of juvenile and female offenders also altered significantly. The reasons behind these changes were complex, and certainly developments in scientific thinking, in popular culture and in the role of the state all played a part. However, although complex, it is important to consider these developments, as the views that prevail in society regarding the essential nature of criminality have a strong influence on the ways in which laws are written and policing is organized.

This chapter will thus initially consider the different ways in which criminals and criminality were conceptualized and represented during the period 1750–1950. It will look at why some groups (particularly among the poor) were often perceived to be inherently 'criminal', while certain types of middle-class ('white-collar') crime were often virtually ignored. It will then propose some broad explanations for the changes which took place in the way criminals were viewed during the nineteenth century, and consider the input of popular culture, scientific debate and crime fiction. Finally, an overview of the interactions between the changing perceptions of criminals and the evolution of Victorian penal policy will be provided.

Introductory reading

Bailey, V. (1993) 'The fabrication of deviance: "dangerous classes" and "criminal classes" in Victorian England', in J. Rule and R. Malcomson (eds), *Protest and Survival: The Historical Experience. Essays for E.P. Thompson*. London: Merlin Press, pp. 221–56.

Emsley, C. (2005) *Crime and Society in England, 1750–1900* (3rd edn). Harlow: Longman, Chapter 3.

Melossi, D. (2000) 'Changing representations of the criminal', *British Journal of Criminology*, 40, pp. 296–320.

Wiener, M.J. (1990) *Reconstructing the Criminal. Culture, Law, and Policy in England, 1830–1914*. Cambridge: Cambridge University Press, Introduction and Chapter 1.

Changing perceptions of crime and criminals

Consider the following two quotations. Both are drawn from the work of nineteenth-century writers seeking to understand criminality and to define the typical 'criminal'. Written at different ends of the nineteenth century, however, they propose very different versions of the causes of crime.

> Idleness is a never-failing road to criminality [...] And when it has unfortunately taken hold of the human mind, unnecessary wants and improper gratifications, not known or thought of by persons in a course of industry, are constantly generated: hence it is, that crimes are resorted to, and every kind of violence, hostile to the laws, and to peace and good order, is perpetrated. (Colquhoun 1800: 94–5)

> Many unfortunate persons have bequeathed to them by their parents morbid affections of the brain which compel some to homicide, some to suicide, some to drunkenness and its consequent vicious and degraded mode of life, reducing others to idiocy or raving madness. In this sad class of cases, it is obvious enough to any one that the criminal should be no less an object of our deep commiseration than the man who has been seized by a loathsome and painful disease. (Rylands 1889: 35)

Patrick Colquhoun was one of the first stipendiary magistrates. His influential *Treatise on the Police of the Metropolis* went through numerous editions, and he has frequently been cited as a key thinker behind the 'New Police' (Neocleous 2000). It is clear from the above quotation that, for Colquhoun, crime was primarily a *moral* issue. He connects criminality with 'idleness' and 'unnecessary wants'. By implication, criminals are individuals with deficient 'character' or 'moral fibre', who are lazy, greedy and unable to stick to 'a course of industry'. He felt that 'offences of every description have their origin in the vicious and immoral habits of the people, and in the facilities which the state of manners and society, particularly in vulgar life, afford in generating vicious and bad habits'. While Colquhoun readily connected crimes of all kinds with the 'poorer classes', there is little recognition in his works of the ways in which poverty might lead to crime through need. Rather, criminals are seen as rational individuals who 'choose' to commit crime rather than work for a living.

The quotation from Gordon Rylands stands in complete contrast. Rylands was one of the first generation of 'criminological' writers, who were interested in taking a 'scientific' approach to crime and its causes. Rather than seeing crime as a 'moral issue', it had become increasingly common by the end of the nineteenth century to focus less on the will and personality of the criminal offender and more on the impersonal conditions from which he was manufactured. As Martin Wiener (1990) notes, the criminal thus became 'less a moral actor and more a point of conjunction of forces larger than individuals, a sign of weak spots in the human (and, to a lesser degree, social) constitution. Far from being rational actors 'choosing' the easy life of crime, criminals, for Rylands and other early criminologists, were thus 'destined' to a life of crime by deficient breeding or degenerating living conditions. As we will see, such changing perceptions had important implications for criminal justice policy, which was of course not made in an intellectual vacuum but rather drew upon such implicit, contemporary assumptions. First, however, we should perhaps further investigate these changing perceptions outlined above.

An initial point to note is that it is certainly *not* the case that crime was seen solely as an individual, moral issue between 1750 and 1850 and as a wider social, environmental problem thereafter. There was, of course, some overlap. It is possible to find early writers aware of the social pressures which could prejudice some individuals to a crime, and equally possible to unearth late nineteenth-century commentators who insisted that criminals were fully responsible individuals who could simply 'choose' not to commit crime. As a general rule, however, it is broadly correct to state that the earlier the period under consideration, the more likely we are to encounter a 'moral' view of crime, based initially on a religious view of crime as 'sin' – the inability to resist temptation. The further we move towards 1950, the greater the prevalence of quasi-scientific explanations of criminality, which focus less on apportioning individual blame and more on the role of physiology, environment and social pressures in predisposing certain individuals to crime. We must be wary, of course, of viewing this evolution as 'progress'. Explanations of crime

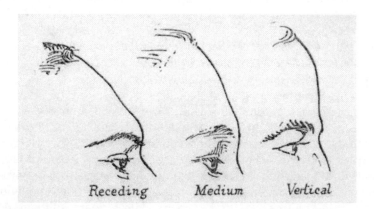

During the nineteenth century, it was common for instructional texts to focus on the physical attributes of criminals.
Source: J.K. Ferrier (1928) *Crooks and Crime*. London: Seeley.

are always rooted in the cultural and scientific paradigms of the time and, indeed, it might be argued that we still have no solid understanding of the way in which criminology as a discipline has 'colluded' from its inception in 'a definite set of political assumptions and policies' (Garland 1985b: 109–37).

Initially, though, during the latter half of the eighteenth century and the first half of the nineteenth, crime was seen as essentially a moral issue and the stereotypical criminal was poor and indolent. While Victor Bailey (1993) has claimed that the notion of 'the dangerous classes' and the threat of social revolution found limited purchase in England, it is certainly the case that the responsibility for the bulk of crime was readily associated with the poor. The 1839 Royal Commission on a Constabulary Force, for example, concluded that 'the notion that any considerable proportion of the the crimes against property are caused by *blameless* poverty we find disproved at every step'.[1] Immorality and vice (particularly alcoholism) were seen to lead the poor inexorably towards crime. As one prison chaplain noted, 'the passion for intoxicating drink is the cause of almost all the crime and misery done or suffered by the working classes' (Clay 1853: 34).

However, from the mid-nineteenth century, prevalent attitudes began to undergo modification. Individualistic explanations of poverty and crime were increasingly ceding ground to more collective theories of 'degeneration' and urban decay. Although most commonly associated with the work of the Italian criminologist Cesare Lombroso, Daniel Pick (1989) has demonstrated that this diffuse and ill-defined discourse had a European-wide impact. Initially associated with the work of the French doctor Morel on cretinism, degeneration theory came to place emphasis on the detrimental effects of modern, urban life (both the effete luxury of the aristocracy and the squalid, filthy existence of the poor) on the physical and mental health of individuals. Adverse environmental conditions not only led individuals towards physical and mental infirmities, but also predisposed them to criminality and vice. Moreover, many late nineteenth-century scientists and criminologists came to believe that such defects could then become hereditary, leading to an inexorable decline in the overall health of the nation. As Pick (1989: 21) expressed it, 'degeneration was increasingly seen by medical and other writers not as the social condition of the poor, but as a self-reproducing force; not the effect but the cause of crime, destitution and disease'. Attention gradually shifted, therefore, from the will/culpability of the individual criminal to the hereditary influences or environmental factors which shaped his/her destiny. As Henry Maudsley, who emerged in the 1870s as the leading psychologist of the era claimed, 'No one can escape the tyranny of his organisation; no one can elude the destiny that is innate in him, and which unconsciously and irresistibly shapes his ends' (Wiener 1990: 169).

One important point which you might already have noticed is that, while the period *c.*1800–*c.*1900 was one of particular concern in regard to crime and criminals, most of the discourse on the topic discussed above relates primarily to adult, male criminals. Certainly, many of the key criminal stereotypes belonged to this group – the 'sturdy beggars' seen to terrorize farmers, the 'dangerous classes' demanding political reform and wealth redistribution, the 'habitual criminals' and 'ticket-of-leave men', mobile and vicious – all were male and adult. While views regarding *criminality* (why individuals committed crimes) may have changed over time, there was a strong degree of continuity in perceptions of *criminals*. In particular, fears over a secretive, professional 'criminal class' endured throughout the nineteenth century. The use of the term 'criminal classes' was widespread during the latter half of the nineteenth century, although it was probably most common during the 1860s. The Leeds reformer, Thomas Plint, in his 1851 book *Crime in England* described them succinctly thus:

> The criminal class live amongst [...] the operative [working] classes, whereby they constitute so many points of vicious contact with those classes – so many ducts by which the virus of a moral poison circulates through and around them. They constitute a pestiferous canker [an infectious sore] in the heart of every locality where they congregate, offending the sight, revolting the sensibilities, and lowering, more or less, the moral status of all who come into contact with them. (Himmelfarb 1984: 387)

While hard to define precisely, the term generally referred to a rather nebulous group of individuals (not just the poor or the working classes *en masse*, but rather a sub-group of these) who made their *living* from crime. The criminal classes were those who had foresworn the world of labour totally and dedicated themselves wholly to crime and vice of all kinds. Very often seen to be steeped in criminality from childhood, it was often claimed that the criminal classes had their own *argot* (or slang language), their own meeting places and their own customs and rituals. They were thus, in every sense of the word, 'separate' from respectable society – 'the enemies of the human race' as the *Times* put it. While alienated from the society within which they lived – '*in* the community, but neither *of* it, nor *from* it', as Plint (1851: 153) put it – it was nonetheless a common fear that the deep-rooted criminality they embodied would spread to other groups at the lower end of the social spectrum. Metaphors of contagion (note Plint's use of the terms 'pestiferous canker' and 'moral poison', for example) were common, and it can be argued that anxieties over the 'criminal classes' were readily transformed into policy. The Habitual Criminals Act of 1869 and the Prevention of Crime Act of 1871 both identified repeat offenders as the primary threat to law and order, and Edmund du Cane (director of the convict prison service) noted in 1875 that 'we have in principle recognised the existence of a criminal class, and directed the operations of the law towards checking the development of that class, or bringing those who belong to it under special control' (Bailey 1993: 246).

However, the existence of such widely held ideas about a criminal class should not be taken to mean that such a 'class' ever actually existed. In fact, most historians would now argue, as Bailey (1993: 246) does, that 'whatever Victorians thought, very few Victorian criminals were full-time "professionals"'. Emsley (2005a: 177) agrees that 'the more historians probe the reality of such a class, the more it is revealed to be spurious'. Rather than the bulk of crime being committed by small, professional gangs, it is far more probable that most crimes were committed by ordinary working people who needed to supplement their paltry wages. It is also unlikely that most offenders were culturally or socially very different from other members of the working class.

This does not, of course, mean that we should discount and ignore the whole Victorian notion of a 'criminal class'. As with many issues in the sphere of crime and policing, *perceptions of crime* (on the part of the public and government officials) were just as important for the formation of policy (and for our subsequent investigations of this) as 'reality'. The notion of a separate 'class' of criminals allowed crime to be defined as 'other'; in other words, as divergent from, and not really a product of, respectable society. An examination of the evolution of the concept can therefore tell us a lot about both patterns of crime and theories of deviance. For example, it is perhaps instructive that, while the 'criminal classes' were always drawn from the poor in nineteenth-century discourse, the perceived relationship between the two groups (as well as the terminology used to describe them) changed over time. While at the end of the eighteenth century, the 'dangerous classes' were virtually synonymous with the poor, gradually more and more elements of the working class were accepted into respectable society, and the 'criminal classes' shrunk to a small and easily managed 'residuum' – a term which passed into common usage from the 1880s onwards. The 'residuum' was seen to be comprised of the lowest and most unproductive members of society – criminals, but also vagrants, lunatics and paupers – who were seen as 'inherently unable to help themselves, because of biological and physical degeneracy' (Harris 1995: 67). There are debates over the extent to which the 'residuum' was seen by late nineteenth-early twentieth-century commentators as 'redeemable', but the idea of an unproductive 'social problem group' which included the mentally ill, the criminally divergent and the physically disabled continued in one form or another up until the Second World War. For example, the Wood Committee on Mental Deficiency concluded in 1929 that, while 'low grade defectives' (defined as idiots and imbeciles) were evenly distributed throughout society, what it termed 'higher-grade feeble minded' were concentrated at the bottom of society, in a 'social problem group' clearly distinct from the bulk of the working class (Macnicol 1987: 302).

Aside from notions of a 'criminal class', changing stereotypical perceptions of other two supplementary criminal 'types' are also noteworthy. Neither juvenile delinquency nor female criminality fitted neatly into nineteenth-century perceptions of crime as primarily associated with the adult, male poor. Both are dealt with more fully in the following chapter, but it will suffice to note that both attracted periodic public concern during the period 1750–1950. Crime committed by children is currently regarded as somewhat separate legally from that perpetrated by adults, and it is generally agreed that children should be treated differently before the law. This was, of course, not always the case. At the start of our period (the end of the eighteenth century), while it was presumed that children under the age of seven could not knowingly commit crime, individuals over that age could be (and were) treated harshly by the law, and subjected to transportation or even execution. However, during the early- to mid-nineteenth century, partly due to changes taking place in the way childhood was conceptualized, there was a massive upsurge in concern over the issue of juvenile delinquency, which was seen to be spiralling out of control. Geoffrey Pearson (1983) has argued that there was an element of 'moral panic' in this anxiety, and that many of the 'causes' attributed to cyclical fears of 'hooliganism' (for example, deficient parental control, inadequate discipline at school, a general decline in public morality) have been cited continually for at least the last 150 years! Compare, for example, the following quotations from works concerned with juvenile crime, the first published in 1849 and the second in 1961 (Pearson 1984: 168, 15). The similarities between the two are obvious, despite their separation by more than a century. Clearly, the interlinked themes of moral decline, of rapid social change and of unruly and criminal youth are somewhat perpetual.

> Any candid judge will acknowledge the manifest superiority of the past century; and in an investigation of the causes which have conspired to produce such an unhappy increase of juvenile crime, which is a blot upon the age, the altered relations of village life cannot be overlooked [...] and [...] the working classes [...] have generally deteriorated in moral condition.

> The society in which today's adolescents find themselves is one of bewildering change [...] the whole face of society has changed in the last 20 years [...] a decrease in moral safeguards, and the advent of the welfare state has provided a national cushion against responsibility and adversity.

Like juveniles, women were not always present in the criminal justice system to the same extent. However, rather than an increase in convictions and arrests, the nineteenth century saw a steady fall in the numbers of women passing through the courts. As Emsley (2005a: 155) notes, 'from the late seventeenth to the early twentieth centuries the percentage of women tried at the Old Bailey fell from roughly forty-five to twelve per cent'. A number of different theories have been postulated to account for this which are discussed in the following chapter. It seems likely, however, that there was (in line with the changing perceptions of criminality discussed above) a broad shift from a perception of women criminals as morally corrupt to a view of them as mentally weak and in need of medical/psychiatric assistance. In other words, female offenders who had once been classified as 'bad' now came to be seen as 'mad'. There is certainly much evidence to support Lucia Zedner's (1991) contention that a shift in the control mechanisms surrounding women (from the law and the courts, to the hospital/psychiatrist's couch) meant that they steadily vanished from the criminal statistics. While often described popularly during the first half of the nineteenth century (roughly speaking) as wicked and unruly, the very antithesis of respectable and acceptable womanhood, female criminals were (by the end of the century) more commonly characterized as weak-willed, and in need of medical help rather than retributive punishment.

It can be seen, therefore, that prevalent perceptions of the causes or reasons behind crime changed significantly over time but that certain stereotypes, such as that of a 'criminal class' of poor, adult males, proved enduring. Other stereotypes, particularly those associated with juveniles and with women, provoked periodic public outrage. Why did these changes take place? Given that they clearly changed over time, just how were attitudes towards crime and criminals formed? It is not sufficient simply to outline and track changing views about crime and criminals. It is possible, although complicated, to investigate some of the wider social trends and pressures that may have shaped the changes in perceptions outlined above.

Factors influencing perceptions of crime and criminals

So, why did the changes outlined above in the way in which crime and criminals were perceived occur? What are the main factors which might be considered in explaining patterns of continuity and change in perceptions of crime and criminals between 1750 and 1950? Initially, of course, it is important to consider the immense social and economic developments of the period. From the late eighteenth century the twin forces of industrialization and urbanization had generated tremendous wealth for some, and standards of living during the nineteenth century were such that England often served as an example to other countries. Indeed, in 1833 the French commentator de Tocqueville (1997: 49) referred to England as the 'Eden of modern civilisation'. However, this transformation had also entailed vast disruption in the living conditions of much of the population. In many new urban areas the spread of wage labour and cyclical unemployment, overcrowding and a lack of social infrastructure meant that the problems of poverty were glaringly apparent. Although industrial output had been expanding rapidly in England since the start of the nineteenth century, economic growth and its attendant benefits remained extremely unevenly distributed.

Perhaps more importantly, however, these changes in the structure of the economy were contributing to a decline in traditional, patriarchal views of the poorer classes. For example, a shift from farm workers as 'servants in husbandry', with the traditional obligations this entailed for employers, to mere wage labourers within a rural proletariat meant an increasing shift towards a market-driven economy where traditional rights, duties and deference counted for little. Allied with this, the upheavals caused by a precocious urbanization blurred the boundaries of national society and contributed to increasingly fluid employment patterns in towns and cities. Thus not only did this economic and social turmoil contribute to harsh living conditions for the bulk of the population (at least until around 1860), and hence trail crime and popular unrest in its wake, but the rapid and forced development of new types of social relations clearly led to fears of a breakdown in morality and the erosion of traditional forms of authority.

The wider political context of the period must also be considered as a factor in generating concern over the problems of controlling a newly empowered and restive population. The French Revolution of 1789, the Chartist disturbances of the early nineteenth century and the continental revolutions of 1848 all raised the spectre that the lawless and vicious 'dangerous classes' would burst the bounds of traditional control. Concern over the putative criminality of the poor was not a new development, as Jim Sharpe (1999) has clearly demonstrated, but the breakdown of traditionally static social relations certainly meant that the late eighteenth and early nineteenth centuries were a period during which 'the crime problem' was particularly hotly debated. The new 'mobility' which industrialization granted the poor, rapid changes in social relations and the continued strength of religious sentiment meant that concerns over crime initially focused primarily on issues of morality. Important contemporary 'scientific' works like Malthus's *Essay on the Principle of Population* (1798) also seemed to reinforce perceptions of the poor as unable to control their more primitive urges and in danger of bursting the boundaries of traditional control methods.

However, as we have already outlined, such perceptions of both poverty and crime changed radically over the next century or so. Concerns over the problem of crime and how best to suppress it remained, and if anything were strengthened by the advent of the new science of statistics and the reports of numerous Royal Commissions. However, the perceived nexus of these concerns changed. Rather than a rampaging member of the 'dangerous classes', unable to control his/her base instincts and heedless of traditional authority, notions of a 'typical' criminal shifted to that of a mentally and physically debilitated individual, buffeted by hereditary and environmental pressures beyond his/her control. What can account for this fundamental shift?

It is likely that the impact of new forms of 'knowledge' and 'expertise' – characterized by developments in the fields of science, medicine and the novel discipline of criminology – had a key role to play in the evolution of social representations of crime and criminals. There is not space to investigate these matters fully here, but some brief comments will perhaps help to illustrate this. In the field of science, for example, the publication of Charles Darwin's *On the Origin of Species* (1859) demolished established certainties. By suggesting a biological path of human development rather than one of 'divine creation', it undoubtedly contributed to a decline in a religious world-view, and hence perhaps a 'moral' approach to crime. Darwin's assertion of the importance of hereditary and environmental factors in the sphere of biology implied that such factors were potentially more important than 'the will of the individual' in the development of humanity, too. Thus notions of untramelled free will and rational choice, which early 'moral' views of crime were based upon, came to be undermined. As Oscar Wilde (Morton 1984: 149) was later to note:

> By revealing to us the absolute mechanism of all action, and so freeing us from the self-imposed and trammelling burden of moral responsibility, the scientific principle of Heredity has become, as it were, the warrant for the contemplative life. It has shown us that we are never less free to act than when we try to act.

There was a second, even more worrying, implication extrapolated by some from Darwin's theories. If the course of human history was not divinely ordained, then 'progress' was not assured. If mankind could evolve, could it not also 'degenerate'? The establishment of the Second Law of

Thermodynamics in 1851, and the concomitant discovery of 'entropy' (the idea that the universe had a finite life, and that energy could eventually be dissipated), while obviously having no immediate implications for Victorian society, did perhaps augment the notion both that 'progress' was not assured in human affairs and that the 'will of the individual' was insignificant when set against the environmental constraints acting upon him or her. Certainly, the impact of the development of notions of 'degeneration' is vital to an understanding of changing perceptions of criminals in the nineteenth century. Degeneration theory (already mentioned briefly above) was a diffuse current of social thought. It was, broadly speaking, concerned with the underbelly of progress, with the notion that modern, urban, industrial life was inherently unhealthy (both mentally and physically) and would eventually produce a 'degenerate' race of humans, weak, debilitated, morally corrupt and incapable of decisive social interaction.

As an idea, degeneration wove itself through fiction, popular discourse and political and scientific thought. For example, medical writings, in particular within the new discipline of psychiatry, often referred to the notion of declining genetic stock and the influence of hereditary factors in mental deficiency and criminality. The psychologist Henry Maudsley (1873: 76) noted, for example:

> [...] in consequences of evil ancestral influences, individuals are born with such a flaw or warp of nature that all the care in the world will not prevent them from being vicious or criminal, or becoming insane [...] No one can escape the tyranny of his organisation; no one can elude the destiny that is innate in him, and which unconsciously and irresistibly shapes his ends, even when he believes that he is determining them with consummate foresight and skill [...]

Writers from the new 'science' of criminology often also sought to forge links between modern living, vice and crime (Garland 1985b). The intention of the individual was downplayed and the force of 'hereditary impulses' stressed. For example, William Morrison (1896: 109–10) claimed, when writing about juvenile delinquents, that:

> We may [...] say on the grounds of heredity that a considerable proportion of juvenile offenders come into the world with defective moral instincts, and that their deficiencies in this respect, combined with external circumstances of a more or less unfavourable character, have the effect of making these juveniles what they are.

Martin Wiener (1990: 12) argues that these developments in scientific discourse led to a fundamental change in the prevalent image of the individual. As we have seen, at the start of the nineteenth century the individual was perceived as a rational, responsible being who could be held accountable for his own 'moral' choices. However, Wiener argues that 'as technology and economic advances kept extending the scale and complexity of life [...] the Victorian image of the individual weakened'. Individuals in the late nineteenth century were more commonly described by science as weak and unable to break free from the hereditary and environmental influences shaping their actions. Consequently, Wiener argues, fears of crime as a wave of 'dam-bursting anarchy' were replaced by anxiety over a 'society of ineffectual, devitalised, and over-controlled individuals moulded by environmental and biological forces beyond their control'.

While we are discussing these kinds of changes in knowledge and popular perception, it is probably worth noting that they were both mirrored and reinforced by the development of crime fiction as a specific genre and by the portrayal of criminals in fiction generally (Ousby, 1976; Kayman 1992). The emergence of the 'novel' as a literary form during the eighteenth century became linked to growing concerns over crime and criminality, and it was not long before nineteenth-century forms of 'crime fiction' began to develop. This process was aided in the latter half of the century by the expansion of primary school education, which created a 'reading public' non-existent before this time. After all, it was only in 1870 that Trollope testified that 'We have become a novel-reading people. Novels are in the hands of all us: from the Prime Minister down to the last-appointed scullery-maid' (Kayman 1992: 172).

It could be argued that the enormous narrative production of the nineteenth century, and particularly crime fiction and policing memoirs, reflects a culmination of anxiety at the loss of what Brooks (1984: 27) has termed 'providential plots'. As he notes:

> the emergence of narrative plot as a dominant mode of ordering and explanation may belong to the large process of secularisation [...] which marks a falling-away from those revealed plots [...] that appeared to subsume transitory human time to the timeless.

In other words, with no 'divine plan' to order human affairs, the actions of individuals or institutions take on a new importance in literature (see also Leps 1992). It may well have been that, in a period of acute social turbulence, crime fiction and other such writings (for example, policing memoirs) may have helped readers (and authors) to explore/reinforce the lines demarcating acceptable and anti-social behaviour (Lawrence 2003). Certainly, too, the depictions of crime and criminals in fiction shows a close correlation to the broader representations of the individual discussed above. In Dickens's *Oliver Twist*, first published in 1838, Sikes's murder of Nancy shows him to be a ruthless, calculating thug, as the extract below indicates:

> Without one pause, or a moment's consideration; without once turning his head to the right, or left, raising his eyes to the sky, or lowering them to the ground, but looking straight before him with savage resolution [...] He [...] freed one arm, and grasped his pistol. The certainty of immediate detection if he fired, flashed across his mind even in the midst of his fury; and he beat it twice with all the force he could summon, upon the upturned face that almost touched his own. [...] It was a ghastly figure to look upon. The murderer staggering backward to the wall, and shutting out the sight with his hand, seized a heavy club and struck her down. (Dickens 1999: 383).

By contrast, Wiener (1990: 227) notes that late Victorian serious social novelists, such as George Gissing, 'tended to locate individuals tightly embedded within larger structures, with little room to maneuver [sic] either physically or morally'. In *New Grub Street*, for example, the criminal Milvain explains his selfishness as a function of his poverty, noting that 'Selfishness – that's one of my faults [...] If I were rich, I should be a generous and good man; so would many another poor fellow whose worst features come out under hardship' (Gissing 1891).

It can be seen, therefore, that when considering changing representations of crime and criminals, we must be aware that these were not constructed in a vacuum. Cultural trends, scientific developments and economic and social changes all have an impact on the construction of criminality. However, having delineated some of the causes of these changing perceptions, what about their effects? Can we make any assertions regarding the likely impact of changing representations of crime and criminals on the actual operation of the criminal justice system?

The effects of changing representations of crime and criminals

The changing perceptions of crime and criminals outlined above, and particularly the prevalence of the idea that crime was on the increase in the period 1780–1850, may well have had a bearing on the introduction of the New Police and on the nature of their early duties. In regard to the setting up of the New Police, as noted in Chapter 2, there is considerable controversy over the extent to which the older systems of policing in place at the end of the eighteenth century were actually failing (Reynolds 1998), and also over the degree to which Sir Robert Peel and other reformers (such as Edwin Chadwick) actively distorted the available evidence to serve their own agenda (Philips and Storch 1999). However, it might be argued that Peel and others would not have been able to mobilize the necessary support for the introduction of what was, after all, quite an unpopular new institution without the existence of a widespread perception that crime was on the increase and that the working classes were becoming steadily more unruly.

Certainly, the anxiety felt by many in England during the 1820s and 1830s over a newly mobile and potentially criminal 'dangerous class' must have had important ramifications for the duties of the new police forces. As Clive Emsley (2005a: 60) notes, while 'counterfactual history is fraught with danger', we cannot help but speculate that:

If legislators and commentators on crime had concentrated on the few big thefts or embezzlements as their benchmark for crime, rather than on the very many small thefts and incidents of disorders, then the overall perception of criminality and of the criminal class would have been very different.

The continual focus on crime as primarily located within the lower end of the working class meant that middle-class, white-collar crime was consistently marginalized. It was common for most commentators during the nineteenth century to associate crime with the poorer classes, and to frame their arguments accordingly, largely disregarding the offences (such as fraud, blackmail and insider trading) more usually perpetrated by the middle classes (Sindall 1983). It was arguably not until the advent of motoring that the middle classes came into regular contact with the police, and certainly stereotypical representations of criminality (and hence the focus of the judicial system) concentrated almost exclusively on the lower classes until well into the twentieth century (Emsley 1993). Thefts perpetrated by complex stock market frauds had far less law and legislation surrounding them than more simple forms of property crime. It would appear that laws regarding appropriation by devious means were disproportionately focused on the lower end of society until well into the twentieth century. In addition, even the legislation which was in place was either not enforced uniformly (as is evidenced by clerks being treated more severely by the courts than directors), or sometimes not enforced at all. The reliance on action by the victims certainly influenced the way that police acted in relation to the frauds and thefts collectively known as 'white-collar crime'. Complex stock market frauds (such as occurred throughout the nineteenth and twentieth centuries) demanded highly trained and knowledgeable police officers, yet the vast majority of police officers, even detectives, knew very little about the rules governing the financial services industry.

The perceptions of many influential individuals that the poor were responsible for the bulk of crime undoubtedly helped to shape the course of much police activity. Much police endeavour, particularly in the period up to 1880, was directed towards 'policing the poor and the very poor' (Lawrence 2000: 64). As Robert Storch (1976) and others have shown, perceptions of crime as a 'class issue' may well have led to the development of patterns of policing which were directed particularly towards the lower classes.

The perceptions of crime and criminals held by police officers themselves must also be considered. For much of the nineteenth century, for example, most senior officers (and many junior ones, too) were convinced that all vagrants were potential criminals. Not only did the English police 'share the distaste of the middle classes for "tramps and suspicious looking characters"', they were also 'more than willing to act against them' (Lawrence 2004: 215). Chief Constable Edwin Chadwick (1900: 128), for example, referred to tramps as 'this social blot on our civilisation', and 'the scum which floats on the surface of our civilisation'. Towards the end of the century, however, many officers had begun to imbibe welfarist notions of the role of environment in shaping criminals, and were beginning to modify such strident views and act accordingly. For example, Edmund Henderson, Chief Commissioner of the Metropolitan Police, writing in 1875 about juvenile delinquents, noted that 'with reference to the evils arising from overcrowding in the dwellings of the poor, I would remark that children born in such places are generally puny and delicate, many of them growing up unfit for manual labour, and are driven either to crime or begging for a livelihood'.[2] It seems likely that the perceptions police officers had of potential criminals affected the way in which they carried out their duties, just as the perceptions held by government officials and ratepayers dictated the precise tasks they required of the police.

Martin Wiener (1990) has put forward a similar, although much more wide-ranging, argument in relation to Victorian criminal policy – in particular the development of the prison and the gradual growth of dissatisfaction with it. Rather than approach criminal policy from an *internalist* standpoint (looking at it primarily from a legal perspective) or from a *pragmatic* viewpoint (taking the view that policy was constructed by pragmatists merely responding to events as best they could), Wiener has argued for a *cultural* approach to the study of criminal policy. In other words, he believes that society's broad views of the 'individual' and of the 'criminal type' frame the formation of criminal justice policy.

As has been outlined above, it is possible to argue (as Wiener does) that the period to *c.*1850 was marked by a view of crime as primarily caused by 'deficiency of character' – in particular, a failure of certain individuals to defer gratification and to control their more primitive and selfish desires. A perceived need for legislation to deal with this problem arose and hence:

> By the 1860s, therefore, both criminal and civil law were placing greater stress upon impersonal rules defining, and insisting upon, individual responsibility. Law was being employed with increasing consistency as an instrument for developing self-disciplining and gratification-deferring personalities in the population at large. To counter the crime wave and immorality wave of the first half of the century stood a newly character-building law. (Wiener 1990: 91)

More specifically, there was a transformation in punishment. Arbitrary retribution actioned on the body (such as execution) came to be seen firstly as ineffective in preventing crime and secondly as likely to corrupt those watching (public executions were the norm until the 1860s). Thus a new system of penal punishment arose, in which routine activity and solitary confinement were the norm. Punishment was still arduous, but the intention was that good habits had to be learnt under guidance. As a member of the 1853 Select Committee on Gaols expressed this:

> Human nature is so constituted that when a man has been long addicted to a life of crime or sensual indulgence it requires a severe affliction to force him to reflect – he must be providentially deprived of those sources of animal pleasure and excitement which have hitherto enabled him to silence his conscience and to shut out from his mind all thoughts of the future – there must be something external to afflict, to break down his spirit, some bodily suffering or distress of mind, before the still small voice will be heard and the man brought to himself. (Ignatieff 1978: 199).

However, with the development of new discourses of criminality and of the individual which focused more on the wider 'net' of social and genetic influences producing crime than on the apportioning of 'blame' to individuals, this 'moral imperative' began to fade from punishment theory. Psychologists and criminologists began to stake their claim for expertise in 'treating' certain types of offenders. The Police Court Missionary system gradually developed into the probation service and the provision of welfare systems to prevent reoffending came to be seen as at least as important as notions of retribution and moral regeneration (Garland 1985).

Conclusion

In some ways, perceptions of both crime and criminals clearly changed radically during the period 1750–1950. Fears of the 'dangerous classes', the disorderly poor and the morally weak (but ultimately rational) criminal gradually gave way to notions of criminals as 'degenerate' and weak-minded. While criminality continued, in large part, to be associated with the poorer classes, the links made between poverty and criminality changed considerably. The reasons behind these changing perceptions and manifestations were multiple and can perhaps never be fully delineated. However, the role of developments in the scientific and medical spheres, the impact of new forms of criminological knowledge and the subtle yet pervasive influence of fictional writings must all be acknowledged. The cumulative impact on policy of these changing perceptions was massive. The gradual shift from the 'Bloody Code' of the late eighteenth century through the harsh Victorian penal system to the more welfare-orientated mix of punishment and assistance available by 1950 cannot be fully understood without an adequate grasp of such issues.

Key questions

1. In what ways did perceptions of the causes of crime change during the nineteenth century, and why?

Obviously, the assessment of public opinion is a problematic and difficult exercise. At any one point in time there are likely to be a number of different currents of thought in the public sphere, whatever the topic being considered. However, broadly speaking, it is possible to discern a gradual change in the prevalent perception of crime and its causes in the United Kingdom during the course of the nineteenth century.

At the start of the century, crime was viewed by many as primarily a 'moral' issue, an issue of 'character'. Criminals were those (primarily among the poor), who chose not to rein in their more primitive desires and who were unable to delay their gratification. Such views were based on a conception of the individual as a self-aware and informed actor. Criminals knew what they were about to do was wrong but (perhaps due to alcoholism, perhaps due to the lack of a proper upbringing or perhaps simply due to laxity in the criminal justice system) chose to commit crime anyway. Such views were not universal, of course, and a number of reformers felt that there must be more to criminality than simple wilfulness, but it is probably fair to say that this was the majority view.

Later on in the century, and particularly from the 1870s onwards, a much more impersonal view of criminality came into vogue, based largely on early criminological theories of degeneration. Many came to believe that the harsh physical conditions prevalent in the large, new industrial cities were leading to a degradation of the mind and body of many (poorer) individuals. Exhausted both mentally and physically, criminals were thought to be those who could not cope with the demands of modern life. Rather than wilful and cunning, they came to be seen as sick and weak – often more in need more of medical help than harsh discipline. The reasons for this change are manifold, but scientific developments (such as the publication of Darwin's *On the Origin of Species*), the genesis of the criminological and psychiatric professions, and the role of fiction writing and the media all had a part to play.

2. What evidence is there that the 'fear' of a criminal class far outstripped its 'reality' during the nineteenth century?

For the nineteenth century and earlier, specific reading on this topic should include Vic Bailey's 1993 essay 'The fabrication of deviance: "dangerous classes" and "criminal classes" in Victorian England', Randall McGowan's 'Getting to know the criminal class', Jennifer Davis's 1980 essay on the Garotting Panic of 1862 and Rob Sindall's work (1987, 1990). For the end of the nineteenth century and the start of the twentieth, begin with Harris (1995), Macnicol (1987) and Davis (1989).

3. Why was so-called 'white-collar' crime marginalized by the criminal justice system for so long?

On this topic see the historical work of Robb (2002), Godfrey and Locker (2001) and Sindall (1983). There also exists a rather more voluminous criminological literature. On this, see Croall (2001), particularly chapters 1 to 4, Nelken (2002) and Sutherland (1983).

Notes

1. Royal Commission on a Constabulary Force, *Parliamentary Papers* (1839), XIX, 73, (paragraph 65).
2. Henderson, 'Report of the Commissioner of Police of the Metropolis, 1875', *Parliamentary Papers*, 1876.

Further reading

The references for this chapter can be found in the Bibliography at the back of the book. If you wish to do some further reading, you should investigate these first. However, below is a list of publications which could also be consulted.

Becker, P. (1999) 'Weak bodies? Prostitutes and the role of gender in the criminological writings of nineteenth-century German detectives and magistrates', *Crime, Histoire et Sociétés*, pp. 45–70.

Feeley, M. (1994) 'The decline of women in the criminal process: a comparative history', *Criminal Justice History*, 15, pp. 235–74

Hanway, J. (1772) *Observations on the Causes of dissoluteness which reigns among the low Classes of the People*. London.

Ignatieff, M. (1978) *A Just Measure of Pain: The Penitentiary in the Industrial Revolution 1750–1850*. New York: Pantheon.

Lawrence, P. (2003) "Scoundrels and scallywags, and some honest men ..." Memoirs and the self-image of French and English policemen, *c.*1870–1939', in C. Emsley, B. Godfrey and G. Dunstall (eds), *Comparative Histories of Crime*. Cullompton: Willan Press.

Lawrence, P. (2004) 'Policing the poor in England and France, 1850–1900', in C. Emsley, E. Johnson and P. Spierenburg (eds), *Social Control in Europe 1800-2000*, Columbus, OH: Ohio State University Press, pp. 210–25.

Peek, F. (1883) *Social Wreckage – A Review of the Laws of England as they Affect the Poor*. London.

Reynolds, E. (1998) *Before the Bobbies: The Night Watch and Police Reform in Metropolitan London, 1720–1830*. London: Macmillan.

Sindall, R. (1990) *Street Violence in the Nineteenth Century: Media Panic or Real Danger?* Leicester: Leicester University Press.

Worsley, H. (1849) *Juvenile Depravity*. London: Gilpin.

8. Criminal others: women and children[1]

Introduction

Home Office figures published in 2004 suggest that men are responsible for 80 per cent of crime – indeed one-third of men will have a conviction by their thirtieth birthday (and that does not include motoring offences). Historically, too, men have been arrested, prosecuted, convicted and imprisoned in far greater numbers than women. While the numbers of women caught up in the criminal justice system are far smaller than those of men (although female prison numbers were still rising sharply at the end of the twentieth century), this is not a universal 'law', and the proportions of female and male offenders, and proportions of juvenile and adult offenders, are not somehow 'fixed'. For example, during the nineteenth century indictments against women fell from 27 per cent of all cases in 1857 to 19 per cent in 1890 while prosecutions for minor offences were around 20 per cent (Emsley 2005: 93–4, also see Zedner 1991: 36). There was also a trend during the late nineteenth century and early twentieth centuries that reduced the proportion of offending women even further by diverting them away from the criminal justice system and placing them in semi-carceral institutions such as inebriates reformatories, and asylums (Barton 2005; Morrison 2005). Juvenile crime statistics were moving in the opposite direction, as changes in the criminal justice system brought more and more children before the courts during the nineteenth century.

So, was it the propensity of women and children to commit crime, or their opportunities to do so, which altered the figures? Or is it the way that offending women and children were policed and punished which had the major impact? These issues are critical because the differential treatment they received throws light not only on conceptions of female and child criminals, but on the status of all women and children in society, and how their positions have changed over time. Not that we can assume that all women or all female offenders were treated alike. The respectability, ethnicity and age of child (male and female) offenders too might have mitigated or aggravated the treatment of individual children by the police and the courts – though this is not so often explored. In addition to considering the 'reality' of juvenile and female offending, therefore, this chapter will discuss how conceptions of `respectable femininity' and `ideal childhood' conditioned criminal justice responses.

Introductory reading

Emsley, C. (2005) *Crime and Society in England 1750–1900* (3rd edn). Harlow: Longman, chapter 4.

Heidensohn, F. (2002) 'Gender and crime', in M. Maguire, R. Morgan and R. Reiner (eds), *Oxford Handbook of Criminology*. Oxford: Oxford University Press.

King, P. (1999) 'The rise of juvenile delinquency in England 1780–1840', *Past and Present*, clx, pp. 17–41.

Zedner, L. (1991) *Women, Crime and Custody in Victorian England*. Oxford: Oxford University Press, chapters 1 and 2.

Changing patterns of juvenile and female criminality

Adult men have been the main preoccupation of the criminal justice system for the last two hundred years. They have not only been over-represented as participants in the criminal justice process (as defendants, police officers, advocates and sentencers) but also dominate criminological literature. Until around twenty years ago, the study of criminality meant the study of adult male criminality, and to an extent women and children are still conceived as 'non-adult men' in criminological and penal discourse. It is important, however, not only to explore the involvement of women and children in crime, but also to assess in particular the ways in which the problem of 'deviant' females and 'juvenile delinquency' has been historically constructed.

From the fourteenth century there existed in law a presumption that children below a certain age were incapable of evil and could not, therefore, be held responsible for their actions. This is known as *doli incapacitas* and during the eighteenth century was set at seven years of age. Above the age of seven children were granted the same status as adults: they could drink alcohol and gamble, but were often expected to work and were not spared the legal consequences of their actions. Indeed, in the eighteenth century, child offenders could be imprisoned, transported or executed – youth was not considered a defence in law although it could be used in *mitigation*.[2] In the nineteenth century, changes in the conception of childhood forced a change to the law relating to criminal responsibility: the principle of *doli incapacitas* remained but added to it was that of *doli incapax* whereby children between the ages of seven and 14 were presumed in law to be incapable of criminal intent *unless it could be proved otherwise*. At the same time as the law was adapting, a rise in juvenile offending was observed. Shore shows that indictments in Middlesex of juveniles under 16 years of age rose from 3 per cent in 1797 to 15 per cent in 1847 with the sharpest rise occurring between 1807 and 1817 (Shore 1999: 17). However, does this rise in the recorded number of prosecutions equate to a genuine rise in juvenile crime?

Concern about a supposed rise in young people and crime was most heightened in the period immediately following the Napoleonic Wars. In May 1816 a government report gave rise to the concept of juvenile delinquency. The report found that: 'Juvenile Delinquency existed in the metropolis to a very alarming extent; that a system was in action, by which these unfortunate Lads were organised into gangs; that they resorted regularly to houses, where

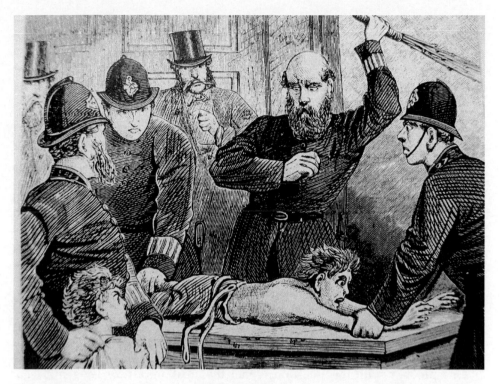

Two 'ragged and helpless urchins' aged nine and eleven were given ten strokes of the birch for stealing pigeons in Yorkshire (*The Police Illustrated News*, 19 February 1877). It was usual for the largest police officer in the station to be selected for this task.

they planned their enterprises, and afterwards divided the produce of their plunder' (*1816 Report of the committee for investigating the causes of the alarming increase of juvenile delinquency in the metropolis*, cited in Shore 1999: 6). In the same period, a number of developments in the supervision of young people – especially outside the home – contributed to the notion of a moral crisis in early industrial Britain. In many ways these concerns reflected wider issues surrounding the process of industrialization and the changing position of young people both in the home and in the productive or industrial process. Traditionally, children had gone from the parental home directly into an apprenticeship. This cycle was less common by the end of the eighteenth century as new modes of production shifted the industrial emphasis from small-scale but highly skilled producers to larger mechanized factories where labour did not need the same high degree of training. Apprenticeships were in decline and by the early nineteenth century they ceased to form any part of the life-cycle for the majority of young people.

This in turn affected family composition as more young people remained at home or moved into cheap rented accommodation rather than 'living-in'. The altered dynamics of home life focused concerns about the ability of certain families to deal with their unruly youth and the 'unattached' young workers who lived in lodging houses. Apprenticeships did remain, but often in a very different form to the traditional one. A report of 1843 drew attention to the depravity and hardship suffered by children, often orphans, who were legally bound to their employer until the age of 21 even though many did not receive wages and the apprenticeship taught no skills (*The Second Report of the Children's Employment Commission 1843*: 196). Whether the decline of the traditional apprenticeship system was a root cause of a rise in delinquency or whether both were merely characteristics of broader social change remains open to debate.

The focus on 'juvenile delinquency' provoked closer scrutiny from a news-hungry press and other media forms. Of course, the best-known portrayal of juvenile thieves is a fictional one. The popularity of Charles Dickens's *Oliver Twist* (1837) – and its depiction of a gang of young thieves run by Fagin and led by the Artful Dodger – together with increased press attention led to an even greater awareness of juvenile crime. This has all prompted many historians to regard juvenile crime as an 'invention' of the conceptualization process. One eminent authority has remarked that the 'concept of the juvenile offender, with all that implies for penal policy, is a Victorian creation' (Radzinowicz and Hood 1990: 133). Other historians are less convinced and point to earlier concerns with youth crime and also to problems associated with the recording of crime (or lack of surviving records of certain types of crime: see, for example, Griffiths 1996: 126–31). There does appear to be a noticeable rise in the *prosecution* of juveniles at this time. However, did these rates reflect crime committed by juveniles with an acceptable degree of accuracy?

One problem with this question is that the creation of new laws and legal procedures in themselves could affect the statistics substantially. For example, the Vagrancy Act 1824 allowed for 'disorderly' apprentices to be brought before a magistrate and other acts passed in the 1820s brought more disorderly or delinquent young people to the attention of the law. Similarly, the Malicious Trespass Act 1829 empowered magistrates to deal with damage or trespass on private and public property – behaviour some have argued that was particularly associated with the young (Margarey 1978: 11–27; King and Noel 1993). Whether this legislation was specifically aimed at young delinquents is contentious, but other acts certainly were. The Juvenile Offenders Act 1847 removed a number of obstacles to the prosecution of young people by allowing for those under 14 years of age to be tried in petty sessions. This resulted in a huge rise in prosecutions of juveniles – a phenomenon often mistaken for evidence of a rise in juvenile crime. This was increased further when the 1850 version of the Act raised the ceiling to 16 years of age and at a stroke augmented what appeared to be a youth crime wave. Furthermore, prior to the 1847 Act there had not existed any systematic recording of youth 'crime' (or rather prosecutions, to be more accurate). No wonder, then, that delinquency was perceived as an increasing problem. It might equally be argued that this legislation was merely a reaction to a real phenomenon – problematic youth behaviour – but in either case, what is beyond doubt is that the public *perception* of rising delinquency was very real.

Like juvenile delinquency, the outcry about women's involvement in crime was far larger than the statistics of female criminality warranted. Feeley and Little (1991) suggest that from the late eighteenth and early nineteenth centuries, women's social role engendered low involvement in crime. They cite the marginalization of women to the manufacturing base, and the growing social control of women within private spheres (through increasing patriarchal control and perhaps through greater surveillance in the new forms of work organization: see Godfrey 1999). If we add to this Zedner's contention that women (mainly in higher social groups) were removed from criminal proceedings in the period preceding the First World War by the process of the medicalization of 'deviant' women, then women's involvement in criminal justice fell markedly from the eighteenth to the twentieth centuries (see also Smith 1981; Emsley 2005). However, some remain sceptical, believing that the general move towards summary processes in the mid to late nineteenth century took female offenders out of the records consulted by Feeley and Little (the Old Bailey session papers) and replaced them in the records of the minor courts. Also, as King (1996) reveals, the starting point for Feeley and Little's statistical run was a period when large numbers of men were abroad fighting wars and therefore the proportion of female offenders would have been artificially inflated. This discussion relates to property offences – for violent offences the rates are very different. Zedner maintains that women convicted of violence (or other 'masculine offences' such as drunkenness) had a greater presence in the courts – with women making up a third of assault prosecutions in the late nineteenth century.

Women's offending overall may have been lower than men's offending, but many women were still convicted of both violent and property crimes (for example, the Pawnbrokers Act whereby the goods appropriated in minor thefts were then lodged with a pawnbroker in return for cash).[3] But there were certain crimes – such as infanticide, abortion, poisoning and prostitution (discussed in more detail later in the chapter) that became *associated* with women. Many of these reflected contemporary ideas and concerns about femininity, and as such were subject to change over time.

Infanticide was specifically a female crime. By legal definition it was an offence that could only be committed by a mother. Despite the moral overtones (the 1624 Act specified that it was an offence committed by an unmarried woman) and the seriousness of the offence, eighteenth-century juries could often take a sympathetic line. So much so, in fact, that the position became untenable and so, in 1803, a new act was passed that placed on the prosecution the burden to prove that the child had been killed by its mother rather than the child dying of unintentional neglect. Nineteenth-century juries remained sympathetic to the (usually) poor, young women in the dock, and were reluctant to convict even when the evidence was overwhelming. Many blamed the bastardy laws for creating a situation that drove desperate women to such extreme acts in order to preserve their jobs or reputation. The effect of this was that prosecutions for infanticide dropped by roughly 40 per cent during the nineteenth century and by the early twentieth century it was widely recognized that new mothers often acted out of character because of post-natal depression. The Infanticide Act of 1938 acknowledged this by separating infanticide from the more serious crime of murder on the grounds that mothers guilty of the offence were often 'disturbed by reason of not having fully recovered from the effect of giving birth'.

There was also a surprisingly tolerant attitude towards abortion. Abortion was not legalized in Britain until 1967, but the law turned a blind eye to its illicit practice at least until the late nineteenth century when a scandal forced Parliament to act against some of the worst cases. This revolved around the practice of so-called 'baby farming' whereby women would pay a fee for another person (usually women) to keep their unwanted new-born in their own home. The 'keeper' would then allow the baby to die through lack of food or care. The extent of this cannot be known but revelations about baby-farming in South London and the execution of Mary Waters in 1870 forced the government to pass the Infant Life Protection Act 1872, which required the registration of more than a single infant in any one household. Juries were equally lenient with baby farmers as they were with mothers accused of infanticide. Abortion itself, though, appears to have been quite widespread and attracted little in the way of legal intervention. This might have been partly because strict anti-abortion laws were virtually impossible to enforce: chemists sold purgatives for all sorts of ailments and many of these could be used to remove 'obstructions' such as unwanted foetuses. Abortionists were available for those who were otherwise unsuccessful. In working-class communities unqualified 'wise' women were widely used while the better off could afford to pay for a medical practitioner. Abortion was more common among the lower socio-economic groups, but, despite the beliefs of contemporary commentators, this was not due to moral decrepitude. It must be remembered that, with no welfare system to support families, a disabling or fatal accident to the main breadwinner (usually the husband) or simply one more child to feed could be financially crippling. The widespread practice of abortion – and its apparent acceptance – should be viewed in this context.

Poisoning was also often regarded as a peculiarly female crime. Again, this reflected prevailing ideas about women and femininity, which explains why the discourse far outstripped the actual incidence of this particular crime. Women, after all, were generally thought to be incapable of killing a man through direct confrontation. Not only was it believed that a woman lacked the physical strength, but also that she would have to carry out the act in a cowardly manner – at a distance and by stealth rather than strength. The usual scenario, it was believed, was that a woman would add poison to her husband's food, thereby also reinforcing the ascribed domesticity of her position and role in the family. Poisoning became *the* crime most associated with a murderess and some high-profile cases fuelled the popularity of this idea. One such case was that of Florence Maybrick in 1889. The notoriety and interest generated by cases such as Florence Maybrick's was out of all proportion to the actual incidence (approximately one conviction in every three years during the nineteenth century). But it was what the case stood for that is of most significance. Poisoning epitomized the idea of the murderess. It was cowardly and deceitful. It was a crime committed in the home – a domestic crime that subverted ideas about the dutiful housewife. More worrying for the chattering classes, though, it was not confined to the uncontrollable lower stratum of society, but was also perceived as a middle-class crime.

Thus far we have been discussing women and child offenders as if they were discrete categories. We should remember that young women also committed crimes, although as with adult offenders, they were outnumbered by men, as can be seen in Figure 8.1.[4]

Godfrey's (2005: 34) explanation for the figures presented above, is that:

The socialization of girls, and the restrictions placed on their liberty whilst living at home with parents, meant that women in their late teens were less likely to be seen in the public streets (especially at night). During the day when girls played skittles, skipping and other street games they were not considered as problematic as boys playing football or cricket. Nor was their behaviour scrutinized for signs of future disorder. Boys were expected to be rough, and it was no surprise when roughness strayed over into intolerable aggression, and the police stepped in. Girls, however, were denied this conceptual space ... and consequently they were also kept out of the cycle of repeat offending that seems to have affected young lads.

When girls became young women, however, the picture changed somewhat. Despite the extraordinary levels of social and familial control exerted over young women in the Victorian period, there was still considerable anxiety that girls were developing masculine characters and behavioural attributes. It appears that this anxiety was fuelled by women's entry into the labour market. The young women employed in mills, factories and shops may not have needed to heed the dictates of home quite so closely, and their financial

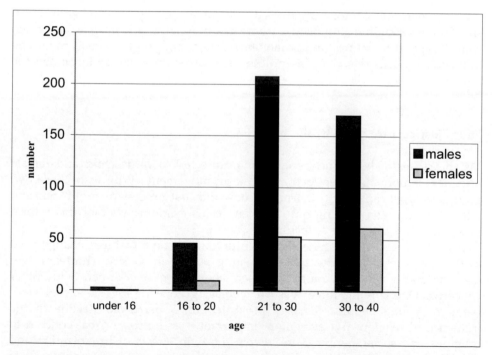

Figure 8.1 Assaults, number of offenders within age brackets, North-West English cities, 1900–20.
Source: Chief Constables' Reports, Liverpool, Chester and Manchester.

contributions to the family budget allowed some measure of freedom from the routines of domestic dicta. Like young male workers, they spent some of their wages on new clothes and frequenting the cinema (which was entering its 'Golden Age' in the 1920s and 1930s) and enjoyed the nightly colonization of the public streets.

So, all that might all be true for 'normal' crime, but what about 'the gang', that most potent of criminal symbols? Although there has been very little written in this area, girls and young women in London and the industrial cities did group together in what contemporaries called 'gangs'. They seem to have participated in rituals of display, and (probably under pressure from young male gang members) were mainly confined to peripheral activities (Davies 1999, 2000). So, girls were again denied the full opportunities their male friends enjoyed, but still encountered considerable risks by playing some part in 'the gang':

> The young women partners draped on the arm of 'Hooligan Harry' or 'Larrikin Larry', by choosing to associate themselves with men for whom society had not a good word to say, virtually removed themselves from respectable society. Therefore, in risking their health, reputation and future economic security, the many thousands of young women who may have chosen 'unsuitable' partners, or to experiment sexually before marriage, proved the equal of men as risk takers – even if that route did not carry them into the courts.' (Godfrey 2004: 36)

As the nineteenth century progressed, the contemporary concern with youth and female offending provoked various institutional and legal reforms which were designed to control and rehabilitate delinquent youths and women. The following sections describe this process, and question what underpinned the reform process.

Youth justice: care or control?

The processes of legal and penal change directed towards child and female offenders is normally described as a 'reform movement'. Why were these two groups thought capable of reform and how did that process play out? Starting with children, then moving onto women, let us examine whether this reform process can be described so benignly.

As we have seen, the nineteenth century was a time of great change both in the law and in attitudes towards young people in society. The fears over the criminality of the young discussed above also overlapped with other concerns. One driving force was an increasing concern for the moral well-being of young people – largely prompted by a perceived decline in the influence of religion. But ever more important – and also of great concern to religious and social campaigners – were the twin effects of urbanization and industrialization. This was a broad concern that impacted on many aspects of society. For example, the Factory Act 1819 banned children under nine years of age from working in cotton mills and introduced a restriction to 12 hours a day for children over nine. Other Acts followed: in 1833 night work was forbidden for children and further restrictions placed on the permitted hours to be worked by children between nine and 13; in 1844 these hours were further reduced and by 1864 similar restrictions were extended to workshops. But reform was equally visible in the area of penal reform. The foundation of the Society for the Improvement of Prison Discipline and the Reformation of Juvenile Offenders was founded in 1817 and campaigned for juvenile penal institutions separated from hardened adult prisons *to prevent the moral contamination of the young*. The first such institution was established at Parkhurst in 1838, though this was solely for boys.

Why did children become the focus of reform? We have already mentioned the impact of industrialization and urbanization, and we should bear in mind that these were revolutionary times. Revolution continued to plague much of Europe and even Britain – whose relative stability many thought would make her immune from such chaos – faced widespread unrest for much of the nineteenth century. In this volatile climate the moral character of the next generation was regarded as an essential ingredient for the future well-being of the nation (and its growing Empire). A very visible sign of morality was church attendance – and that appeared to be in decline.

The perceived decline in religion had been an ongoing concern since at least the early modern period. Once again children were not just the problem, they were also the solution. In 1788 'The Philanthropic Society for the Prevention of Crimes and the Reform of the Criminal Poor; by the Encouragement of Industry and the Culture of Good Morals, among those children who are now trained up to Vicious Courses, Public Plunder, Infamy and Ruin' was formed. Through a programme of religious and industrial instruction, the society sought to rescue delinquent and destitute children from 'the vices of the street'. The establishment of a separate place of safety for children was the key to reversing the moral decline. But the central tenets of the society – improvement through religious adherence *and* industry – were themselves characteristics of eighteenth-century ideas that linked poverty to idleness and immorality. These ideas remained persistent in the minds of many during the nineteenth century and by 1849 the Philanthropic Society had established its own agricultural farm at Redhill in Surrey where delinquents and young vagrants were 'rescued' with a diet of religion, exercise and self-denial.

These ideas were further developed by a number of Victorian philanthropists including Mary Carpenter. The daughter of a Unitarian minister, Carpenter was one of a new wave of mid-nineteenth-century 'humanitarian' reformers who were highly critical of the penal system – including the Parkhurst establishment. However, Carpenter did not separate her wider concerns from the 'moral crisis' that she believed was the blight of many young people in working-class families. The primacy of the family was central to her argument – an argument that would exert considerable influence on government policy in the 1850s.

Carpenter regarded immoral boys as potential criminals, and immorality in girls, she believed, made them especially vulnerable to prostitution. She further identified two 'classes' among the immoral poor: the 'perishing' (or destitute) and the 'dangerous' (or delinquent). While she believed that those in the perishing class could be put to useful work in industrial schools, the dangerous class needed to be reformed. Carpenter's ideas, which echoed earlier Philanthropic Society practices of placing orphans in the Manufactory and delinquents in the Reform, were soon formalized in legislation: the Youthful Offenders Act 1854 and the Industrial Schools Act 1857. Approximately 4,000 young offenders were housed in 48 reformatories by 1860 and by 1900 over 30,000 young people were held in over 200 state reformatories or industrial schools.

Where it was believed that the parents had failed to provide for the moral well-being of their children, therefore, the state had intervened. This amounted to one in every 230 juveniles (Radzinowicz and Hood 1990: 181). Britain, it seemed, had come a long way from the *laissez-faire* ideology of the eighteenth century. Despite the growth of state involvement it would be a mistake to view the nineteenth century as being characterized by progressive initiatives aimed at 'improving' working-class morals. Many opposed the ideas of reformers and the government could not afford to alienate this body of opinion. Accordingly, the new legislation did not supersede the existing more punitive measures and magistrates retained the *option* of prison or reformatory. In any case before entering a reformatory, juveniles were required to serve a 14-day prison sentence. Again, the importance of the legislation, from the historian's perspective at least, is that it further consolidated and formalized the *idea* of juvenile delinquency.

Whatever the cause, measures were deemed necessary to prevent the evolutionary problem from occurring. Increasingly the state, through both public (state initiatives) and private (philanthropic and charitable) means, sought to intervene where it saw the danger signs. These varied from perceived bad parenting, to the exposure of children to immorality, to insanitary living conditions, to cases of extreme poverty, to what might be interpreted as the first steps towards a career in crime and so on. In this way, ideas about children who were in danger (and therefore in need of care) or children who were a danger to society (and therefore in need of control) became conflated.

As we have seen, many of the concerns of nineteenth-century reformers were driven by society's response to young offenders. This was equally true of youth justice where reformers focused on what they saw as an inherent contradiction: that normal modes of punishment (especially imprisonment) actually contributed to the growing problem of juvenile crime. Coupled with this was the increasingly accepted view that children should be treated differently: that they could not be held responsible for their actions and needed nurturing rather than punishing.

In 1817, just one year after the publication of the report into 'the alarming increase in juvenile delinquency in the metropolis' (see above), the Society for the Improvement of Prison Discipline and the Reformation of Juvenile Offenders was established. Its purpose was to establish a separate system for juvenile offenders where they could be reformed and reclaimed as useful members of a future society away from the pernicious influence of adult criminals. The argument was a simple one: that moral improvement was only possible if boys (again, we are dealing with gender-specific ideas at this point) were isolated from the contaminating effects of men's prisons.

The establishment of the first such institution at Parkhurst did not happen until 1838, but pressure did lead to the separation of boys from adults within the existing prison system. This necessitated a new approach which led to the classification of prisoners into either juveniles or adults – a process that consolidated the conceptualization of juvenile delinquency.

Once this new category of prisoner had been established it was surely only a matter of time before this was formalized through legislation. However, it took until the Children Act 1908 for this to occur. The Act established the principle that young offenders should be dealt with separately in juvenile courts. Juvenile courts differed from other courts in three main areas. Firstly, proceedings were held *in camera* – so the public was excluded – reflecting the idea that young offenders should not be stigmatized or publicly castigated for acts that they might not be wholly responsible for. Secondly, there was no jury which enabled justice to be handled less formally and with greater speed. Again, this removed the young person from a legal process that might be damaging. Finally, there was no right to legal representation. This also distanced the child or young person from the legal process while also placing on the court an additional welfare responsibility.

But the changes introduced by these courts should not be overstated and important continuities arguably had an even greater impact. Juvenile courts remained criminal courts in all but name. Children and young people were still taken before the courts with a view to punishment and correction. This was reflected in the nature of sentences handed out by juvenile courts such as fines, probation orders, commitment to industrial schools and, if over 14 years old, whipping and/or imprisonment.

The new juvenile courts also enabled the state to intervene where it considered there might be a 'moral crisis'. In other words, if a child was found to be begging, vagrant, associating with reputed thieves or even if the parents were deemed unworthy. In these circumstances the juvenile court was empowered to act in the name of welfare. As with earlier concerns about moral crises that we have already noted, ideas about how to deal with both the *troublesome* and the *troubled* were blurred, distinctions were confused and solutions, therefore, became merged with little or no differentiation in 'sentencing'.

One solution that emerged during the late nineteenth and early twentieth centuries was the scouting movement and similar organizations such as the sea scouts and girl guides. The purpose of such organizations was to remove children from the unhealthy cities – albeit temporarily – and take them to the countryside where they could partake of healthy pursuits such as hiking, cycling and camping. This was not only motivated by fears about crime – there had also been grave concerns over the physical fitness of volunteers for the British army during the Boer War (1898–1902). But the two issues were linked because of the supposed degeneration or poor evolution of city dwellers. In fact, Baden-Powell expressed a preference for hooligans – 'the best sort of boy' – for his scouting movement (however, when the courts labelled a child a 'hooligan' he was likely to be carted off to Borstal not the Boy Scouts).

While society was comfortable with the punishment of those who were fully responsible for their actions it remained less convinced in cases where there might be an underlying welfare issue that mitigated the level of criminal responsibility. Clearly, many juvenile cases fell into the latter category. Yet the deterrent argument on which ideas about punishment were based was resilient and infiltrated even those measures intended to deal with welfare problems. This is most clearly illustrated in the approach to child imprisonment. The Children Act 1908 had abolished imprisonment for those under 14 years of age, but the Crime Prevention Act of the same year set up detention centres aimed specifically at those too young for prison. The first of these detention centres, which specialized in providing discipline and work training, was established at Borstal in Kent and this name was then adopted for all subsequent centres. The emphasis of the regime in the 'Borstals' was, as the name of the originating statute implied, to prevent young offenders from setting out on a criminal career. Discipline was designed to reverse the moral crisis and work training to facilitate a more fruitful career. But there is little doubt that Borstal remained at least a form of juvenile imprisonment.

There was renewed concern about delinquency during the First World War. This was caused by fears surrounding the effects of absent fathers who were serving in the armed forces and mothers who were working in munitions factories and driving buses and such like. The Board of Education noted a serious increase in delinquency during the war years, especially among children aged between 11 and 13 (*Report of the Board of Education 1916–17*, cited in Marwick 1991: 158). The disruption to family life and to education caused by the war was to blame according to some while the influence of the cinema was blamed by others. A most notorious case concerned the appearance at court of nine boys calling themselves the Black Hand Gang of St Luke's. Concerns were sufficient to instigate an investigation of the cinema by the National Council of Public Morals, which rejected the suggestion of a pernicious influence and urged the problem of delinquency to be considered in the context of the prevailing social and economic conditions. Other factors also contributed to the rise in juvenile crime during the First World War, as one witness – a probation officer – informed the inquiry:

> There has been a tendency in recent years to increase the variety of offences with which children may be charged. For instance, children are now charged with wandering, with being without proper guardianship, with being 'beyond control'. Our streets are now more rigidly supervised than ever before. There is a large and increasing army of officials whose duty it is to watch over child life. In many cases it has seemed to me that the zeal of those officers was not always tempered by humanity and expediency. (National Council of Public Morals, *The Cinema*, 1917, cited in Marwick 1991: 158)

These comments indicate that some professionals – in this case a probation officer – were aware of the complex relationship between crime rates and the activities of official bodies and agents such as the courts and the police. It should be noted, however, that later in the war the army of officers to which the witness refers dwindled as its members were drawn off to prop up the other army whose numbers were also dwindling because of the carnage of the Western Front. After the war attention turned to improving welfare conditions generally, but especially in the areas of health and education. At a lecture to the London Teachers' Association on 28 November 1924, Prime Minister Stanley Baldwin informed his audience that: 'There are still too many, far too many, insanitary schools, and that there are many ill-nourished and defective children; but let us remember that the standard by which we judge these matters today has risen immeasurably from the standard adopted by our parents' (Baldwin 1926: 161).

Heightened fears about delinquency remained during the interwar period. A new, more permissive, morality (believed to be imported from America) and the economic slump of the 1930s lay behind the perception. Superficially, the emphasis of the response to these 'crises' appeared to shift towards improving the welfare of neglected children and young offenders (or potential young offenders), which provided a possible link between the two. In reality there was little difference beyond the terminology to differentiate between children at risk and children who posed a risk and most who found themselves before a court were treated in much the same manner regardless of how or why they were there. This was underpinned by a rationale that was rooted in the traditional ideas that continued to link crime to immorality and indolence. According to a Home Office Committee of 1927:

> There is little or no difference in character and needs between the neglected and the delinquent child. It is often a mere accident whether he is brought before the court because he was wandering or beyond control or whether he has committed some offence. Neglect leads to delinquency. (Home Office Departmental Committee on the Treatment of the Young Offender, Home Office 1927: 6)

The Children and Young Persons Act 1933, which was spawned by the findings of the 1927 Committee, extended the power of the courts to act *in loco parentis*. This was a major and most significant step because it took away parental control and replaced it with state intervention (via the courts) even in cases where no offence had been committed. The assumption of responsibility for the care of young people (offenders or not) was further cemented by the Act, which directed the court to take primary account of the 'welfare of the child', which in turn led to an expansion of the role of probation and social services.

The government of Clement Atlee that swept to power at the end of the Second World War is largely credited with establishing the welfare state. Certainly, a great swathe of welfare legislation was enacted in the late 1940s. Much of this was directed at young people. In building a new and better Britain, politicians had to take account of the next generation, which represented the future. It also had to deal with the deprivation and poverty that was endemic in many parts of Britain and which had been worsened by the destruction of the war – something that had not been anywhere near as evident during the First World War. Another feature of wartime Britain was the evacuation of city children from their homes and parents to the countryside where, it was thought, they would be safer.

Many of the new welfare measures were in keeping with the recommendations of the Beveridge Report. Commissioned in 1941 at the behest of trade unionists (whose cooperation was needed by the wartime government) the Beveridge Committee, which reported in 1942, suggested a 'comprehensive policy of social progress' to address what Beveridge considered the 'five giants' of Want, Disease, Ignorance, Squalor and Idleness (*Parliamentary Papers* 1942–3, vol. VI, Cmd. 6404, HMSO, London). The language employed here should be familiar – reflecting, as it does, the ideas of the nineteenth-century reformers. This was no coincidence and Beveridge, who had chosen his words carefully, 'borrowed' his five giants from Charles Dickens's *A Tale of Two Cities*.

The measure affecting young people most commonly associated with Beveridge is the Education Act 1944 (actually passed by the Churchill-led wartime coalition government), which was aimed at the giant of `Ignorance'. But broader concerns about society and the relationship between crime and the effects of war also had to be addressed. Two pieces of postwar legislation are of significance here. The 1948 Children Act empowered local authorities to take children into care while the 1948 Criminal Justice Act set up attendance centres and detention centres to retrain young offenders through strict regimes of military-style drill and hard labour. The former, it appears, was aimed at the welfare of young people and the latter at the punishment of young offenders.

Both measures, though, reflected the broader concerns about the impact of war on the family. Thousands of children had been removed from their parents and evacuated. In many families the father had been conscripted into the armed forces and perhaps even killed in action. This, it was widely believed, removed the basis of discipline within the family without which unruliness might follow. Nor was this line of thinking unique to Britain: a recent study found similar concerns existed in France where a perceived rise in delinquency was attributed to the 1.5 million French prisoners of war that had left 600,000 children 'fatherless' in 1940 (Fishman 2002: 141–57). The introduction in 1948 of military-style drill and discipline in British detention centres for young offenders ought to be viewed in this context. Furthermore, many families had also been deprived of the welfare role normally associated with the mother. Many women were drafted into industry or transport work to 'substitute' for conscripted male workers, and we should regard the intervention of the state in matters concerning children's welfare in this context while recognizing also the continuity with prewar developments.

Evidence of the effects of war and concerns about crime, often involving juveniles, can be found in a number of postwar British feature films (as well as elsewhere). *Brighton Rock* (1947), based on the 1938 Graham Greene novel, graphically portrays violence and youth crime through the character of Pinkie (played by Richard Attenborough), the juvenile leader of a vicious gang based in Brighton. But it is the explicit portrayal of violence rather than the plot that was (and remains) so shocking about this film. *Hue and Cry* (1947) – the first of the Ealing comedies – shows the devastation of the war on London and also featured a juvenile gang in a mischievous manner as they take on a criminal gang. In fact it is not unreasonable to speak of these films, together with others such as *Waterloo Road*, as an identifiable genre that emerged from the wartime experience and concerns. Interestingly, the censors (often reflecting government attitudes) were sympathetic to the graphic representation of violence and crime that occasionally characterized some of these films. Eventually, however, there would be a reaction to this permissiveness and it came in the form of the 1950 film *The Blue Lamp*, which also featured a delinquent juvenile. Not only did this film introduce to British audiences a new folk hero, PC George Dixon (played by Jack Warner), it also portrayed a far more sanitized version of crime and violence, and thereby advocated new standards of 'decency'.

Prostitution, social control and reform

In the eighteenth, nineteenth and for much of the twentieth centuries, women were expected to be dutiful housewives, subordinate and subservient to their husbands. Their role in society was a modest, passive and private one, confined to the household and the family. Any behaviour that challenged this position was considered unwomanly. To contemporary observers, women committing

'Shocking cruelty to children' – *The Police Illustrated News*, 15 July 1876, reported on a case of neglect and cruelty to children in Folkestone. The report detailed the filthy conditions of the household, and linked together the neglect of household duties with the lack of care for the children who were suffering from malnutrition. Although the father of the children was prosecuted, it was an effigy of Mrs Upton (the housekeeper/ lover) which was burned in the streets outside the court, and in the illustration the white dress and tidy appearance of the neighbour contrasts with the unkempt and wild appearance (in a symbolically significant black dress) of Mrs Upton.

'masculine' offences, such as violence and drunkenness, indicated something very wrong with society and the state of feminine virtue – but how did they explain female offending?

As the previous sections have demonstrated, the offences that were *associated* with women were taken to be perversions of natural femininity and their domestic role. Early social enquirers such as Acton and Mayhew observed the topic from a mid-Victorian perspective and placed women in a special, separate, category because they believed women to be especially vulnerable to moral corruption in view of their natural purity (Zedner 1991). This was largely informed by the pervasive nineteenth-century idea of women as passive that might have distorted their own observations.

Later in the nineteenth century concerns about degeneration and tainted heredity also permeated studies on women and crime. Most notable here is Lombroso and Ferrero's *The Female Offender*, which was first published in 1895. They regarded women as less evolved than men, which reflected some of the ideas of Charles Darwin (1871) who considered that through greater exposure to competition (or struggle for existence) 'man has ultimately become superior to woman'. Taking as their starting point the idea that criminality was largely a product of bad breeding or tainted heredity which would, they believed, be characterized by physical appearances, Lombroso and Ferrero argued that criminality had effectively been bred out in women through the process of natural selection. This had occurred, they claimed, because criminally inclined women were more masculine in appearance and, consequently, less attractive to men resulting in the failure of criminal women to find sexual partners and pass on their criminal heredity. This theory failed to account for criminal men who, if we follow Lombroso and Ferrero's line of argument, had 'feminine' mothers who presumably were hereditarily untainted.[5] Interestingly, the work of Lombroso and Ferrero was rejected for its conclusions on criminal men long before it was for those on criminal women. Even as late as 1950 we can detect a misogynist rationale underpinning theories on women's apparent absence from crime statistics, for example Pollak's (1950) theory that women – despite being *more* criminal than men – were naturally more devious and avoided detection by exploiting men's innate chivalry. As Garland noted in 1991, 'female offenders are dealt with in gender-specific ways which reflect traditional conceptions of the female role and its pathologies' (1991: 202). But we should also note that Victorian theories of female criminality all expressed the possibility of reform – the malleability of women's wills, the 'weakness' of their minds – all offered to Victorian penal reformers the possibility that women (and children for that matter) were more open to change. For this change to take place they would need to be provided with institutional support, hence the separate women's' prison where they could be uncontaminated by men's criminal traits; the girls' rescue and reform homes that sprang up around the country in the late 1900s; the asylum and inebriates home for drunken and mentally ill women. Barton (2005), Morrison (2005) and McKenzie (2005) have critiqued the view that these penal and semi-penal institutions were somehow 'havens of rest' for women. Indeed, women were subject to more scrutiny and intrusive processes of change than male offenders. In addition, those women who were deemed unsuitable for reform – those who had fallen too far, who

Cesare Lombroso compared the physiological features of 'normal', i.e. women who had not been accused of any crimes, with convicted Russian and Italian prostitutes. He claimed that it was possible to identify criminals by their physical features, and these theories continued to have some influence until the second half of the twentieth century. All these women displayed, for Lombroso, criminal features.
Source: C. Lombroso (1893) *La Donna Delinquente. La Prostituta e la Donna Normale.*

were too confirmed in their behaviour, too masculine, to be saved – were said to be doubly punished for their transgressions. A number of commentators have already discussed the 'double deviancy' stigmatization of women who have offended against both the law and the defining social constructions of femininity (Heidensohn 1981, 1996; Carlen 1983, 1985; Gelsthorpe 1989; Cain 1990; Worrall 1990; Zedner 1991; Lloyd 1995; D'Cruze 1998, 1999). However, recently, the issue of double deviancy has re-emerged. Godfrey, Farrall and Karstedt's (2005) study of men and women convicted of assault between 1880 and 1920 was able to isolate gender from all other contextual factors of the crime (how severe the assault was, the relationship between victim and assailant, and so on) and showed that men rather than women bore the brunt of the civilizing mission and reformative zeal:

> Magistrates might have seen men as the more important gender on whose shoulders the Empire rested, as did its industrial wealth and its capacity to maintain power. Civilising efforts therefore needed to target masculinities. The apparent 'leniency' towards female offenders does not reflect a particular empathy with the situation of working-class women, but to the contrary. It seems to reflect a more 'dismissive' and perhaps 'contemptuous' attitude toward women. (Godfrey, Farrall and Karstedt, 2005)

This study has demonstrated that, when it came to sentencing in the late Victorian and Edwardian period, 'gender counted', but rather than women receiving heavier penalties than men for similar offences, they were dealt with more leniently. But did this hold true for all offences committed by women? Ballinger (2000) has demonstrated the disadvantages faced by women convicted of capital crimes and many commentators have described the disproportionately harsh approach towards prostitution.

The crime most synonymous with disreputable, criminal or sexually provocative women was prostitution. Just as with other crimes discussed above, prostitution was widely regarded as unnatural and not 'feminine'. Again, it was a type of behaviour that amounted to a negation of the idea of womanhood; in this case unnatural sexual urges – a dangerous sexuality – and a growing social problem. By 1857 there were reputed to be 3,325 brothels and 8,600 prostitutes in the Metropolitan Police area alone. However, this is at best a conservative figure because it only accounts for those who were known to the police (Acton 1857). In all likelihood there were many more regular prostitutes in London and even more irregular ones (those who were forced by financial circumstances to one or two desperate acts). This was certainly the picture painted by Henry Mayhew, a journalist, and Samuel Bracebridge whose 1861 study estimated the total number of prostitutes in London at 80,000. Their figures were broadly supported by an article in the medical journal *The Lancet* in 1857, which declared that one in every 16 women was a prostitute and one in every 60 houses was a brothel. If true, then the number of brothels and prostitutes in poorer areas of the capital would have been especially large if, as seems likely, more affluent areas were under-represented because women there had little or no need to resort to prostitution for financial reasons alone. The 'Great Social Evil', as even progressive, liberal-minded commentators referred to it, did spark a huge swathe of social investigation (such as Mayhew, Bracebridge and the doctor William Acton) from which modern-day historians continue to benefit (see, for example, Greg 1850 and Acton 1857).

Who were the prostitutes? Most sources tend to suggest that they were the 'unskilled daughters of the unskilled classes' (Abraham Flexner, cited in Walkowitz 1980: 15). More accurately, they were overwhelmingly the offspring of unskilled and semi-skilled working men and with a background of low-status, low-paid jobs such as servants, laundry and charwomen, and street sellers (Walkowitz 1980: 15–16). Often local variations can be detected such as the preponderance of former mill-workers among Glasgow's prostitutes and street sellers in Liverpool's. Most came from poor families which could not support them and, therefore, they were forced by circumstance to leave home and find their own way in the world. Many came from families with only one living parent – a factor that would often have resulted in poverty. This would then have triggered the need for extra income and pitched the young woman into prostitution – usually at around 18 years of age. Moreover, as a result of employment legislation, both women and children were progressively removed from the factories and other growing sectors of the economy. For some women, the lack of economic opportunities left but one option – prostitution. However, we should guard against overstating this as a causal factor. The majority of prostitutes were young and single with no children and most had given up 'the trade' after only a few years – perhaps when one or all of these factors no longer applied to them. These temporary, part-time and economically marginal women who turned to prostitution were a constant worry to respectable society from the mid-nineteenth century.

As women, of course, they were also regarded as flawed with an unnatural sexuality and lacking in proper restraint. This was often attributed to poor parenting – itself the blight of the working classes according to many social commentators. That the women were also seen as uneducated merely confirmed their putative idleness to many rather than alerting observers to the real problems of the poor. The idea that women could salvage their position through their own industry pervaded public and judicial attitudes alike. Accordingly, penalties were often harsh and were designed to deter women and put them back on the path of self-help rather than idleness.

Attempts to control prostitution and its effects took two forms: deterrence through ever harsher penalties and regulation to eradicate brothels. Another form of regulation appeared in the middle of the nineteenth century. Faced with mounting concerns about syphilis epidemics and continuing fears about the efficiency of the military – which was itself subjected to reforms because of its inability to cope with the mutiny of Indian troops in 1857 – the government resorted to legislation. *The Contagious Diseases Acts* of 1864, 1866 and 1869 provoked a wave of opposition and created some unlikely alliances.

The Act was applied to 18 garrison and port towns. Reflecting the concerns about military efficiency, it required that 'common prostitutes' were identified and registered. They then were subjected to fortnightly examinations and if found to be suffering from venereal disease they could be interned in a 'Lock' hospital for nine months. There was no attempt to extend the same sort of regulation or treatment to male sufferers of venereal disease which remained, therefore, viewed solely as a female problem. This, of course, reflected ongoing double standards on sexuality and behaviour – after all there was no attempt to attach any blame to men for the 'problem' of prostitution. According to a Royal Commission in 1871 men were merely enslaved to 'an irregular indulgence of a natural impulse'. But for prostitutes 'the offence is committed as a matter of gain' (*Report from the Royal Commission on the Administration and Operation of the Contagious Diseases Acts 1866–9*, 1871: 17, cited in Emsley 2005: 105). Attempts in 1869 to extend the Act and make it generally applied across the country caused an outcry and it was eventually abolished in 1883.

Prominent in the campaign to abolish the *Contagious Diseases Act* was Josephine Butler. Butler, whose father had also campaigned against the slave trade, began her work with prostitutes in Liverpool around 1864. She collaborated with a journalist of questionable integrity, William Stead (who later died in the sinking of the Titanic in 1912). The social purity movement, as it was known, consisted of diverse characters including socialists, radicals, early feminists such as Butler and all sorts of religious and political figures. As well as the abolition of the Contagious Diseases Act the movement campaigned against child prostitution and other forms of exploitation. Butler eventually tired of Stead's sensationalist approach and the broader aims of the social purity movement, which also campaigned against homosexuality. Instead, she devoted herself to campaigning for working-class women's rights.

Other attempts at control were equally unimpressive in their originality and impact. In 1885 the government attempted to eradicate brothels. The Criminal Law Amendment Act of that year included a number of measures aimed at curbing what many regarded as unacceptable sexual behaviour. The age of female consent was raised from 13 to 16 (largely as a result of the agitation of William Stead) and all male homosexual acts were outlawed (previously, only the act of buggery had been illegal). Brothels were also outlawed but the act had little effect beyond the formalization of the perceived link between homosexuality and prostitution as depraved acts by immoral people. Prostitution continued but in a more dispersed manner leaving only deterrence as the weapon of control. Harsh penalties for prostitution continued and even as late as 1959 further legislation increasing the penalties available to the courts remained the response of government.

Conclusion

Just as with a history of youth offending, the history of women and crime cannot be separated from the pressures exerted by the processes of industrialization and urbanization in the nineteenth century. Expectations and supposed standards of behaviour underpinned how society at large viewed women and children, and how the lawmakers and the courts treated women who did not meet these 'standards'. Concerns about juvenile delinquency appear to have surfaced periodically at times of national crises: often immediately following wars (crises of youth, crime and authority followed the Napoleonic, First and

Second World Wars). Other factors heightened concerns about delinquency: the fear of revolution that affected most of Europe (including Britain) after 1789; changes in the means of production and employment ranging from the ending of apprenticeships to larger-scale industrialization; the decline in religiosity. Each represented a crisis or upheaval in society to contemporary observers. Underpinning all these concerns was the fear of a moral crisis, much of which was rooted in the process of urbanization and particularly the degradation associated with the city slums.

Moments of crisis within society, it appears, have a tendency to focus concerns on crime. Often it is on juvenile crime that these fears are most heightened. As Pearson has argued, these fears are closely associated with more general concerns about the breakdown of order or the collapse of society (Pearson 1983). Why this should be the case is clear: it is a lingering concern for the future, represented by the next generation. However, by the mid-twentieth century rather than representing different approaches to two different problems affecting young people (the offended or the offender) the two had become synonymous in youth justice. Panics about female offending were more diffuse. In the eighteenth and nineteenth centuries, a woman's role and her social status were clearly stated with primacy attributed to her subordinate position and her domesticity. The suggestion that a woman had a specific role within the family and in society which, if not adhered to, amounted to a negation of her womanhood was consistent with ideas that underpinned the concerns about female crime. As with juvenile offending, moral panics about female criminality came and went, but did not cause the peaks in concern that juvenile crime waves created.

The response to concern was the reform of penal systems to cope with what was perceived as the special circumstances of youth and female criminality. As we have seen, the foundations of the reform process lay in medical, criminological and popular discourses that could not be described as benign. The dominant constructions of femininity, for example, caused drunken women in inebriates reformatories to be dressed, rouged and presented in parodies of respectable femininity, with hands clasped on their laps in domestic passivity. Juveniles brought up in working families, with parents of poor education, poor employment, poor housing and low pay, were expected to conform to ideal images of childhood or else be subject to police scrutiny and public condemnation. It seems that ideas about the proper (or natural) behaviour and position of women and children at this time combined with ideas about respectability and social hierarchy to produce a penal-welfarist system that many found (and find) contentious.

Key questions

1. To what extent was the whole notion of 'juvenile delinquency' an invention of the early nineteenth century?

In the eighteenth century and the centuries preceding it, young people committed crimes. Indeed, the disrespectful, troublesome and dishonest apprentice is a common figure in eighteenth-century literature. However, the combination of legislative acts, procedural changes in the administration of justice in the courts and the changes brought by urbanization/industrialization all contributed to create a new category in the public imagination – the juvenile delinquent. The figure of the juvenile thief was given form in Dickens (the 'Artful Dodger' tutored by Fagin) and other writers, and social investigators such as Mayhew introduced the Victorian public to the world of the half-naked street urchins who roamed the cities causing trouble, picking pockets and stealing purses. Later in the century, delinquents became 'hooligans' and that word, though it has lost the power it held a hundred years ago, is still used today.

Can we say which of the changes in mid-nineteenth century society was the dominant influence? Probably not, because these changes were mutually reinforcing. For example, the movement of minor crimes to the minor courts in 1855 caused many of the offences typically committed by the young to be heard in the petty sessions. Since it was far cheaper and easier for complainants to prosecute in these courts, victims were encouraged to take their cases there and the crime rate grew (particularly the juvenile crime rate). The reporting of so many cases created an impression of a youth crime wave, and public opinion forced the police to look for youth delinquency – creating more arrests and so on. Concern about the lack of parental control in the working-class city districts kept the pot boiling and, as Shore (2002: 3) demonstrated, it has never really stopped:

> A gradual centralization of local judicial and welfare procedures; a gradual separation of children and young people from adults within emerging judicial and welfare systems; an overwhelming concern to publicly (rather than privately) police boys and young men rather than girls and young women; a drawing of distinctions between the reform of boys and girls, between older and younger children, between innocent and depraved children, and often between children of different religious faiths; a belief in the desirability of removing vulnerable children from bad families and a continual search for a workable and often institutional substitute for those families; a need to combine private (notably familial and philanthropic) ways of dealing with delinquency with public (notably statutory educational, medical and penal) ways of so doing; a tendency to explain delinquency in terms of a familiar and contradictory cluster of causes, notably dangerous urban pleasures, poverty, precocity, bad parenting and more general breakdowns in traditions of authority.

2. Was 'respectability' or 'gender' the more important factor in the treatment of women in the Victorian criminal justice system?

You should review the sections on crimes associated with women, and read D'Cruze (1999), Zedner (1991) and Godfrey, Farrall and Karstedt (2005). Compare and contrast the historical with the modern by reading Carlen (1985) and Worrall (1990).

3. Despite their larger involvement in the criminal justice process as police officers, defendants and prisoners, men should no longer form the main focus of criminological research. Discuss.

There are no specific publications that address this point, but you should give a considered overview based on all the reading you have completed for this topic.

Notes

1. The authors are grateful to Chris Williams and Gerry Oram for providing first drafts of this chapter.
2. Executions of children eventually ceased in 1840 because of humanitarian reform and concerns about its effect on the watching crowd.
3. In fact, even middle-class women could attract a reputation for theft as 'kleptomaniacs' (from the Greek *kleptes* meaning thief and *mania* meaning madness). This reflected the growing influence of psychology during the later nineteenth century and implied illness rather than criminality, which 'naturally' remained the preserve of the lower orders.
4. See Godfrey (2004: 27–9).
5. See Darwin (1871).

Further reading

The references for this chapter can be found in the Bibliography at the back of the book. If you wish to do some further reading, you should investigate these first. However, below is a list of publications which could also be consulted.

Bourke, J. (1994) *Working Class Cultures in Britain, 1890–1960*. London: Routledge.
Gattrell, V. A. C. (1996) *The Hanging Tree: Executions and the English People 1770–1868*. Oxford: Oxford University Press.
Lewis, G. (ed.) (1998) *Forming Nation, Framing Welfare*. London: Routledge.
Pick, D. (1989) *Faces of Degeneration: A European Disorder, c.1848–c.1918*. Cambridge: Cambridge University Press.
Wiener, M. (1998) 'The Victorian criminalization of men', in P. Spierenburg (ed.), *Men and Violence: Gender, Honor and Rituals in Modern Europe and America*. Columbus, OH: Ohio, Ohio State University Press.
Wiener, M. (2004) *Men of Blood. Violence, Manliness, and Criminal Justice in Victorian England*. Cambridge: Cambridge University Press.

9. Control in the workplace and the rise of surveillance society

Introduction

The workplace has been a battleground between the rights of custom and tradition and the rights of property. The 'rights' of workers to work at their own pace, take home waste material and have some autonomy over the conditions of their employment have been gradually eroded from the eighteenth century onwards. The introduction of the factory system has been seen as a key weapon in the employers' fight to control the work completed and the 'work time' they believed they had paid for.

In the eighteenth and nineteenth centuries, the workplace proved the battleground for the conceptual battle between the entitlements granted to employees by custom and tradition and the rights of property enjoyed by employers. This chapter therefore begins by describing the customary perquisites (perks) that workers in many industries believed were given to them as a traditional right. It will go on to describe how employers tried to limit and eradicate customary rights in the workplace in the eighteenth and nineteenth centuries. This chapter will outline the legislation that made customary perquisites illegal (particularly the 1777 Worsted Acts which established an Inspectorate to police workplace appropriation or what employers called 'workplace theft'). It will then discuss changes in the organization of work and the establishment of the factory system. In particular it focuses on the possibilities that this new system of production offered employers for increased powers of surveillance over workers. Lastly, the chapter will briefly discuss the general rise in surveillance in society, and pose the questions: 'are we now living in a "Big Brother" society, and if so, how and when did that come about?'

Introductory reading

Dandaker, C. (1990) *Surveillance, Power and Modernity*. Cambridge: Polity Press, pp. 176–92.

Godfrey, B. (1999) 'The impact of the factory on workplace appropriation in the nineteenth-century', *British Journal of Criminology*, 39, 1, pp. 56–71.

Lyon, D. (1994) *The Electronic Eye. The Rise of Surveillance Society*. Cambridge: Polity Press, chapter 7.

Thompson, E. P. (1967) 'Time, work-discipline and industrial capitalism', *Past and Present*, 38, pp. 56–97.

Customary rights in the workplace

In the eighteenth century (and before) many workers considered it a customary right to keep for themselves some part of the materials used in their stage of production.[1] This was viewed as a traditional entitlement passed down through the ages, and may have involved taking pieces of workplace material or some of the waste goods produced in manufacturing, for example the thrums (cloth or woollen waste) produced in textile manufacture. Many traditional rights were gradually criminalized. These included gleaning (collecting corn left after harvesting), firebote (gathering small amounts of wood from forests for the fireplace), the rights of grazing (on common land) and the poaching of small game, rabbits and pheasants. Although the taking of customary perquisites (and their subsequent criminalization) was common to most industries, this chapter concentrates on the textile industry because the factory/mill owners were most active in trying to eradicate customary rights in the workplace both by use of the law and also through the physical/ hierarchical organization of the workplace. The factory facilitated higher levels of surveillance over employees, and allowed employers to use *both* informal punishments and the law to 'police' the behaviour of their workers.

Perhaps the most discussed example of eighteenth-century workplace appropriation is the taking of 'chips' (pieces of wood) from the Royal Dockyards. However, Emsley (2005: 143–73), Styles (1983) and Rule (1981, 1986) have catalogued a series of outworker appropriations – including 'bugging' by hatters and shoemakers (whereby cheap material was substituted for the more valuable material they were supposed to use). Indeed, most industries saw some form of appropriation of finished goods or raw materials. However, the taking of waste materials was also rife, particularly in the textile trades. The creation of waste was an inevitable consequence of most manufacturing processes. In some industries the waste could be valuable, although often it consisted merely of scraps. The property rights to the waste products often rested on unspoken customary agreements between employers and employed, with periodic redrawing of the boundaries. If the waste product itself acquired value, as it did in the textile trade with the growth of the recovered wool industry in the latter half of the nineteenth century, then the redrawing of the customary line usually became final, and in favour of the employers.

Textile manufacturers attempted to use various strategies, including the law, to combat workplace appropriation. Indeed, Linebaugh (1991) and Hobsbawm (1968) have both asserted that both the eighteenth and nineteenth centuries saw the employers attempt to criminalize customary rights within the workplace (see also Davis 1987 and 1989), just as other historians have argued that a parallel process was occurring in the countryside. Marxist historians like Peter Linebaugh place the large body of eighteenth-century legislation against workplace frauds within the context of what they believe was a defining character of eighteenth-century criminal law – the transformation of a large number of infractions that had previously been violations of trust or corporate obligation into criminal offences against property. This view is typified in the work of Hay (1983: 53) who said:

> The custom of ... payment in perquisites, either part of the product or raw materials, became the subject of extensive penal legislation. Employers did not always want to eliminate perks: allowing such appropriation by employees could be a way of escaping employers' wage-fixing agreements in times of labour shortage, and also a way of avoiding monetary wage payment during downturns in the trade cycle. At such times both capital and labour tacitly agreed on the custom, within limits, of taking perks. But those limits were always contested, and in the long term, with expanding inventories, larger workforces, and a sharpening interest in accurate book-keeping, employers requested, and received, criminal legislation that designated such appropriation as theft.

In 1777 the textile manufacturers of Yorkshire persuaded Parliament to enact legislation which outlawed customary perquisites and established the Worsted Inspectorate to patrol the region, search suspects' houses and apprehend those suspected of theft from work. Between 1840 and 1880 this agency (which was controlled by the Worsted Committee made up of leading manufacturers) prosecuted approximately three thousand workers. Moreover, by adapting their detective methods to the context of factory production, they continued as the most important employers' policing/prosecution agency for approximately 200 years (for a history of this organization see Godfrey 2002).

However, when workers were collected together in centralized production areas (factories) it offered the employers the possibility of far greater control over their workers' time and behaviour.

> What an extraordinary spectacle! There stands rows and groups of huge manufactories, each consisting of numerous buildings which are sometimes bound together by one surrounding wall. Sometimes these walls are fortified and guarded like fortresses by vigilant sentinels who allow none to pass but such as have right to enter ... The great factories, which employ 500 or 1000 people, are built in various ways; some piled up storey on storey, others on the straight line system in long successive rows; others like huge greenhouses, all in one floor lighted from the top. From these huge and oddly shaped buildings rise immense chimneys as tall as the steeples of St. Paul's and St. Stephen's and sometimes architecturally ornamented with stone garlands, bas-reliefs and pedestals ... Sometimes the workpeople of each manufactory form a little community by themselves, living together in its neighbourhood in a little town of their own, but in general they occupy particular quarters of the town which contain nothing but long unbroken rows of small, low, dirty houses, each exactly like each other. These quarters are the most melancholy and disagreeable parts of town, squalid, filthy and miserable to a deplorable degree. Here stand the abominable beerhouses,

dram shops and gin palaces which are never without customers. Here streets are filled with ragged women and naked children. (Kohl 1844)

This factory landscape, this 'extraordinary spectacle' and 'monument to the Mechanical Age', was for contemporaries a symbol of change and progress. The factory, too, has become something of a talisman for modern social and economic historians. When Gregory (1982) writes of 'the awesome potency of the factory system', and Joyce describes the factory as 'the most characteristic expression of modernity in nineteenth-century economic organization', it is Kohl's vision of rows of smoke-belching chimneys they refer to (Joyce 1980: xiii). However, the development of the factory system was neither so relentless nor dramatic as Kohl has suggested. The following paragraphs describe the uneven technological and economic progress of the textile factory system both nationally and in West Yorkshire.

In the textile industry, at least by 1820, three systems of industrial organization existed. The first, the 'clothier' or 'domestic outwork' system, had been in existence since the sixteenth century and remained economically and organizationally viable into the 1850s and 1860s. In this system, wool was 'put out' to spinners and weavers in domestic houses/workshops before being returned to the clothier to be sold on to merchants in the marketing centres. The 'manufacturing' system was similar to the domestic/clothier system, but differed in that all of the early processes were 'undertaken in sheds under their [employers'] direct supervision'. Lastly, in ideal 'factory' organizations, all of the processes came under a system of centralized and directly supervised production, usually with managers and foremen looking after the 'shopfloor'.

The size and physical organization of the factories that housed both workers and supervisors changed throughout the 1790–1850 period. Although in the late eighteenth century there were occasionally other small buildings on the mill site, most of the early mill premises seem to have consisted of single buildings in which many of the processes were carried out. In addition, the main building was used for the warehousing of raw materials and finished products, and also under its roof were the counting houses, offices, stabling, workshops and even living accommodation for the employees. However, between 1780 and 1830, many factories established specific buildings for individual processes alongside the main mills. Relatively few factories employed over a hundred people, and only 11 textile factories in Yorkshire employed over 200 people by 1833. Even by 1870, the average woollen firm employed only 70 operatives, which is not to say that the large firm was unknown in Yorkshire, for worsted factories had developed along a different tradition. In Bradford during the 1850s, for example, nine worsted companies had over a thousand employees.

The development of steam power, with the resulting larger and more complicated machinery, allowed the greater employment of adults. The proportion of women employed also increased with the early years of the nineteenth century, although women had always been a significant part of the worsted workforce because of that industry's reliance on the water-frame (which was suitable for female labour). The Factory Act of 1833 and subsequent

Acts which limited the use of child labour increased the proportion of adults in the factory. Finally, with the extensive use of powered machinery in the 1840s, female workers poured into the factory.

In collecting together dispersed workers into one very controlled space the factory offered the possibility of eradicating workplace theft, or at least substantially controlling it. It established a complex and hierarchical system of managers, supervisors, foremen and overseers who could watch over the behaviour of the workers. The factory also had physical boundaries (gatehouses and walls) which helped to prevent theft. Later, mechanization governed the pace of production, and also the start and finish times of shifts, which required a strict control over workers' time and punishments were imposed on those who 'wasted' their employer's time by talking to neighbours and so on (see Thompson 1967). Some employers also attempted to control their workers' time outside of work by establishing factory sports teams or providing workers' outings in order to foster community spirit, but also to emphasize morality, punctuality and sobriety.

Did workers attempt to preserve the traditions of their industry and their right to customary perks? Unfortunately, there is not much evidence to say for sure whether existing or new traditions were defended or were swept aside by the relocation of large numbers of people to factory districts and the shift to mechanized factory production lines. What we do know is that the factory established rigidly organized hierarchies of surveillance, and numerous sets of rules for workers to abide by, together with a list of punishments for those that ignored the rules. For example, below the rules of Calderdale Mill and Stansfield Mill are set out in Figures 9.1 and 9.2.

Rules such as those outlined in the notices in Figures 9.1 and 9.2 governed the use of time and space within the factory and were comprehensive, but they would be little more than rhetorical if there was no one to enforce them.

The prosecution and punishment of 'offending' employees

The people who ensured that factory rules were complied with were called

---

Calderdale Mill Rules

1 All weavers are expected to be at their Loom at the time the Engine begins to work and any weaver who shall come in more than 15 minutes late shall be fined One Penny for every 15 minutes late.

2 All weavers are expected to attend to their own Loom and any one having their Loom and going to Chat or play with their others more than a reasonable time shall be fined Two Pence.

3 Any weaver playing any other weaver mischievous jokes shall be fined One Shilling.

4 Any weaver who shall leave their Loom (but at regular times) without leave from the master shall be fined six pence.

5 When the pieces are wanted to be taken in a Signal shall be placed, and all the weavers shall proceed to deliver them without delay or be fined Two Pence.

Figure 9.1 Calderdale Mill Rules

RULES & LAWS of STANSFIELD MILL (1833)

THE WORK – PEOPLE Are to observe the following RULES, and for every NEGLECT of each of them shall forfeit the PENALTIES annexed thereto; and if any of the HANDS shall be found incorrigible by such FINES, the said FINES to be doubled and trebled according to the number of OFFENCES committed.

I. Waste of every description, and of any value shall be pointed out to the Overlooker.

II. No roving or waste of any kind to be carried out of the room and especially when going to the necessaries.

III. Work people of one room are not to go into any other room unless they have substantial reason for so doing.

IV. No hands to meddle with a machine which is not theirs.

V. Any person found to behave immorally or improperly to the other sex to be expelled from the mill.

VI. It is further hereby made a law, that if it should be found necessary to establish further additional reasonable laws and penalties for offence, the overlooker shall, by direction of the masters, make them known to all hands; or they shall be stuck up in public.

VII. All punishments shall publicly be made known in the mill.

Figure 9.2 Rules and Laws of Stansfield Mill (1833)

overlookers, overseers or foremen. They were (as the last term suggests) invariably male, although in the 1930s it became common in the mills to see a woman acting as overlooker, even if they were not called forewomen. Since the factory system was based in the main on a system of delegated authority rather than direct control, the foreman or overlooker assumed a crucial role in the disciplining of labour.

For those that were caught by the foreman breaking the factory rules, there were three informal punishments: a fine (some mills were fining 600 workers a week), physical punishments or dismissal from employment. Alternatively he could take the offender to the Worsted Inspector for prosecution either in the civil court (where financial damages could be claimed by the employer), or the criminal courts (where the offender could receive a month in prison under the Worsted Acts or even a capital sentence under the larceny acts). The development of anti-appropriation legislation in this period is described in the first sections of Godfrey and Locker (2001: 260–73) and is summarized in Table 9.1.

The legislative framework in existence by 1777 provided easy opportunities for employers to take offending workers to court and to employ the full force of the law in a private arena. But, although the courts did regularly deal with workplace theft, official prosecution was rarely used in comparison with more informal, private sanctions. The criteria that decided whether an offending employee faced a fine, dismissal or the magistrate is outlined below:

Table 9.1 The legislative structure for the punishment of illegal workplace appropriation, 1777–1875

	Act	Offence	1st offence	2nd offence	3rd offence
1777	17 Geo.III c.56 (the Worsted Acts)	Embezzlement/ unexplained possession	£20 fine/ 1 month gaol	£30 fine/ 2 months gaol	£40 fine/ 3 months gaol
		Buying embezzled goods	£20–£40/ 3–6 months	£50–£100/ 3–6 months	£50–£100/ 3–6 months
		Selling embezzled goods	£20–£40/ 3–6 months	£50–£100/ 3–6 months	£50–£100/ 3–6 months
1823	4 Geo.IV c.9	Breaking contract	Damages/ 1 month gaol	Damages/ 1 month gaol	Damages/ 1 month gaol
1827	7 & 8 Geo.IV c.29	Larceny of wool in process of manufacture	4 years gaol/ 7 years transportation	4 years gaol/ 7 years transportation	4 years gaol/ 7 years transportation
1843	6 & 7 Vict. C.40	Frauds by workmen	Restatement of clauses of 17 Geo.III c.56 (1777)		
1861	24 & 25 Vict c.96 s.62	Larceny of wool in process of manufacture	Penal servitude 3–7 years/2 years gaol	Penal servitude 3–7 years/2 years gaol	Penal servitude 3–7 yrs/2 years gaol
1867	30 & 31 Vict c.141	Breaking contract	Damages/ 3 months gaol	Damages/ 3 months gaol	Damages/ 3 months gaol
1875	38 & 39 Vict c.86	Breaking contract	£20 fine/ 3 months gaol	£20 fine/ 3 months gaol	£20 fine/ 3 months gaol

Source: Taken from the series of new statutes enacted published annually.

1. The more serious the offence, the more likely the case was to go to court (i.e. cases of theft were often dealt with by formal prosecution).

2. If unemployment was high, then dismissal and blacklisting would often ensure that the offender went to the workhouse or left the district, and therefore provided a substantial penalty for the offending worker.

3. Higher status workers were prosecuted less often, though, again, if the theft involved cash rather than goods then even higher grades could be prosecuted. For example, Locker (2004) found that the railway companies prosecuted office clerks if they found proof of embezzlement.

4. Those who had already established a good relationship with their supervisor might escape punishment, and some women offered/were forced to give sexual favours in return for no action being taken.

5. Female workers and juveniles were more likely to be physically chastised than prosecuted. These physical punishments could be brutal, but after factories became largely unionized, both the ferocity and the frequency of the physical beatings reduced.

This last point warrants further consideration. Why is it that, whereas men received more formal punishments, foremen favoured more retributive, visible and physical forms of control and punishment for women and child workers, at least until the final quarter of the century when over-physical supervisors began to be prosecuted by their victims in significant numbers (probably as a result of unionization)? It may be that the factory reproduced gender inequalities and patriarchal controls similar to those exercised by husbands in domestic settings – the foremen physically disciplining women in the same way as many men physically (violently) controlled their wives in eighteenth- and nineteenth-century households. Some of the violent assaults on child workers and female employees were taken to court. When they were, some magistrates considered it their duty to protect female workers from physical abuse, others sympathized more with factory management, and even when assaults were proved, female workers could be cautioned on their behaviour. For example, when one foreman was convicted of assault he pleaded for mitigation on the grounds that the victim had provoked him by swearing. The magistrate fined him 2 shillings, but also chastised the woman for using such foul language to her overlooker (Godfrey 1999). There may be other reasons why women were not prosecuted in the numbers that men were: they might have had less opportunity to commit thefts because they were subject to greater surveillance, or they might have been protected from prosecution by legal convention. In the end, the character and personal philosophy of individual foremen may still have been the most influential factor in the decision to prosecute workers. Prosecution remained more likely if the route from detection to prosecution did not involve the foreman, or if he decided that the offence was 'worth' a punishment other than dismissal, a fine or physical assault. The following extracts from interviews/autobiographies about life in the factories illustrate these issues.

It was hard work, it was a chore to get up and go ... I couldn't face it you see love. I hated it, I really hated it ... that's what it is all about, having bits of kids slave away ... that's the history of the mills ... People of my generation will tell you exactly what I've told you: they wouldn't go back in the mills for a thousand pounds a day ... Oh they were rat bags! Oh yes! I worked with one and she was only little, she was the old-fashioned mill type, black stockings and clogs, and if you didn't do something straight away she'd knock you to it. (Kenny 1994)

The woman in the queue put both her hands in front of her and the coins were then put in her hands, she said 'Thank you' turned away, went in front of Alice who ran a pencil through her name on the list. I thought it hilarious to see those hard working women standing in lines with their hands out-stretched to have the money they had worked so hard for tipped into their hands ... (she went on to say that) George the overlooker would walk down the aisles waving his alley-strap and cracking it on the floor ... The alley-strap was a piece of leather about 27 inches long and 10 inches broad; it was fixed to a handle, and when swung round the floor with a violent whack it became a most fearsome thing. I was always afraid of it. I suppose that is why it cracked so often near me when I was least expecting it. I have seen George whang it round the boys when they misbehaved. (Smith 1990)

He'd come and put his hand down your blouse [with] anyone he could do it with. So he did it to me one day ... I hit him and run like hell! ... And he says, 'Tha's going home. I'm giving thee t'sack' ... You see, I thought, 'Well if he does that to me, he might do it to our Clarrie', and she were younger than me, and that were awfu'. [This event occurred in the 1940s when this interviewee was 17 years old.] (Anonymous female worker, A0189/02/53, Bradford Oral History Archive, *Bradford Library*[2])

[In the 1950s] I were doing something with the machine and he [the overlooker] come and put his hand right across my bottom so I turned round, I picked up the bobbin and hit him with it. So this gentleman what were over the overlookers asked me what I'd hit him for, so I told him, 'When he stops touching my arse I'll stop hitting him with bobbins'. (Female worker, tape A0058/02/28, Bradford Oral History Archive, *Bradford Library*)

However, despite the massive use of informal punishments and factory fines, between 1840 and 1880 around three thousand workers were still prosecuted by the Worsted Inspectorate and received hefty punishments (see Table 9.2).

While the punishments handed down to offenders merit attention, it is the conviction rate which is more noteworthy. Approximately eight out of ten defendants were convicted. This is not only a very high rate of conviction, but is also a much higher conviction rate than that of simple theft, which was around 60–70 per cent. How can this high conviction rate be explained?

Table 9.2 Punishments imposed on workplace theft cases, West Yorkshire, 1844–76

Length of imprisonment	Prosecuted at Quarter Sessions		Prosecuted at Petty Sessions	
	No. of cases	% of cases	No. of cases	% cases
One to three months	56	50.0	459	98.5
Four to six months	40	35.7	7	1.5
Seven to twelve months	16	14.2	0	0

Source: Worsted Committee records held at West Yorkshire Archives at Bradford.

There exists today a judicial principle that magistrates should not judge a case with any motivation other than the execution of justice. Self-interest on behalf of the magistrate is, in theory, precluded from the judicial process. However, the vast majority of eighteenth- and nineteenth-century statutes did not include clauses that prevented those magistrates who had an interest in any particular case from acting as judicial arbiters (see Table 9.3). Edward Lister, for example, one of the eighty manufacturers who judged workplace 'theft' cases in West Yorkshire, held petty sessional summary hearings in an extension of his own home. Mr Holdsworth, a member of the Worsted Committee, tried his workers inside his own factory. It is little wonder that these men were concerned with the control of workplace appropriation – their membership of the Worsted Committee proved as much. But were such men blinded to justice inside the courthouse by their own personal interests?

Given that a significant proportion of the magistrates who tried appropriation cases were manufacturers in the same line of business as the prosecutor, sat on a committee which decided whether to prosecute offenders and had an indirect commercial interest in the outcome of the case, it would seem that the legal principle which is adhered to today was not apparent in that period. So, is it possible to find evidence of judicial bias against workers?

The issue of judicial partiality is a slippery one. From the prosecution/conviction statistics, we can see that there appears to be convincing evidence of judicial bias, but still no consistent *causal* link between the occupation of

Table 9.3 Conviction rate by combination of magistrates, 1844–76

Occupation and combination of magistrates	Conviction rate (%)	Number of cases
A textile manufacturer plus one non-textile manufacturer	87.8	123
Both textile manufacturers	82.1	246
Both Worsted Committee members	72.7	22
Neither textile manufacturers	70.2	26
All cases in which magistrate's occupation is known	82.4	417

Source: Figures taken from private Worsted Committee records held at West Yorkshire Archives at Bradford.

the magistrates and the conviction rate of appropriators can be established. Although the occupation of the magistrate had some impact it is not a clear predictor of the likelihood of conviction. For example, the conviction rate when two Worsted Committee members judged the case was actually *lower* than the average. Did more subtle factors exist which affected the statistics (see Godfrey 1999)? Quantitative analysis of prosecution/conviction statistics suggests in the strongest terms that manufacturing magistrates were keen to convict offending workpeople. Yet the laws against workplace appropriation were tightly framed, and the criteria for conviction were easily met compared to other property offences. These factors are, in themselves, sufficient to cast doubt on overdramatic assertions of judicial bias. It may be that the way the legislation was framed made conviction an overwhelming possibility – no matter who the magistrate was.

Did the factory eradicate workplace theft?

The criminal law was clearly an important weapon in the employers' armoury, but some believe that it was changes in the organization of the workplace which had the greatest impact on levels of workplace appropriation. Indeed some have suggested that the factory can be ranked alongside the prison, the asylum and the barracks as a 'total institution' (see Ignatieff 1983). A number of commentators have debated the existence of 'total institutions' (which controlled most aspects of their inhabitants' lives) in the eighteenth and nineteenth centuries, and have drawn out the similarities between the factory and the prison. For Foucault (1991), Melossi and Pavarini (1981) and others, the differences between working conditions and prison conditions were minimal: 'For the worker the factory is like a prison (loss of liberty and subordination); for the inmate the prison is like a factory (work and discipline) ... The ideological meaning of this complex reality can be summarised by the attempt to rationalise and conceptualise a dual analogy: *prisoners must be workers, workers must be prisoners*' (Melossi and Pavarini 1981). They believe that the factory did not consciously imitate the prison, nor the prison the factory, but both evolved from ideas concerning the control of time and space. Giddens (1995) stated that: 'The commodification of time, and its differentiation from further processes of the commodification of space, hold the key to the deepest transformations of day-to-day social life that are brought about by the emergence of capitalism.' Clearly, the factory acted upon the will or the character of the worker in unknown ways, which may have been of benefit to capitalistic society by encouraging workers to be disciplined, compliant, and 'civilized' with middle-class morality.

For these commentators, the employers' search for greater efficiency led both to mechanization and the establishment of centralized production areas in order to facilitate greater control over labour. For example, the development of the factory therefore accomplished four aims in Dickson's (1989) opinion: first, the suppression of 'embezzlement'; second, control over the pace of production; third, the centralization of labour which both facilitated machine technology and allowed the control of the workers' adverse reaction to new machinery; lastly, it made capitalists indispensable to production because the factories needed large and frequent capital investments. Although the first two aims were explicitly concerned with labour control, Dickson, rightly, saw the other aims as also being primarily work discipline measures. The origins of the factory were therefore embedded in the desire to control labour, and this desire inevitably spawned supervisors and surveillance techniques in the workplace. Marglin (1976 and 1984) asserts that this explains why factories were established with the kind of technology already in place in much of the cottage textile industry, and also why many factories did not mechanize until years after their establishment. After all, Gott's mill in Leeds, a huge and highly developed complex, was managed for 25 years without mechanization taking place in any key area of production.

The alternative theory, that factories were developed to increase the pace of production, has been put forward by Landes (1987). He has attacked the 'workplace social control' thesis on a number of grounds. First, he argues that the specialization of labour and the introduction of machinery created a higher level of profits for their owners than any other system. In other words, factories were more profitable and so they made the cottage industry redundant. Second, mechanization became possible once factories had been established, and that as soon as employers could raise the funds, they mechanized. Even Landes, however, believed that mechanization was only possible as long as workers were under the supervision of employers or their agents. Recently, Pollard, Berg and Hudson have adopted a more measured response to the debate, arguing that both mechanization (combined with the specialization and division of labour) and social control were motivating forces behind the move to factory production.

It seems that the debate, which has been presented by the protagonists as 'technology versus discipline', is actually a debate about the *relative* importance of the two main reasons for the growth of the factory system. For example, *all* of the theorists in this debate believe that workplace indiscipline, especially appropriation, was rife in the domestic system, and also that the factory engendered and increased managerial control over the workforce. If the employers had not seen the benefits of centralization in terms of labour control and/or as a way of controlling workplace theft then the domestic system with its unspecialized and dispersed labour force could have continued as the primary form of work organization unhindered for many decades more than it did. However, the assumption that centralization, and the concomitant surveillance systems, were successful in controlling the workers, and eradicating workplace theft must be questioned, particularly since the criminal law continued to be used until the mid-twentieth century, well beyond the point when the factory was supposed to have made the law redundant and workplace theft impossible, as the broadsheet illustrated in Figure 9.3 (issued by the Worsted Inspectorate in 1934) shows.

These cases may be singular or extraordinary, or possibly the most serious cases and thought to deserve prosecution where other minor cases may not. Whatever the case, they do illustrate that the law was still being used to discipline offending workers well into the mid-twentieth century.

Recent Convictions under the Worsted Acts, 1934

At the Wakefield City Police Court –
Nine girls employed at a mill at Ardsley for purloining botany roving were each fined £5 or 31 days' imprisonment.

An important prosecution under the Acts was brought at Wakefield against a rag and waste dealer for receiving waste from an employee without having first obtained the consent of his employers. The weight of the waste involved in this case was very large, namely, 30,728 lbs. The man was fined £50 or two months.

Night Watchman and Fireman charged with being found in possession of belting, canvas, file, bolts, and other tools and failing to give a good account of the same. Discharged under the Probation of Offenders Act and to pay costs.

At the Bradford Police Court –
Three women employed in a mill at Bradford for purloining yarn and roving were each fined £3 or 21 days' imprisonment. A weaver was convicted of purloining botany weft piece ends and spools and was fined £5 or 21 days' imprisonment. For having in her possession a quantity of yarn suspected to have been purloined, a weaver was sent to prison for 21 days. For having in his possession 60 yards of cloth suspected to have been stolen, a man was fined £5.

A man, who it was suspected had received from some person employed at Manningham Mills a quantity of silk and cotton yarn, was fined £10. A weft room man was convicted of stealing a quantity of woollen, cotton and worsted yarn, and was sent to prison for 6 months. The goods recovered were valued at over £1,400. Two warehousemen purloining 1,800 lbs of camel hair tops, the property of their employers. Each fined £14 or two months' imprisonment. A waste dealer charged with receiving 1,200 lbs. of the above camel hair tops from persons employed without the consent of the employer. Fined £30 or two months' imprisonment.

At the West Riding Police Court, Bradford –
A dyer was charged on three counts, viz: For secreting certain worsted pieces, failing to return to the owners, and with having in possession botany serge pieces suspected to have been purloined or embezzled. A fine of £10 was imposed in each case, and £10 10s. for costs, amounting altogether to £40 10s. Thirty-four pieces of the value of £1,000 were restored to the owners.

Figure 9.3 Broadsheet issued by the Worsted Inspectorate, 1934.

Conclusion

In this chapter, we have been considering two main questions. First, how was the criminal law used within private spaces such as the workplace? Second, did the factory end the customary perquisites enjoyed by the workers? In conclusion, it seems that the factory did not bring about the end of workplace appropriation. Factory masters used a plethora of measures against workplace indiscipline, including specific legislation, private police agencies, internal supervisory structures and the physical layout of the workplace. These measures had great symbolic importance, and were arguably effective in combating time-wasting and helping to shape a factory culture in which work indiscipline was disapproved of by workers and employers alike. Nevertheless, workplace appropriation remained and ebbed and flowed with economic conditions. It seems clear that the factory system is not, and has never been, sufficient by itself to eradicate workplace 'theft'. Although systems of supervision and surveillance increased the likelihood that wrong-doing would be detected, that possibility was not sufficient to deter appropriation from taking place. Indeed there is a mass of newspaper and oral evidence to suggest that workplace appropriation continued as an occasional or routine practice for many workers. For example, surviving Worsted Committee minute books suggest that, until at least 1951, employers still used the criminal law to punish workplace offenders. Moreover, modern studies by Ditton (1977) and Mars (1983) and others show that appropriation continues in factories today.

In considering these questions, more spring to mind. For example, is workplace appropriation really criminological 'property'? The subjects of criminological research are diverse, but can be listed thus: law-breaking, the construction and contravening of normative orderings (normal rules of behaviour), and the operation of both the administration of the law and the state's instruments of control and punishment. Appropriation would seem to have a resonance in many of those areas of research, except in one important respect. The behaviour of criminological subjects – those who break the law, or who deviate from societal norms – are marked out as 'special', extraordinary and deviant. Yet factory appropriation was endemic to that production system. The appropriation of materials was as likely to have accorded with the internal belief systems constructed by the workforce as to have contravened them. People who were seen, and saw themselves, as normal, committed the 'offence'. Thompson (1972) said, of the eighteenth century, that, 'Crime – in the sense of being on the wrong side of the law – was, for vast numbers of undifferentiated people, normal.' Studies of workplace appropriation are similarly studies of ordinary people in everyday work situations, a history of, what many might consider, routine human activity.

Lastly, does the growth in surveillance at work fit within a general societal pattern of social control? Are we living in a Big Brother society? This is a phrase that, despite being coined over fifty years ago (Orwell 1948), has some currency today. Indeed some allege that the introduction of closed-circuit television (CCTV), credit, cashpoint and identity cards, and the myriad number of forms that need to be filled in with personal biographical information on a weekly basis, all point to a growing control by the state over the lives of ordinary people. George Orwell's Big Brother was a system rather than a person who exerted omnipotent power over the general population:

> At the apex of the pyramid comes Big Brother. Big Brother is infallible and all-powerful ... Nobody has ever seen Big Brother. He is a face on the hoardings, a voice on the telescreen. We may be reasonably sure that he will never die, and there is already considerable uncertainty as to when he was born ... in the past no government had the power to keep its citizens under constant surveillance. [Now] every citizen, or at least every citizen important enough to be worth watching, could be kept for

twenty-four hours a day under the eyes of the police and in the sound of official propaganda, with all other channels of communication closed. The possibility of enforcing not only complete obedience to the will of the State, but complete uniformity of opinion on all subjects, now existed for the first time. (Orwell 1948, chapter 9)

For Lyon (1994) and Dandaker (1990), there has been a growing sophistication of surveillance techniques since the crude attempts to oversee factory labour. Indeed these authors chart a long history of surveillance. Let us examine how such a history might be constructed: in the modern period patronage and personal favour as a form of control was largely replaced with impersonal bureaucratic power; the nation states formed not only armies to guard their borders, but also domestic forces of control to watch over their subjects; the processes of manufacture required the collecting together of thousands of workers, controlled with a hierarchy of supervisors; the protection of citizens from harm required the new sciences of psychology and criminology to categorize and identify the potentially dangerous; electronic technology enabled massive amounts of information not only to be stored, but also quickly processed and shared between the powerful bureaucracies; and the information age which defines modernity is born, or as Lyon said:

Organizations of many kinds know us only as coded sequences of numbers and letters. This was once worked out on pieces of paper collated in folders and kept in filing cabinets, but now the same tasks – and many others, unimaginable to a Victorian clerk – are performed by computer. Precise details of our personal lives are collected, stored, retrieved and processed every day within huge computer databases belonging to big corporations and government departments. This is 'surveillance society'. (Lyon 1994: 3)

Few would doubt that the capacity of the government and private enterprise to know more about 'us' has increased and that those agencies do regularly take advantage of this capacity. But perhaps the routine transfer of information from the citizen to the state is part of participatory democracy? For example, many agree that a certain level of personal freedom must be sacrificed in dangerous times, and with the justification of avoiding terrorist outrages, governments across the western world now feel able to claim more and more information about the daily activities of ordinary people. Moreover, the ease with which people give over personal information is a demonstration of increased trust in society, not fear.

In any case, as this chapter has demonstrated, the demand for information on the powerless by the powerful is not new, but many will feel that the historical road from the factory foreman in private businesses to the anonymous controller of CCTV cameras on public streets is a long and uncomfortable one.

Key questions

1. How was the criminal law used in the workplace, and did the rise of the factory end workplace appropriation?

We have to be careful with the term 'workplace'. Before the factory system became established, there were laws which attempted to prevent the theft of employers' property by their workers, but this was in the domestic or workshop system. For example, the 1777 Worsted Acts were passed by Parliament when the main form of production was cottage industry, not factory based. The legislation was most effective, however, when the workers were collected and supervised centrally. This allowed the internal supervisory hierarchy of foremen/overseers to detect workplace appropriations and summon a Worsted Inspector. The approximately three thousand prosecutions over a forty year period and the length of time the Worsted Inspectorate continued to prosecute offending workers shows that the law played an important role, but research shows that informal discipline was also very evident. The foremen could decide who and which acts of appropriation were worthy of prosecution rather than a fine, dismissal from employment or physical punishment. In practice, the gender and age of the 'offender' was critical. So was the employment situation at the time – times of high unemployment made dismissal as harsh a penalty as formal prosecution (without all the expense for the employer). Neither the use of formal or informal codes manages to eradicate appropriation, however. Indeed, it was so ingrained to most industries in the nineteenth and twentieth centuries, and is still as evident today in the taking of 'customary perks', that it is doubtful that the practice will ever end, since it is (to the majority of employers) normal.

2. Why were men and women punished differently in the factory?

See Godfrey (1997) for a discussion of this topic.

3. Has there been a general rise in surveillance in society over the last two hundred years?

See Lyon (1994) and Dandaker (1990) who both take a broad historical view of surveillance, both inside the workplace and in the public sphere.

Notes

1. The taking home of workplace materials by employees has various labels attached to it – some refer to the practice as workplace appropriation, pilfering, 'fiddling' or 'embezzlement'. The terms reflect that some considered the practice a customary right established by tradition, others as a form of theft (see Hobsbawm 1968).
2. These extracts are from the Bradford Heritage Recording Unit, which carried out hundreds of interviews with former mill workers.

Further reading

The references for this chapter can be found in the Bibliography at the back of the book. If you wish to do some further reading, you should investigate these first. However, below is a list of publications which could also be consulted.

Ashton, T. (1955) *An Economic History of England. The Eighteenth Century*. London: Methuen.

Ditton, J. (1995) *Natural Criminology: An Essay on the Fiddle*. Glasgow: Press Gang.

Du Guy, P. (1996) *Consumption and Identity at Work*. London: Sage.

Gregory, D. (1984) *Regional Transformation and the Industrial Revolution: A Geography of the Yorkshire Woollen Industry*. London: Macmillan.

Hay, D. and Snyder, F. (1989) 'Using the criminal law, 1750–1850: policing, private prosecution, and the state', in D. Hay and F. Snyder, *Policing and Prosecution in Britain, 1750–1850*. Oxford: Clarendon.

Heaton, H. (1965) *The Yorkshire Woollen and Worsted Industries from the Earliest Times up to the Industrial Revolution*. Oxford: Clarendon.

Ignatieff, M. (1979) *A Just Measure of Pain. The Penitentiary and the Industrial Revolution*. London: Macmillan.

Jenkins, P. (1987) 'Into the upperworld? Law, crime and punishment in English society', *Social History*, 12, 27–53.

Johnstone, P. (1998) 'Serious white collar fraud: historical and contemporary perspectives', *Crime, Law and Social Change*, 30, 2, 107–30.

Koditchek, T. (1990) *Class Formation and Urban Industrial Society, 1750–1850*. Cambridge: Cambridge University Press.

Locker, J. (forthcoming) 'Quiet thieves, quiet punishment: private responses to the "respectable" offender, c.1850–1930', *Crime, Histoire et Sociétés/Crime, History and Societies*.

Morris, R. J. (1990) *Class, Sect and Party: The Making of the British Middle Class: Leeds 1820–50*. Manchester: Manchester University Press.

Pinchbeck, I. (1930/1969 reprint) *Women Workers and the Industrial Revolution, 1750–1850*. London: Cass.

Robb, G. (1992) *White Collar Crime in Modern England: Financial Fraud and Business Morality, 1845–1929*. Cambridge: Cambridge University Press.

Simon, D. (1954) 'Masters and servants', in J. Saville (ed.), *Democracy and the Labour Movement. Essays in Honour of Dona Tore*. London: Lawrence & Wishart.

Sindall, R. (1983) 'Middle class crime in nineteenth century England', *Criminal Justice History. An International Annual*, Vol. IV, pp. 23–40.

Snyder, F. and Hay, D. (1987) 'Comparisons in the social history of the law, labour and crime', in F. Snyder and D. Hay, *Labour, Law and Crime: An Historical perspective*. London: Tavistock.

Thompson, E. P. (1972) 'Eighteenth-century crime, popular movements and social control', *Bulletin of the Society of Social and Labour History*, 52, 4–5.

Wiener, M. (1994) *Reconstructing the Criminal: Culture, Law and Policy in England, 1830–1914*. Cambridge: Cambridge University Press, Chapter 6.

Woods, D. (1982) 'The operation of the master and servant act in the Black Country, 1858–1875, *Midland History*, 7, 93–115.

10. Conclusion

By selecting particular topics for discussion in this book – the development of policing and punishment; how criminality, victims of crime and offenders have been conceived; violence; and the rise of surveillance – we have added to the literature which has helped to define a body of knowledge which can be described as 'crime history' (together with, for example, Taylor 1998; Rawlings 1999; Emsley 2005). While it is true that a comprehensive study of crime history would be incomplete without most if not all of these topics, the broad boundaries that have been constructed around this subdiscipline will surely expand over time. Crime history (if we can use that term for the large and somewhat sprawling collection of historical studies of criminal justice agencies, offences, legislation and individual offenders that has developed over the last twenty or thirty years) is at a crossroads. The methods used, the approaches taken and the intellectual preoccupations of those who have written on the subject are recognizable to all social historians. The subject would fit seamlessly into a history degree programme, or help to make an academic contribution to modern understandings of social life and political thought in the 1750–1950 period. The acceptance of both qualitative and quantitative approaches (or a mix of both), and the willingness to share sources and ideas, do, perhaps, mark out the crime history community as a distinct group within social historians. However, the concern with rigorous method, the correct appreciation and use of difficult sources, the attempt to understand complex contemporary situations and the motivations of historical actors, all place the subdiscipline under the broad subject banner of 'history'.

However, the focus of history moves ever forwards, and although historical studies of criminality from the end of the First World War to the post-Second World War period are few and far between at the moment, they are beginning to grow in number. Those studies will not only need to interact with sociological theory, but will indeed use sociological data as a source material. For example, the interviews with young offenders growing up in the 1950s and 1960s by Fyvel (1961) or Willmott (1966) have now become historically significant material. Those interviews carried out with those young men in the 1950s, or Cyril Burt's carried out in the 1920s, if handled carefully, provide the means to successfully carry out secondary analysis. Similarly, George Orwell's journey down *The Road to Wigan Pier* (1937); Richard Hoggart's (1955) study of working-class life in Leeds in the 1950s, or Stan Cohen's (1973) study of youth gangs provide not only a study of criminality or leisure in a particular period, but also prevailing theories of social life when the books were originally published. Can these works (or the many others that we could have named) really be left as part of a 'history of sociological theory' course?

As historical investigation begins to more meaningfully interact with sociological enquiry, two things will happen. First, crime history will continue to evolve and probably adopt a more sociological language and methodology. Second, sociologists and criminologists are more likely to take an interest in historical materials. These outcomes are to be welcomed, but they will inevitably provide a constant and engaging set of challenges to all of those who work in the field of deviance, crime and policing.

Further reading

The references for this chapter can be found in the Bibliography at the back of the book. If you wish to do some further reading, you should investigate these first. However, below is a list of publications which could also be consulted.

Burt, C. Sir (1925) *The Young Delinquent*. London: London University Press.
Cohen, S. (1973) *Folk Devils and Moral Panics: The Creation of Mods and Rockers*. St Albans: Paladin.
Fyvel, T. (1961) *The Insecure Offenders. Rebellious Youth in the Welfare State*. London: Penguin Books.
Hoggart, R. (1955) *The Uses of Literacy. Aspects of Working-Class Life with Special Reference to Publications and Entertainments*. London: Penguin Books.
Orwell, G. (1937) *The Road to Wigan Pier*. London: Victor Gollancz.
Willmott, P. (1966) *Adolescent Boys of East London*. London: Routledge & Kegan Paul.

Glossary

Assize Courts – The highest form of regional court between medieval times and the twentieth century. Assize judges, based in London, went round the country on various circuits trying serious crimes in front of a trial jury. Most offences tried at the assize had at one time carried the death penalty. Most counties held assizes twice a year.

Bentham, Jeremy – As one of the most influential exponents of Utilitarianism, Jeremy Bentham (1748–1832) had maintained that social organization had to be adjusted in such a way as to maximize human happiness, and that the best way to effect this was via a series of specialized government departments controlling public administration from Whitehall.

Bloody Code – A long series of statutes (over 200 in 1820) under which the death penalty could be applied. Many applied to relatively minor offences, and the existence of the 'Bloody Code' led early historians of crime to conclude that justice in the late eighteenth century was excessively harsh. However, more recent research indicates that judges used their discretion a great deal, and the practical operation of the code was less harsh than might at first be imagined.

Borstal – An institution for the detention and training of young offenders. First introduced in 1908 and replaced in 1982 by Young Custody Centres.

Bow Street Runners – Formed by the magistrate Henry Fielding in London in 1749, the Bow Street Runners consisted originally of eight constables. Initially nicknamed Robin Redbreasts because of their scarlet waistcoats, their functions included serving writs, detective work and arresting offenders. The Bow Street Runners could on occasion travel around the country and were engaged by magistrates and private individuals.

Capital crimes – Any crime carrying the death penalty as punishment. While most crimes of theft were capital before the 1820s, more than 90 per cent of death sentences for property crime were never carried out but replaced by transportation for life. These kinds of crimes were originally termed 'felonies'.

Charivari – The use of a rude cacophony of sound and simple dramatic performance to ridicule or express hostility towards those who had offended against communal values and moral standards. Also known as 'rough musicking'.

Chartism – A popular movement of the 1830s and 1840s directed towards political reform. Advocating the 'People's Charter', Chartists sought (via a series of demonstrations and protests) to extend the vote to all men over the age of 21 and to abolish the property qualifications which barred the working class from the House of Commons.

Constable – The most junior level of law enforcement official. Constables are sworn in to maintain the monarch's peace and to enforce the law. They have legal obligations to arrest criminals, enforce warrants and enter property. Before 1800, most were part-time householders; after this point, an increasing number were part of uniformed police forces. In recent years, the proportion of police employees who are not constables has increased substantially.

Court Leet – A court deriving its power from old feudal legislation, presided over by the Lord of the Manor or his representative, which met annually and appointed local office-holders. Courts Leet were superseded in the nineteenth century.

Degeneration – This idea was popular towards the end of the nineteenth century. The theory suggested that, just as Darwin had proposed that species evolved into more sophisticated forms over time, it was also possible that some people were degenerating into lower, more animalistic forms of being. Typically the criminal classes were identified as degenerate, although there were some fictional representations of upper-class degenerates. See, for example, Stevenson's *Dr Jekyll and Mr Hyde* or Disraeli's *Sybil*.

Eugenics – The term 'eugenics', first coined in 1883 by Francis Galton, was inspired by discoveries in genetics and biology. Soon scientists, reformers and professionals were asserting that the human race could and should be improved through the breeding out of deficiencies such as mental retardation and inheritable diseases – some even included poverty, crime, alcoholism and prostitution.

Fabians – British socialists aiming at gradual social change through democratic means. The Fabian Society was founded in 1884 by a group of intellectuals who believed that new political pressures were needed to achieve social reforms. It was one of the socialist societies that helped found the Labour Representation Committee, the origin of the Labour Party, in 1900.

Felony – A serious crime, as distinct from a misdemeanour. In the past, felony crimes were those which had carried the death penalty, and the power of the law against people accused of them was far greater than against those who committed other crimes. Felonies were often tried at assizes in front of a judge. The distinction is now obsolete in UK law, but aspects of it survive in the definition of a 'serious arrestable offence'.

Fenian outrages – The Fenians were members of a group of Irish nationalists committed to the overthrow of English rule in Ireland by physical force.

Force majeure – A legal term referring to the settlement of an issue by the application of irresistible force or overwhelming power.

French Revolution – Taking place in 1789, the French Revolution marked the end of the *ancien régime* (the monarchy) in France and the birth of the Republic. Now, ostensibly at least, 'the people' were in charge of the nation rather than a privileged ruler. Many of the nobility were executed publicly and this caused a frisson of fear across Europe that similar events might unfold in other countries.

Grande Peur – A period during the French Revolution of 1789 *before* the fall of the monarchy. Poverty and unemployment made living conditions very harsh in much of the country, and militias were formed in case the King should attempt to dissolve the Estates-General, a kind of fledgling parliament.

Justice of the Peace – The name Justice of the Peace is the official title of a magistrate. JPs were (and still are) unpaid volunteers from the local community. These officials preside over the lowest courts in the UK's criminal system. Before the twentieth century, magistrates were invariably prominent local people, usually landowners or industrialists, heavily involved in local government. Since 1750 there has been an increase in the number of paid or stipendiary magistrates, usually appointed to the larger urban areas.

Laissez-faire – Meaning allowing people to do as they think best, it usually describes a philosophy where government does little to interfere or regulate (depending on your point of view) industry or trade.

Luddite disturbances/Luddism – The Luddite disturbances took place in the counties of Nottinghamshire, Lancashire, Cheshire, Derbyshire, Leicestershire and Yorkshire during the period 1811–13. Led by a fictional leader called 'Ned Ludd', the Luddites attacked new machinery and mills in an attempt to maintain the price (money) paid to them as textile workers and control over their work practices.

Magistrate – See *Justice of the Peace.*

Misdemeanour – A less serious crime than a felony, for which the law has fewer powers than it does in a case of felony. These crimes were usually tried in the lower (magistrates') courts. The distinction no longer has force in UK law, but to an extent it survives in the form of 'non-arrestable offences'.

Petty sessions – A court operated by between one and three justices of the peace, sitting between once a week and daily. Petty sessions began as informal but were formalized in the nineteenth century. Felonies (i.e. serious crimes of violence and most crimes of theft) could not be tried at these sessions. By the early twentieth century petty sessions were normally referred to as magistrates' courts.

Police Courts – London's Metropolitan Police Courts assumed their final form in 1839. Staffed by stipendiary (salaried) magistrates, these summary courts dealt with a wide range of minor offences such as drunk and disorderly charges, vagrancy offences and petty theft. While handling mostly cases brought by the police, they were also an arena wherein the working class could seek justice.

Quarter sessions – A court sitting four or six times a year, often moving round the county. Any member of the county bench of Justices of the Peace could sit on quarter sessions, whose members tried offences and dispensed punishment without a jury.

Residuum – A late-nineteenth-century term for the poorest, roughest and most unproductive element of the working class, akin to Marx's notion of the *lumpenproletariat*. Some believed the residuum could be reclaimed, others believed their situation was hopeless.

Serve (as in 'serve a warrant') – Serving a warrant involves a law officer (usually a bailiff or constable) going to the place or person to which the warrant applies and, if necessary, producing it to justify court-ordered actions (such as arrest, search or seizure) which would otherwise be unlawful.

Special Constables (Specials) – Volunteers from the public (normally the middle-class) sworn into the police force for a limited period to assist with special duties. The 'specials' could be armed and were often used to help maintain public order during periods of popular disturbance. Special constables still exist today.

Ticket of leave system – This was an early form of probation, introduced by the Penal Servitude Act of 1853, whereby tickets were issued to convicts on release, licensing them to free movement but only within set terms. For example, the ticket might specify they had to travel home from prison by a specific route or by a set day. Ticket-of-leave men were often suspected of committing crimes as soon as they were released rather than seeking work.

Vagrancy/vagrants – The word used for the wandering about of homeless people. A number of parliamentary acts passed since the fifteenth century (such as the Vagrancy Act of 1824) have specified that vagrancy (i.e. merely being of no fixed abode) was actually a criminal offence, for which short prison sentences were often applied.

Warrant – A legal document issued by a court, or by a law officer such as a magistrate or judge, which mandates or allows an action which would otherwise be outside the law. The most important of these are arrest warrants asking the police to take a suspect into custody and search warrants which authorize them to enter and search private premises without the permission of their occupants in order to look for fugitives or illegally obtained goods.

Watch/night watch – An urban force, initially of householders but later of (badly) paid employees, whose job it was to watch the streets at night, stop suspicious persons and enforce curfews. Watchmen did not have the legal powers of constables. From the early nineteenth century, they were replaced by the new police forces.

Timetable of significant events

1750–1800

1750s	First salaried police: 'Bow Street Runners' introduced in London by magistrates Henry and John Fielding. Growth of provincial newspapers carrying crime advertising.
1760s	Associations for the Prosecution of Felons set up in many parts of the country.
1775	Marylebone Watch introduces a three-tier command structure.
1777	Worsted Acts create an Inspectorate, controlled by the Worsted Committee, a group of prominent Yorkshire employers, to find and prosecute workplace theft. John Howard's *The State of the Prisons* initiates prison reform debate.
1787	First convicts transported to Botany Bay.
1789	French Revolution inspires fears of similar disorder in Britain.
1792	Bow Street Police offices created.
1798	Malthus publishes his views on population growth and poverty.
1799	Thames Police introduced by Patrick Colquhoun as a uniformed professional patrolling force.

1800–50

1803	Lord Ellenborough's Act makes shooting with intent to kill a capital crime.
1811–13	Luddite disturbances.
1812–27	Several parliamentary inquiries into policing London are carried out.
1815	Napoleon defeated at Waterloo.
1816	Report of the committee for investigating the causes of the alarming increase of juvenile delinquency in the metropolis is published and is the first official recognition of 'juvenile delinquency'. Millbank prison, the largest in Europe, opens.
1818	Peterloo Massacre.
1819	Factory Act bans children under nine years old working in the cotton mills.

Select Committee on Criminal Laws criticizes the costs of attending court.

1822   Cruelty to livestock made illegal.
        Select Committee on the Police investigates the possibility of police reform.

1826   Criminal Justice Act provides for the paying of witness expenses.

1829   Home Secretary Robert Peel creates the London Metropolitan Police.
        Malicious Trespass Act passed.

1832–34 Death penalty abolished for shoplifting.

1833   Factory Act restricts child labour in factories.

1835   Municipal Corporations Act obliges towns outside London to set up police forces.

1837   Charles Dickens publishes *Oliver Twist*.
        Select Committee on Transportation hears criticism from Australian lobby groups.

1838   Parkhurst Prison established for boys.

1839   Metropolitan Police Act abolishes the last 'old' police.

1839–40 County Police Acts allow rural counties to set up police.

1842   Opening of Pentonville prison.
        Formation of the Detective Department of the Metropolitan Police.

1844   Factory Act further restricts child labour in factories.

1847   Juvenile Offenders Act allows under 14 year olds to be prosecuted in magistrates' courts.

1848   Jervis Acts increase the number of summary offences.
        Continental revolutions again raise the spectre of public disorder.

1849   The Philanthropic Society establishes a reformatory for boys at Redhill in Surrey.

1850–1900

1850   Juvenile Offenders Act allows under 16 year olds to be prosecuted in magistrates' courts.

1851   Henry Mayhew publishes his social investigation of the London poor.

1853   Criminal Procedure Act increases punishment for assaults against women and children.

1854   Youthful Offenders Act establishes a reformatory system.

1855   Criminal Justice Act expands the jurisdiction of the summary courts.

1856   County and Borough Police Act means all local governments must set up a police force.
        Industrial Schools Act created institutions across the country.

1857   End of transportation as a judicial sentence.

1861   Offences against the Persons Act enables common assaults to be tried summarily in magistrates' courts (this Act is still in force today).

Henry Mayhew and Samuel Bracebridge estimate there are 80,000 prostitutes in London.

The Malthusian League is formed.

Number of capital crimes reduced to four.

1863   Security from Violence Act allows whipping for those convicted of robbery from the person.

1864   Factory Act restricts child labour in workshops.

First Contagious Diseases Act passed to control venereal disease.

1866   Second Contagious Diseases Act increases police supervision of unattached women in public places.

1868   End of public executions.

1869   Habitual Criminals Act increases supervision of released prisoners and creates a national register of habitual criminals.

Third Contagious Diseases Act passed, and accelerates increasing opposition to these acts.

1870   Baby-farmer Mary Waters executed.

1871   Second Habitual Offenders Act increases the penalties for habitual offenders, and allows 12 months' imprisonment for ex-prisoners who are found in public with no means of support or in any suspicious circumstances.

Report from the Royal Commission on the administration and operation of the Contagious Diseases Act published.

1874   Police Expenses Act.

1875   First Offenders Act allows some children to be diverted away from imprisonment.

1878   The Matrimonial Causes Act allows magistrates to order a separation.

1879   Habitual Drunkards Act passed.

Prosecution of Offences Act sets up a public prosecutor for the first time.

1885   The age of consent is raised to 16 by the Criminal Law Amendment Act, and homosexual acts between males are outlawed.

1888   The Whitechapel murders are attributed to Jack the Ripper.

1889   Florence Maybrick's prosecution creates moral panic about female poisoners.

1890   Police Act grants all police officers a pension.

1895   Summary Jurisdiction (Married Women) Act grants divorce (or a separation order with maintenance payments) if the husband is found by a magistrate to be 'persistently cruel'.

1898   Inebriates reformatories established.

1899   Anglo-Boer War begins.

1900–50

1901   Queen Victoria dies.

1902   Boer War ends.

1908   Children's Act makes violence to children under 16 punishable by a maximum of two years imprisonment or £100 fine. It also establishes a separate juvenile court system.

Crime Prevention Act sets up detention centres (Borstals) for those offenders too young to be sent to prison.

1910   Tonypandy strike disturbances.

1911   Britain introduces first compulsory unemployment insurance scheme.

1914   First World War begins; Defence of the Realm Act (DORA) passed.

1917   Report of the Board of Education published.

Report of the National Council of Public Morals considers the effect of cinemas on youth behaviour.

Bolshevik Revolution in Russia.

1918   First World War ends.

1919   After a successful strike, Police Act sets national rates of pay and a representative Federation is created.

Sex Disqualification (Removal) Act allows women to become magistrates.

1920   Emergency Powers Act.

1922   First female barrister appointed.

1926   General Strike.

1933   Children and Young Persons Act enables the state to intervene in family affairs and take any child into care.

1934   First in a series of Firearms Acts passed (also 1936 and 1937).

1936   Public Order Act grants new police powers in controlling demonstrations.

1938   Infanticide Act acknowledges post-natal depression as a mitigating factor in prosecutions.

1939   Second World War begins.

1942   Beveridge Report published.

1944   Education Act passed.

1945   Second World War ends.

First female judge appointed.

1947   Graham Green's *Brighton Rock* reaches the cinema screen.

1948   Military drill and physical labour introduced at detention centres.

George Orwell publishes *1984*.

Women accepted into the police federation.

1949   Legal Aid and Legal Advice Act passed.

1950   *The Blue Lamp* introduces Dixon of Dock Green to the public.

Useful websites

There are some useful websites that will give you access to governmental statistics on crime and policing, newspaper comment and reports, reports from criminal justice agencies, and also the opinions of pressure and activist groups. The addresses we list below are the ones which are most stable and which should stay in place for a long time. If you find that the addresses do not link to the site you are looking for, try putting a keyword (such as 'National Probation Service' or 'Home Office statistics') into a search engine such as Google and you should be able to locate the sites you are looking for. All of the websites listed here are freely accessible. If you have access to a university or college library, they will be able to advise you as to the journals and resources to which they subscribe.

The Internet for Historians

www.vts.rdn.ac.uk/tutorial/history

This link will take you to the Resource Discovery Network 'Internet for Historians' tutorial. Part of the RDN Virtual Training Suite, this is an interactive tutorial for historians aiming to provide information skills training and guidance on using the Internet. It features links to websites, quizzes and a 'basket' to store links to which you can return. Internet for Historians has been written by Frances Condron and Grazyna Cooper, Humanities Computing Unit, Oxford University Computing Services, University of Oxford.

The National Archives Learning Curve

www.learningcurve.gov.uk/candp/default.htm

This is a site hosted by the National Archives at Kew – the repository where all governmental (and many other) papers are deposited. Basic information about the development of the British criminal justice system, and about crime trends, is provided. This site is primarily aimed at A-level school pupils, but will be of some use at degree level. You will be able to view digitized versions of some actual historical records. This will give you a feel for the way in which historians use documents to reconstruct the past.

The Old Bailey Sessions Papers

www.oldbaileyonline.org

This project provides online, searchable versions of the sessions papers of the Old Bailey from 1674–1834. This was a period of great change in judicial culture and this massive project – a joint venture between Sheffield University, Hertfordshire University and the AHRB – offers a wealth of opportunities for primary research. Probably the best way to proceed is click first on 'About the Proceedings' and 'Historical Background' on the left hand menu bar. Then, once you have familiarized yourself with the aims of the project, proceed to 'Search the Proceedings'.

Home Office Crime Statistics

www.homeoffice.gov.uk/rds

On this site you will be able to search for and download recent and historical crime statistics. You should first of all click on the 'About RDS' button, and read about what this department actually does. Then the easiest way to locate the crime statistics is by clicking on 'Subjects' and then 'Crime'. As well as the historical statistical sets, you may be interested in the contemporary British Crime Survey. Note, however, that some of these sets have very large file sizes and hence correspondingly long download times.

Project Gutenberg

www.gutenberg.org

Project Gutenberg is the brainchild of Michael Hart, who in 1971 decided that it would be a really good idea if lots of famous and important texts were freely available to everyone in the world. Since then, he has been joined by hundreds of volunteers who share his vision. This site is particularly good if you are researching literary depictions of criminality. You could download Conrad's *The Secret Agent* or Dickens's *Oliver Twist*, for example.

The Metropolitan Police

www.met.police.uk/history

This link will take you to the 'History' page of the current Metropolitan Police website. While the information provided here is largely accurate, you will notice that it is mostly factual. Discussion of the reasons behind the setting up of the Metropolitan Police in 1829, or the 'purpose' of the New Police is largely absent. Why do you think this is? Does this give a 'Whig' view of the police, i.e. does it assume that their advent was largely a part of 'progress'? How much use do you think this site might be to you as a historical criminologist?

Charles Booth Police Notebooks

http://booth.lse.ac.uk

The Charles Booth Online Archive is a searchable resource giving access to archive material from the Booth collections of the British Library of Political and Economic Science (the Library of the London School of Economics and Political Science) and the University of London Library. The archives of the British Library of Political and Economic Science contain the original records from Booth's survey into life and labour in London, dating from 1886 to 1903. The archives of the University of London Library contain Booth family papers from 1799 to 1967. Click on the link 'Browse the Digitised Police Notebooks' to view some digitized excerpts from walks that Booth's team did with police officers, recording their comments on prostitution. The handwriting in the notebooks is hard to read, but this is a skill that historians gradually develop. This site is well worth taking the time to explore.

Online newspapers

The *Sun* – www.thesun.co.uk
The *Daily Mail* – www.dailymail.co.uk
The *Times* – www.timesonline.co.uk
The *Guardian* – www.guardian.co.uk

Most national newspapers now have online versions which can be browsed electronically. Some have archives (of varying sizes) via which you can search back issues for articles on specific topics. The *Times* has all back issues digitized, but this is a subscriber service. If you belong to a university or college, this may well be available via their library website. Obviously, as historical criminologists, you will be using newspapers primarily as evidence of public attitudes, perceptions and stereotypes rather than as sources of raw data. Hence, you should consider a wide range of newspapers. You could, perhaps, try comparing the way in which the same events are reported in newspapers with different political bias or different readerships.

Bibliography

Acton, W. (1857) *Prostitution Considered in its Moral, Social and Sanitary Aspects in London and Other Large Cities; with Proposals for the Mitigation and Prevention of its Attendant Evils*. London: Frank Cass.

Anderson, J. (1929) 'The police', *Public Administration*, VII: 192–202.

Archer, D. and Gartner, R. (1984) *Violence and Crime in Cross-national Perspective*. New Haven, CT: Yale University Press.

Archer, J. (1999) 'The violence we have lost? Body counts, historians and interpersonal violence in England', *Memoria y Civilización*, 2: 171–90.

Archer, J. and Jones, J. (2003) 'Headlines from history: violence in the press, 1850–1914', in E. Stanko (ed.), *The Meanings of Violence*. London: Routledge, pp. 17–31.

Bailey, V. (1993) 'The fabrication of deviance: "dangerous classes" and "criminal classes" in Victorian England', in J. Rule and R. Malcomson (eds), *Protest and Survival: The Historical Experience. Essays for E. P. Thompson*. London: Merlin, pp. 221–56.

Baldwin, S. (1926) *On England and Other Addresses*. London: Philip Allen.

Ballinger, A. (2000) *Dead Woman Walking*. Chippenham: Ashgate.

Barton, A. (2005) *Fragile Moralities and Dangerous Sexualities: Two Centuries of Semi-penal Institutionalisation for Women*. Aldershot: Ashgate.

Beattie, J. (1986) *Crime and the Courts in England 1660–1800*. Oxford: Clarendon Press.

Beattie, J. M. (2001) *Policing and Punishment in London, 1660–1750*. Oxford: Oxford University Press.

Berg, M. (1984) 'The power of knowledge: comments on Marglin's "Knowledge and Power"', in F. Stephen (ed.), *Firms, Organization and Labour: Approaches to the Economics of Work Organization*. London: Routledge, pp. 165–75.

Blackstone, W. (1982) *Commentaries on the Laws of England, in four books* (first published in 1765, 15th edition published in 1809 with notes and additions by Edward Christian). London: Professional Books.

Brewer, J. and Styles J. (eds) (1980) *An Ungovernable People: The English and Their Law in the Seventeenth and Eighteenth Centuries*. London: Hutchinson.

Brooks, P. (1984) *Reading for the Plot. Design and Intention in Narrative*. Oxford: Clarendon Press.

Brown, A. (2003) *English Society and the Prison: Time, Culture and Politics in the Development of the Modern Prison, 1850–1920*. London: Boydell Press.

Cain, M. (1990) *Growing up Good*. London: Sage.

Carlen, P. (1983) *Women's Imprisonment*. London: Routledge.

Carlen, P. (1985) *Criminal Women*. Cambridge: Polity.

Chadwick, W. (1900) *Reminiscences of a Chief Constable*. Manchester: J. Heywood.

Clay, Revd J. (1853) *Chaplain's Report on the Preston House of Correction*. Preston.

Colquhoun, P. (1800) *A TREATISE on the POLICE of the METROPOLIS*. London: C. Dilly.

Conley, C. (1991) *The Unwritten Law: Criminal Justice in Victorian Kent*. New York: Oxford University Press.

Cox, P. and Shore, H. (eds) (2002) *Becoming Delinquent: British and European Youth 1650–1950*. Aldershot: Ashgate.

Critchley, T. A. (1967) *A History of Police in England and Wales, 900–1966*. London: Constable.

Critchley, T. (1970) *The Conquest of Violence. Order and Liberty in Britain*. London: Constable.

Croall, H. (2001) *Understanding White-Collar Crime*. Buckingham: Open University Press.

D'Cruze, S. (1998) *Crimes of Outrage: Sex, Violence and Victorian Working Women*. London: University College London Press.

D'Cruze, S. (1999) 'Sex, violence and local courts: working-class respectability in a mid-nineteenth-century Lancashire town', *British Journal of Criminology*, 39, 1: 39–55.

Dandaker, C. (1990) *Surveillance, Power and Modernity*. Cambridge: Polity Press.

Daniels, K. (1998) *Convict Women: Rough Culture and Reformation*. St Leonards: Allen & Unwin.

Darwin, C. (1871) *The Descent of Man and Selection in Relation to Sex*. London: John Murray.

Davies, A. (1999) 'These viragoes are no less cruel than the lads: young women, gangs and violence in Late Victorian Manchester and Salford', *British Journal of Criminology*, 39, 1: 72–89.

Davies, A. (2000) 'Youth gangs, gender and violence, 1870–1900', in S. D'Cruze, *Everyday Violence in Britain, 1850–1950*. Harlow: Longman Pearson.

Davies, A. and Pearson, G. (1999) 'Introduction', *British Journal of Criminology*, 39, 1: 1–9.

Davis, J. (1980) 'The London garotting panic of 1862', in V. A. C. Gatrell *et al.* (eds), *Crime and the Law: The Social History of Crime in Western Europe since 1500*. London: Europa.

Davis, J. (1984) 'A poor man's system of justice? The London Police Courts in the second half of the nineteenth century', *Historical Journal*, 27, 2: 309–35.

Davis, J. (1987) 'The thief non-professional: workplace appropriation in nineteenth-century London' (summary of paper), *Bulletin of the Society for the Study of Labour History*, 52: 41.

Davis, J. (1989a) 'From rookeries to communities: race, poverty and policing in London, 1850–1985', *History Workshop Journal*, 27: 65–85.

Davis, J. (1989b) 'Prosecutions and their context: the use of the criminal law in later nineteenth-century London', in D. Hay and F. Snyder (eds), *Policing and Prosecution in Britain, 1750–1850*. Oxford: Clarendon Press, pp. 397–426.

De Tocqueville, A. (1997) *Memoir on Pauperism* [1833], trans. Seymour Drescher. Chicago, IL: Ivan R. Dee.

Dickens, C. (1999) *Oliver Twist*. Oxford: Oxford University Press.

Dickson, D. (1989) *Alternative Technology*. London: Fontana.

Dikötter, F. (1998) 'Race culture: recent perspectives on the history of eugenics', *American Historical Review*, 103, 2: 467–78.

Ditton, J. (1977) *Part-Time Crime. An Ethnography of Fiddling and Pilferage*. Basingstoke: Macmillan.

Duffield, I. and Bradley, J. (1997) *Representing Convicts. New Perspectives on Convict Forced Labour Migration*. Leicester: Leicester University Press.

Dunstall, G. (1999) *A Policeman's Paradise? Policing a Stable Society 1918–1945*. Wellington: Dunmore Press in association with the New Zealand Police.

Eisner, M. (2001) 'Modernization, self-control and lethal violence – the long-term dynamics of European homicide rates in theoretical perspective', *British Journal of Criminology*, 41: 618–38.

Elias, N. (1978/2000) *The Civilizing Process. Sociogenetic and Psychogenetic Investigations*. Oxford: Blackwell.

Emsley, C. (1985) '"The thump of wood on a swede turnip": police violence in nineteenth-century England', *Criminal Justice History*, 6: 125–49.

Emsley, C. (1993) '"Mother, what did policemen do when there weren't any motors?" The law, the police and the regulation of motor traffic in England 1900–1939', *Historical Journal*, XXXVII: 357–81.

Emsley, C. (1996) *The English Police: A Political and Social History*. Harlow: Longman.

Emsley, C. (2002) 'The history of crime and crime control institutions', in M. Maguire, R. Morgan and R. Reiner (eds), *The Oxford Handbook of Criminology* (3rd edn). Oxford: Oxford University Press.

Emsley, C. (2005a) *Crime and Society in England, 1750–1900* (3rd edn). Harlow: Longman.

Emsley, C. (2005b) *Hard Men: Violence in England since 1750*. London: Hambledon & London.

Emsley, C. (ed.) (2005c) *The Persistent Prison. Problems, Images and Alternatives*. London: Francis Boutle.

Emsley, C., and Clapson, M. (1994) 'Recruiting the English Policeman, c.1840–1940', *Policing and Society*, 3: 269–86.

Emsley, C. and Clapson, M. (2002) 'Street, beat and respectability: the culture and self-image of the late Victorian and Edwardian policeman', in L. Knafla (ed.), *Policing and War in Europe: Criminal Justice History*, 16: 107–31.

Feeley, M. and Little, D. L. (1991) 'The vanishing female: the decline of women in the criminal process, 1687–1912', *Law and Society Review*, 25, 4: 719–59.

Fishman, S. (2002) 'Absent fathers and family breakdown: delinquency in Vichy France', in P. Cox and H. Shore (eds), *Becoming Delinquent: British and European Youth 1650–1950*. Aldershot: Ashgate, pp. 141–57.

Foucault, M. (1991) *Discipline and Punish*. London: Penguin. (First published as *Surveiller et Punir: Naissance de la Prison* (1975).)

Fry, M. (1951) *Arms of the Law*. London: Gollancz.

Garland, D. (1985a) *Punishment and Welfare: A History of Penal Strategies*. Aldershot: Gower.

Garland, D. (1985b) 'The criminal and his science: a critical account of the formation of criminology at the end of the nineteenth century', *British Journal of Criminology*, 25, 2: 109–37.

Garland, D. (1990) *Punishment and Modern Society: A Study in Social Theory*. Oxford: Clarendon Press.

Garland, D. (2002) 'Of crimes and criminals: the development of criminology in Britain', in M. Maguire, R. Morgan and R. Reiner (eds) *The Oxford Handbook of Criminology* (3rd edn). Oxford: Oxford University Press, pp. 7–50.

Gatrell, V. A. C. (1980) 'The decline of theft and violence in Victorian and Edwardian England', in V. A. C. Gatrell, B. Lenman and G. Parker (eds), *Crime and the Law: The Social History of Crime in Western Europe since 1500*. London: Europa, pp. 238–337.

Gatrell, V. A. C. (1990) 'Crime, authority and the policeman-state', in F. M. L. Thompson (ed.), *The Cambridge Social History of Britain 1750–1950*, Vol. 3: *Social Agencies and Institutions*. Cambridge: Cambridge University Press, pp. 243–310.

Gatrell, V. A. C. (1994) *The Hanging Tree: Execution and the English People, 1770–1868*. Oxford: Oxford University Press.

Gatrell, V. A. C. and Hadden, T. B. (1972) 'Nineteenth-century criminal statistics and their interpretation', in E. A. Wrigley (ed.), *Nineteenth-Century Society: Essays in the Use of Quantitative Methods for the Study of Social Data*. Cambridge: Cambridge University Press.

Gatrell, V. A. C., Lenman, B. and Parker, G. (eds) (1980) *Crime and the Law: A Social History of Crime in Early Modern Europe*. London: Europa.

Gelsthorpe, L. (1989) *Sexism and the Female Offender*. Aldershot: Gower.

Giddens, A. (1992) *The Nation-State and Violence*. Cambridge: Polity Press.

Giddens, A. (1995) *A Contemporary Critique of Historical Materialism* (2nd edn). Basingstoke: Macmillan.

Gissing, G. (1891) *New Grub Street, Vol. 1*. London: Smith, Elder.

Godfrey, B. (1997) 'Workplace appropriation and the gendering of factory "law": West Yorkshire, 1840–1880', M. Arnot and C. Usborne (eds), *Crime and Gender in Modern Europe*. London: University College London Press.

Godfrey, B. (1999a) 'The impact of the factory on workplace appropriation in the nineteenth century', *British Journal of Criminology*, 39, 1: 56–71.

Godfrey, B. (1999b) 'The use of the criminal law against labour: the West Riding magistracy and the sentencing of workplace appropriators, 1840–80', *Crime, History and Societies*, 3, 2: 56–71.

Godfrey, B. (2002) 'Private policing and the workplace: the Worsted Committee and the policing of labour in Northern England, 1840–1880', in L. Knafla (ed.), *Policing and War in Europe: Criminal Justice History*. London: Greenwood Press, pp. 87–107.

Godfrey, B. (2003a) 'Counting and accounting for violence', *British Journal of Criminology*, 43, 2: 340–53.

Godfrey, B. (2003b) '"Dear reader I killed him": ethical and emotional issues in researching convicted murderers through the analysis of interview transcripts', *Oral History*, 31, 1: 54–64.

Godfrey, B. (2004) 'Rough girls: a "recent" history of violent young women, 1900–1930', in C. Alder and A. Worrall (eds), *Criminal Girls*. New York: State University of New York Press, pp. 1–30.

Godfrey, B. and Locker, J. (2001) 'The nineteenth-century decline of custom and its impact on theories of "workplace theft" and "white collar" crime', *Northern History*, 38: 261–73.

Godfrey, B. and Richardson, J. (2003) 'Towards ethical practice in the use of transcribed oral interviews', *International Journal of Social Research Methodology*, 6, 4: 200–14.

Godfrey, B., Farrall, S. and Karstedt, S. (2005) 'Explaining gendered sentencing patterns for violent men and women in the late Victorian and Edwardian period', *British Journal of Criminology online*, advance access 31 March.

Greg, W. R. (1850) 'Prostitution', *Westminster Review*, no. 53.

Gregory, D. (1982) *Regional Transformation and Industrial Revolution: A Geography of the Yorkshire Woollen Industry*. Basingstoke: Macmillan.

Griffiths, P. (1996) *Youth and Authority: Formative Experience in England 1560–1640*. Oxford: Oxford University Press.

Gurr, E. (1981) 'Historical trends in violent crime: a critical review of the evidence', *Crime and Justice: An Annual Review of Research*, 3: 295–353.

Harris, A. (2003) 'Policing and public order in the City of London, 1784–1815', *London Journal*, 28, 2: 1–20.

Harris, J. (1995) 'Between civic virtue and Social Darwinism: the concept of the residuum', in D. Englander and R. O'Day (eds), *Retrieved Riches*. Aldershot: Scolar Press, pp. 67–88.

Hart, J. (1955) 'Reform of the borough police, 1835–1856', *English Historical Review*, LXX: 411–27.

Hay, D. (1975) 'Property, authority and the criminal law', in D. Hay, P. Linebaugh, J. Rule, E. P. Thompson and C. Winslow, *Albion's Fatal Tree: Crime and Society in Eighteenth-Century England*. London: Allen Lane, pp. 17–63.

Hay, D. (1983) 'Manufacturers and the criminal law in the later eighteenth-century', *Past and Present Colloquium on Police and Policing*, conference proceedings, Birmingham University.

Hay, D. (1989) 'Using the criminal law, 1750–1850: policing, private prosecution, and the state', in D. Hay and F. Snyder (eds), *Policing and Prosecution in Britain, 1750–1850*. Oxford: Clarendon Press.

Hay, D. and Snyder, F. (eds) (1989) *Policing and Prosecution in Britain 1750–1850*. Oxford: Clarendon Press.

Hay, D., Linebaugh, P., Rule, J., Thompson, E. P. and Winslow, C. (1975) *Albion's Fatal Tree: Crime and Society in Eighteenth-Century England*. London: Allen Lane.

Heidensohn, F. (1981) 'Women and the penal system', in A. Morris and L. Gelsthorpe (eds), *Women and Crime*. Cambridge: Cropwood Conference Series 13.

Heidensohn, F. (1989) *Crime and Society*. Basingstoke: Palgrave Macmillan.

Heidensohn, F. (1996) 'Feminist perspectives and their impact on criminology and criminal justice in Britain', in N. Rafter and F. Heidensohn (eds), *International Feminist Perspectives in Criminology*. Buckinghamshire: Open University Press.

Heidensohn, F. (ed.) (2002) 'Gender and crime', in M. Maguire, R. Morgan and R. Reiner (eds), *The Oxford Handbook of Criminology* (3rd edn). Oxford: Oxford University, pp. 491–535.

Himmelfarb, G. (1984) *The Idea of Poverty: England in the Early Industrial Age*. New York: Alfred Knopf.

Hobsbawm, E. (1968) 'Customs, wages and workload', in *Labouring Men: Studies in the History of Labour*. London: Weidenfield & Nicolson.

Hohenberg, P. and Lees, L. (1985) *The Making of Urban Europe, 1000–1994*. Cambridge, MA and London: Harvard University Press.

Howard, J. (1929) *The State of the Prisons*. London: Dent & Sons.

Hudson, P. (1992) *The Industrial Revolution*. London: Edward Arnold.

Hughes, R. (1987) *The Fatal Shore: A History of the Transportation of Convicts to Australia 1787–1868*. London: Collins Harvill.

Iggers, G. (1997) *Historiography in the Twentieth Century*. Hanover, NH and London: Weslyan University Press.

Ignatieff, M. (1978) *A Just Measure of Pain. The Penitentiary in the Industrial Revolution, 1750–1850*. New York: Columbia University Press.

Ignatieff, M. (1983) 'State, civil society and total institutions: a critique of recent social histories of punishment', in D. Sugarman (ed.), *Legality, Ideology and the State*. London: Academic Press.

Jackson, L. (2003) 'Care or control? The Metropolitan Women Police and child welfare, 1919–1969', *Historical Journal*, 46, 3: 623–48.

Jewkes, Y. (2004) *Media and Crime*. London: Sage.

Joyce, P. (1980) *Work, Society and Politics the Culture of the Factory in Later Victorian England*. New Brunswick, NJ: Rutgers University Press.

Karstedt, S. (2000) 'Emancipation, crime and problem behaviour of women: a perspective from Germany', *Gender Issues*, 18, 3: 21–58.

Kayman, M. (1992) *From Bow Street to Baker Street: Mystery, Detection and Narrative*. Basingstoke: Macmillan.

Kenny, C. (1994) *Cotton Everywhere*. Bolton: Aurora Press.

King, P. (1996) 'Punishing assault: the transformation of attitudes in the English courts', *Journal of Interdisciplinary History*, 27, 1: 43–74.

King, P. (1999a) 'Locating histories of crime: a bibliographical study', *British Journal of Criminology*, 39, 1: 161–74.

King, P. (1999b) 'The rise of juvenile delinquency in England 1780–1840', *Past and Present*, CLX: 17–41.

King, P. (2000) *Crime, Justice and Discretion in England, 1740–1820*. Oxford: Oxford University Press.

King, P. and Noel, J. (1993) 'The origins of "the problem of juvenile delinquency": the growth of juvenile prosecutions in London in the late eighteenth and early nineteenth centuries', *Criminal Justice History: An International Annual*, 14: 198–207.

Kohl, J. G. (1844) *Ireland, Scotland and England*. London.

Landes, D. (1987) 'What do bosses really do?', *Journal of Economic History*, 46: 585–623.

Langbein, J. (1983) 'Albion's fatal flaws', *Past and Present*, 98–101: 96–120.

Langbein, J. (2003) *The Origins of the Adversary Criminal Trial*. Oxford: Oxford University Press.

Lawrence, P. (2000) 'Images of poverty and crime: police memoirs in England and France at the end of the nineteenth century', *Crime, Histoire et Sociétés / Crime, History and Societies*, 4, 1: 63–82.

Lawrence, P. (2003) '"Scoundrels and scallywags, and some honest men ..." Memoirs and the self-image of French and English policemen, *c*.1870–1939', in B. Godfrey, C. Emsley and G. Dunstall (eds), *Comparative Histories of Crime*. Cullompton: Willan Press, pp. 125–44.

Lawrence, P. (2004) 'Policing the poor in England and France, 1850–1900', in C. Emsley, E. Johnson and P. Spierenburg (eds), *Social Control in Europe 1800–2000*. Columbus: Ohio State University Press, pp. 210–25.

Leps, M.-C. (1992) *Apprehending the Criminal: The Production of Deviance in Nineteenth-Century Discourse*. Durham, NC and London: Duke University Press.

Levi, M. and Maguire, M. (2002) 'Violent crime', in M. Maguire, R. Morgan and R. Reiner (eds), *The Oxford Handbook of Criminology* (3rd edn). Oxford: Oxford University Press.

Linebaugh, P. (1991), *The London Hanged: Crime and Civil Society in the Eighteenth-Century*. Cambridge: Cambridge University Press.

Lloyd, A. (1995) *Doubly Deviant, Doubly Damned*. London: Penguin.

Locker, J. (2004) '"This most pernicious species of crime": embezzlement in its public and private dimensions, *c*.1850–1930'. Unpublished PhD thesis, Keele University.

Lombroso, C. and Ferrero, W. (1895) *The Female Offender*. London: T. Fisher Unwin.

Lyon, D. (1994) *The Electronic Eye: The Rise of Surveillance Society*. Cambridge: Polity Press.

Macnicol, J. (1987) 'In pursuit of the underclass', *Journal of Social Policy*, 16, 3: 293–318.

Malcolm, J. L. (1996) *To Keep and Bear Arms: The Origins of an Anglo-American Right*. Cambridge, MA: Harvard University Press.

Malcolm, J. L. (2002) *Guns and Violence: The English Experience*. Cambridge, MA: Harvard University Press.

Malthus, T. (1832) *Essay on the Principle of Population* [first published 1798].

Margarey, S. (1978) 'The invention of juvenile delinquency in early nineteenth-century England' *Labour History*, 34: 11–27.

Marglin, S. (1976) '"What do bosses do?" The origins and function of hierarchy in capitalist production', in A. Gorz (ed.), *The Division of Labour: The Labour Process and Class Struggle in Modern Capitalism*. London: Allen Lane.

Marglin, S. (1984) 'Knowledge and power', in F. Stephen (ed.), *Firms, Organization and Labour, Approaches to the Economics of Work Organization*. Basingstoke: Macmillan, pp. 148–80.

Mars, G. (1983) *Cheats at Work: An Ethnography of Workplace Crime*. London: Allen & Unwin.

Marwick, A. (1991) *The Deluge: British Society and the First World War*. Basingstoke: Macmillan.

Masterman, C. (1901) *The Heart of the Empire: Discussions of Problems of Modern City Life in England*. London: Fisher Unwin.

Maudsley, H. (1873) *Body and Mind*. Basingstoke: Macmillan.

McGowan, R. (1983) 'The image of justice and reform of the criminal law in early nineteenth-century England', *Buffalo Law Review*, 23: 89–125.

McGowan, R. (1987) 'The body and punishment in eighteenth-century England', *Journal of Modern History*, 59 (December): 651–79.

McGowan, R. (1990) 'Getting to know the criminal class in nineteenth-century England', *Nineteenth Century Contexts*, 14, 1: 33–54.

McGowan, R. (1999) 'From pillory to gallows: the punishment of forgery in the age of the financial revolution', *Past and Present*, 165: 107–40.

McGowan, R. (2005) 'The Bank of England and the policing of forgery 1797–1821', *Past and Present*, 186: 81–116.

McKenzie, A. (2005) '"Saving our unfortunate sisters"? Establishing the first separate prison for women in New Zealand', in B. Godfrey and G. Dunstall (eds), *Crime and Empire 1840–1940*. Cullompton: Willan.

McLevy, J. (1975) *The Casebook of a Victorian Detective*. Edinburgh: Canongate.

Melossi, D. (2000) 'Changing representations of the criminal', *British Journal of Criminology*, 40: 296–320.

Melossi, D. and Pavarini, M. (1981) *The Prison and the Factory: The Origins of the Penitentiary System*. Basingstoke: Macmillan.

Miers, D. (1978) *Responses to Victimisation*. Abingdon: Professional.

Miers, D. (1990) *Compensation for Criminal Injuries*. London: Butterworth.

Morgan, G. and Rushton, P. (1998) *Rogues, Thieves and the Rule of Law: The Problem of Law Enforcement in North-East England, 1718–1800*. London: UCL Press.

Morris, L. (1994) *Dangerous Classes: The Underclass and Social Citizenship*. London: Routledge.

Morrison, B. (2005) 'Ordering disorderly women: female drunkenness in England *c.*1870–1920'. Unpublished PhD thesis, Keele University.

Morrison, W. (1896) *Juvenile Offenders*. London: Allen.

Morton, P. (1984) *The Vital Science: Biology and the Literary Imagination 1860–1900*. London: Allen & Unwin.

Neal, D. (1987) 'Free society, penal colony, slave society, prison?', *Historical Studies*, 22, 86: 497–518.

Nelken, D. (2002) 'White-collar crime', in M. Maguire, R. Morgan and R. Reiner (eds), *The Oxford Handbook of Criminology* (3rd edn). Oxford: Oxford University Press.

Neocleous, M. (2000) 'Social police and the mechanisms of prevention: Patrick Colquhoun and the condition of poverty', *British Journal of Criminology*, 40: 710–26.

Nicholas, S. (ed.) (1988) *Convict Workers: Reinterpreting Australia's Past*. Cambridge: Cambridge University Press.

Orwell, G. (1948) *1984*. (Originally written in 1948, but reprinted in many editions to the present day; the full text is now available online at http://www.online-literature.com/orwell/1984/).

Ousby, I. (1976) *Bloodhounds of Heaven: The Detective in English Fiction from Godwin to Doyle*. London: Harvard University Press.

Oxley, D. (1997) *Convict Maids: Forced Migration of Women to Australia*. Cambridge: Cambridge University Press.

Palmer, S. (1988) *Police and Protest in England and Ireland 1780–1850*. Cambridge: Cambridge University Press.

Pearson, G. (1983) *Hooligan: A History of Respectable Fears*: Basingstoke: Macmillan.

Philips, D. (1977) *Crime and Authority in Victorian England: The Black Country 1835–1860*. London: Croom Helm.

Philips, D. (1980) 'A new engine of power and authority: the institutionalizaton of law-enforcement in England 1780–1830', in V. A. C. Gatrell, B. Lenman and G. Parker (eds), *Crime and the Law: The Social History of Crime in Western Europe since 1500*. London: Europa.

Philips, D. (1989) 'Good men to associate and bad men to conspire: associations for the prosecution of felons in England, 1760–1860', in D. Hay and F. Snyder (eds), *Policing and Prosecution in Britain 1750–1850*. Oxford: Clarendon Press, pp. 113–70.

Philips, D. and Storch, R. (1999) *Policing Provincial England: The Politics of Reform*. London: Leicester University Press.

Pick, D. (1989) *Faces of Degeneration: A European Disorder, c.1848–1918*. Cambridge: Cambridge University Press.

Pollak, O. (1950) *The Criminality of Women*. New York: Barnes/Perpetua.

Pollard, S. (1965) *The Genesis of Modern Management: A Study of the Industrial Revolution in Great Britain*. London: Edward Arnold.

Pratt, J. (2002) *Punishment and Civilization*. London: Sage.

Radzinowicz, L. (1948–86) *A History of the English Criminal Law and Its Administration from 1750*, 5 vols (Vol. 5 with Roger Hood). London: Stevens & Sons.

Radzinowicz, L. and Hood, A. (1990) *A History of the English Criminal Law and Its Administration from 1750, Vol. V: The Emergence of Penal Policy*. Oxford: Clarendon Press.

Rawlings, P. (1999) *Crime and Power: A History of Criminal Justice 1688–1998*. Harlow: Longman.

Rawlings, P. (2002) *Policing: A Short History*. Cullompton: Willan.

Reith, C. (1943) *British Police and the Democratic Ideal*. London: Oxford University Press.

Report of the Select Committee on the Police of the Metropolis (1822) London: HMSO.

Reynolds, E. (1998) *Before the Bobbies: The Night Watch and Police Reform in Metropolitan London, 1720–1830*. Basingstoke: Macmillan.

Robb, G. (2002) *White-Collar Crime in Modern England: Financial Fraud and Business Morality 1845–1929*. Cambridge: Cambridge University Press.

Rock, P. (1990) *Helping Victims of Crime: The Home Office and the Rise of Victim Support in England and Wales.* Oxford: Clarendon Press.

Rock, P. (2004) 'Victims, prosecutors and the state in nineteenth-century England and Wales', *Criminal Justice*, 4, 4: 331–54.

Rule, J. (1981) *The Experiences of Labour in Eighteenth-Century Industry.* London: Croom Helm, pp. 124–46.

Rule, J. (1986) *The Labouring Classes in Early Industrial England, 1750–1850.* Harlow: Longman, pp. 107–38.

Rusche, G. and Kirchheimer, O. (1968) *Punishment and Social Structure.* New York: Russell & Russell (first published 1939, New York: Columbia University Press).

Rylands, G. (1889) *Crime: Its Causes and Remedy.* London: T. Fisher Unwin.

Sanders, W. B. (1974) *The Sociologist as Detective. An Introduction to Research Methods.* New York: Praeger.

Sayers, A. (1997) 'Michael Evans, village constable, tailor and smuggler', *Devon Historian*, 54: 24–6.

Schubert, A. (1981) 'Private initiative in law enforcement: Associations for the Prosecution of Felons, 1744–1856', in V. Bailey (ed.), *Policing and Punishment in Nineteenth Century Britain.* London: Croom Helm, pp. 25–41.

Sharpe, J. A. (1999) *Crime in Early Modern England, 1550–1750* (2nd edn). London: Longman.

Shaw, A. G. L. (1966) *Convicts and the Colonies.* London: Faber.

Shore, H. (1999) *Artful Dodgers: Youth and Crime in Early Nineteenth Century London.* Woodbridge, Suffolk: Boydell Press.

Shpayer-Makov, H. (2002) *The Making of a Policeman.* Aldershot: Ashgate.

Sindall, R. (1983) 'Middle-class crime in nineteenth-century England', *Criminal Justice History: An International Annual*, IV: 23–40.

Sindall, R. (1987) 'The London garrotting panics of 1856 and 1862', *Social History*, 12, 3: 351–9.

Sindall, R. (1990) *Street Violence in the Nineteenth Century: Media Panic or Real Danger?* Leicester: Leicester University Press.

Skidelsky, R. (1990) *Oswald Mosley.* Basingstoke: Macmillan.

Smith, R. (1981) *Trial by Medicine.* New York: St. Martin's Press.

Smith, V. (1990) *All Muck and Nettles: The Early Life of Burler and Mender No. 57.* Huddersfield: Amadeus Press.

Soothill, K. and Walby, S. (1991) *Sex Crime in the News.* London: Routledge.

Spierenburg, P. (1991) *The Prison Experience.* New Brunswick, NJ: Rutgers University Press.

Spierenburg, P. (1998) *Men and Violence: Gender, Honor, and Rituals in Modern Europe and America.* Columbus, OH: Ohio State University Press.

Spierenburg, P. (2000) 'Violence and the civilizing process: does it work?', *Crime, History and Societies*, 5, 2: 87–105.

Spierenburg, P. (2005) 'The origins of the prison', in C. Emsley (ed.), *The Persistent Prison: Problems, Images and Alternatives.* London: Francis Boutle.

Steedman, C. (1984) *Policing the Victorian Community: The Formation of English Provincial Police Forces, 1856–80.* London, Routledge & Kegan Paul.

Stone, D. (2001) 'Race in British eugenics', *European History Quarterly*, 31, 3: 397–425.

Storch, R. (1975) 'The plague of blue locusts: police reform and popular resistance in northern England 1840–57', *International Review of Social History*, 20: 61–90.

Storch, R. (1976) 'The policeman as domestic missionary: urban discipline and popular culture in Northern England, 1850–1880', *Journal of Social History*, IX: 481–511.

Storch, R. and Philips, D. (1999) *Policing Provincial England, 1829–1856: The Politics of Reform*. London: Leicester University Press.

Styles, J. (1983) 'Embezzlement, industry and the law in England, 1500–1800', in M. Berg, P. Hudson and M. Sonescher (eds), *Manufacture in Town and Country before the Factory*. Cambridge: Cambridge University Press.

Sugden, P. (1995) *The Complete History of Jack the Ripper*. London: Carroll & Graf.

Sutherland, E. H. (1983) *White-Collar Crime: The Uncut Version*. New Haven, CT: Yale University Press.

Taylor, D. (1997) *The New Police in Nineteenth-Century England: Crime, Conflict and Control*. Manchester: Manchester University Press.

Taylor, D. (1998) *Crime, Policing and Punishment in England, 1750–1914*. Basingstoke: Macmillan.

Taylor, H. (1998a) 'Rationing crime: the political economy of criminal statistics since the 1850s', *Economic History Review*, 49, 3: 569–90.

Taylor, H. (1998b) 'The politics of the rising crime statistics of England and Wales', *Crime, Histoire et Sociétés/Crime, History and Societies*, 1, 2: 5–28.

Thompson, E. P. (1967) 'Time, work-discipline and industrial capitalism', *Past and Present*, 38: 56–97.

Thompson, E. P. (1975) *Whigs and Hunters: The Origins of the Black Act*. London: Allen Lane.

Tobias, J. J. (1972) *Nineteenth-Century Crime: Prevention and Punishment*. Newton Abbot: David & Charles.

Tomes, N. (1978) 'A torrent of abuse: crimes of violence between working-class men and women in London, 1840–1875', *Journal of Social History*, 11: 328–45.

Vanstone, M. (2004) 'Mission control: the origins of a humanitarian service', *Probation Journal*, 51, 1: 34–47.

Vogler, R. (1991) *Reading the Riot Act: The Magistracy, the Police and the Army in Civil Disorder*. Buckingham: Open University Press.

Walkowitz, J. (1980) *Prostitution and Victorian Society: Women, Class and the State*. Cambridge: Cambridge University Press.

Walkowitz, J. (1992) *City of Dreadful Delight: Narratives of Sexual Danger in Late-Victorian London*. London: Virago.

Weaver, J. (1995) *Crimes, Constables and Courts: Order and Transgression in a Canadian City, 1816–1970*. Montreal: McGill-Queen's University Press.

Weinberger, B. (1988) 'The police and the public in nineteenth-century Warwickshire', in V. Bailey (ed.), *Policing and Punishment in Nineteenth-Century Britain*. London: Croom Helm, pp. 67–93.

Weinberger, B. (1991) *Keeping the Peace: Policing Strikes in Britain 1906–1926*. Oxford: Berg.

Weinberger, B. (1995) *The Best Police in the World: An Oral History of English Policing*. Aldershot: Scolar Press.

Welshman, J. (2005) *Underclass: A History of the Excluded, 1880–2000*. London: Hambledon & London.

Wiener, M. (1987) 'The march of penal progress?', *Journal of British Studies*, 26, 1: 83–96.

Wiener, M. (1990) *Reconstructing the Criminal: Culture, Law and Policy in England, 1830–1914*. Cambridge: Cambridge University Press.

Wiener, M. (1998) 'The Victorian criminalization of men', in P. Spierenburg (ed.), *Men and Violence: Gender, Honor, and Rituals in Modern Europe and America*. Columbus, OH: Ohio State University Press.

Wiener, M. (1999a) 'Judges *v.* jurors: courtroom tensions in murder trials and the law of criminal responsibility in nineteenth-century England', *Law and History Review*, Fall: 467–506

Wiener, M. (1999b) 'The sad story of George Hall: adultery, murder and the politics of mercy in mid-Victorian England', *Social History*, 24, 2: 174–95.

Wiener, M. (2004) *Men of Blood: Violence, Manliness and Criminal Justice in Victorian England*. Cambridge: Cambridge University Press.

Williams, C. A. (1998) 'Police and crime in Sheffield, 1818–1873'. Unpublished PhD thesis, Sheffield University.

Williams, C. A. (2004) 'Review of guns and violence, the British experience by Joyce Lee Malcolm', *Journal of Modern History*, March: 168–9.

Wood, J. C. (2003) 'Self-policing and the policing of the self: violence, protection and the civilising bargain in Britain', *Crime, Histoire et Sociétés/Crime, History and Societies*, 7, 1: 109–28.

Wood, J. C. (2004) *The Shadow of Our Refinement. Violence and Crime in Nineteenth-Century England*. New York: Routledge.

Worrall, A. (1990) *Offending Women: Female Lawbreakers and the Criminal Justice System*. London: Routledge.

Zedner, L. (1991) *Women, Crime and Custody in Victorian England*. Oxford: Oxford University Press.

Zedner, L. (2002) 'Victims and crime', in M. Maguire, R. Morgan and R. Reiner (eds) *The Oxford Handbook of Criminology* (3rd edn). Oxford: Oxford University Press.

Index